Victim

Victim

THE OTHER SIDE OF MURDER

Gary Kinder

ATLANTIC MONTHLY PRESS NEW YORK

Copyright © 1982 by Gary Kinder

Originally published by Delacorte Press
Published simultaneously in Canada
Printed in the United States of America

FIRST ATLANTIC MONTHLY PRESS EDITION

Library of Congress Cataloging-in-Publication Data

Kinder, Gary.
    Victim, the other side of murder / Gary Kinder.
       p.   cm.
    Originally published: New York : Delacorte Press, 1982.
    ISBN 0-87113-735-6
    1. Naisbitt, Cortney, 1957– . 2. Andrews, William. 3. Pierre,
Dale, 1953– . 4. Murder—Utah. 5. Murder victims—Utah.
I. Title.
HV6533.U8K56   1999
364.15'23'0979228—dc21   98045612

Design by MaryJane DiMassi

Atlantic Monthly Press
841 Broadway
New York, NY 10003

99 00 01 10 9 8 7 6 5 4 3 2 1

ACKNOWLEDGMENTS

The characters who appear by name in this book have been thanked before, but I would like to thank them again. The value of their time and consent to explore an event in their lives that was sometimes painful to recall cannot be measured. In addition I would like to thank the doctors, nurses, medical technicians, teachers, police officers, citizens of Trinidad and Tobago, and friends and neighbors of the Naisbitt family whose names do not appear in the book but whose contributions were essential to my understanding of the story. A special thanks to Assistant Chief of Police Dave Reed and nurse Bonnie Judkins.

I welcome this opportunity to thank personally and publicly my agents Arthur and Richard Pine for taking on a new writer with a first book and offering encouragement during the years when there was little to be encouraged about; my editor Morgan Entrekin whose enthusiasm, sensitivity, and integrity are what every writer dreams of finding in an editor; my friends Jim and Shera Arango, and their daughters, Melinda, Valerie, Lisa, and Samantha, who during my frequent research trips to Ogden provided me with the warmth of a home away from home; Becky Dittmer and Chris Jensen, not only for their typing of countless transcript and manuscript pages but for their spirit of cooperation; Becky Valasek, who read the original manuscript and offered insight for its improvement; Patrick Chookolingo, owner and publisher of Trinidad and Tobago's newspaper, *The Bomb,* for his patronage and for making available to me James Ramlogan, a thorough reporter and good companion whose street wisdom was invaluable to my work in the West Indies; Irving and Sylvia Wallace for their genuine interest in new writers and for introducing me to the Pines; Peter Schwed for holding my head above water while I learned more about swimming; Gil Athay and Robert Van Sciver for letting an outsider tag along; Earl Dorius and Craig Barlow of the Utah Attorney General's office for their patient explanations and ready availability; Geoff Irvin of Blue Cross–Blue Shield who assisted me in compiling medical costs; Fred Montmorency, a private citizen who offered me his research on the cost of the Hi-Fi Murder trial; Tony Bair for his cooperation in arranging prison visitations; the Ernest Evans family for their faith and support; and Randy, my brother and friend, who has been as encouraging and hopeful as if the book were his own.

ACKNOWLEDGMENTS vi

Last I would like to thank my wife, Alison, who has never known me when I was not working on this book, and who shared me with it for seven years. Without her love and understanding and sacrifice it would never have been completed. Now we can get on with our lives together.

This book is dedicated with love
To the two people whose influence
Long ago prepared me for writing it—

My mother and my father

The story itself
Belongs to the Naisbitt family,
And I am indebted to each of them
For sharing their part of it with me

AUTHOR'S NOTE

Victim is a true story. No names or facts have been changed. All material not derived from my own experience is taken from police, hospital, and Air Force records; trial transcripts; correspondence; or extended interviews with those persons directly involved.

In some instances I have assumed the physical consequences of a particular action I know from interviews or records took place.

With the exception of the perpetrator Dale Pierre none of the characters appearing in this book was promised payment for his or her cooperation. Pierre has been provided with perhaps twenty-five books, plus pens, pencils, paper, and other educational materials in return for his agreement to answer questions and provide information on his past.

GARY KINDER

THE VICTIMS

St. Benedict's Hospital sat high on the east bench overlooking Ogden, Utah. It was an old three-story structure made of red brick, and from its rooftop shone a fluorescent white cross. At night the panorama spreading before it was a city of one hundred thousand, the lights streaking and twinkling in the distance all the way to the shores of the Great Salt Lake.

That Monday evening, April 22, 1974, was warm and darkness had settled over the city. The St. Benedict's emergency room was quiet. At 10:40 emergency physician Dr. Jess Wallace was in the hallway talking to Dr. James Allred, when a loud buzzer sounded. Wallace ran into the ER office and flicked on the emergency receiver, a hotline between the hospital and emergency ambulance units. The driver calling in was talking so fast Wallace could hardly understand him. Seconds later the driver had signed off and Wallace knew only that an ambulance was coming in with two people shot in the head. They would be at the hospital in three minutes.

Wallace said to Allred, "Stick around, I may need you."

Then he flipped a switch, lighting a large red flasher on the switchboard upstairs. Immediately, "ER alert" reverberated over the hospital intercom. Far below, in the middle of town, the flashing red lights of the ambulance began whirling silently in the night.

The glass doors to the emergency room were propped open, and the two doctors were joined in the hallway by nurses from Intensive Care and Coronary Care, a medical technician, a respiratory technician, an X-ray technician, and the nursing supervisor. They waited by the open doors for an ambulance they were certain carried two bodies from Ogden's notorious Twenty-fifth Street. Winos from the street were rushed to the hospital regularly to have their heads sewn up or a knife wound closed or to be pronounced DOA from one cause or another. Someone standing by the door said that this time one of them had probably shot his old lady then turned the gun on himself. Each of the crew feared only that he or she would be assigned to peel off the shoes or the socks or the underwear of one of the victims.

As the crew waited by the ER doors, the ambulance zigzagged through the grid of city blocks, moving steadily toward the hospital. Traffic was light, and the few cars on the streets cleared away at the sound of the approaching sirens. The motorcycle escort passed first; then a hundred yards behind it came the ambulance at a steady fifty miles an hour. Eight blocks from town they swung right onto Harrison, sped up for a few blocks, then braked and swung left at the high school. Behind the motorcycle the ambulance driver shot straight up the hill, turned right, shut down the siren, and raced the last two blocks to the neon orange EMERGENCY.

The ambulance circled beneath the red brick portico, its flashing red light ricocheting off the walls, splashing over the waiting crew like an eerie red strobe. They saw the driver spring from the front seat. But he moved without that controlled sort of quickness the ambulance attendants usually exhibited. He was shouting, but no one could understand him. He sprinted to the rear of the ambulance and flung open the doors. Two attendants kneeling in back were frantically trying to squeeze oxygen into the victims. They looked frightened. The crew realized then what they had only sensed watching the driver. Something had gone awry.

Then suddenly all three of the attendants were yelling to them at once. Disjointed bits and pieces of torture and mass murder. Of a girl raped. Of a man strangled. Of a ball-point pen driven into a victim's ear. Of five people bound on their hands and knees and shot through the head, blood and vomit everywhere, the most sickening thing any of them had ever seen. They shouted that there were still more bodies in the basement of the Ogden Hi-Fi Shop.

The attendants shoved the stretchers out of the ambulance, and the emergency crew moved in quickly to help. Hands reached out and lowered the bodies into the wash of red light.

On the first stretcher, in a red dress, was a petite blond woman, a large diamond ring on her left hand, an ornate jade ring on her right. Behind her was a teen-age boy dressed in jeans and a brown-check shirt, his longish blond hair cut in a neat shag. He was gulping for air like a dying fish. His skin was bright blue, his blond hair spattered with blood and flecks of vomit. From his mouth bright red scars trailed away across his cheeks and chin. The woman's hair was soaked with sweat, making her appear almost bald. In the back of her head, her blond hair was matted around a bloody hole, and the same curious red scars encircled her mouth. Both bodies stank of blood and vomit.

The group that not sixty seconds earlier had dreaded only gummed socks and stained underwear were now staring at two bodies, not from the remote gutters of Twenty-fifth Street, but from their own safe world.

The confusion spilled through the doorway and hurtled twenty feet down the corridor to the trauma room. Dr. Wallace ran alongside. For an instant he thought the woman looked familiar. He yelled to the driver.

"Any idea who they are?"

"No!" the driver yelled back.

"What about these scars around the mouth?"

The driver hadn't even noticed them.

"I don't know," he said.

An attendant kept pace with the boy, trying to squeeze oxygen from a black Ambu bag into the boy's lungs. Wallace grabbed his arm.

"Hold off for a minute," he said. "Let's see what we've got here, first."

Wallace ran ahead to the trauma room, turned around, and stared in disbelief at the bodies coming through the door.

"For Christ's sake, since when do you bring them in here backwards!" he yelled. "Get them turned around so we can work on them!"

He scanned the bodies quickly with his eyes. The boy was trying to breathe, but the woman made only an occasional effort. Wallace began shouting orders.

"Jim, see what you can do for the woman. Chad, you go with Jim. Get a tube in her as fast as you can. Andy, you and Vicky stay with me. Ginny, shoot two pictures of each, the woman first."

Dr. Allred and respiratory technician Chad Nielsen wheeled the woman across the hall to the other room. In the trauma room, nurse Vicky Moyes yanked the curtain closed. The boy's body was swung in a sheet hammock from the ambulance cart onto the trauma table. Vicky scissored off the boy's shirt and removed his pants.

From the time Wallace's eyes made contact with the boy's body, he had been reflexively cataloging his injuries and life signs: bullet hole right rear of head; body flaccid, bright blue; red scars around mouth—no explanation. The boy's body now lay naked and unconscious on the table. Wallace began a closer, rapid examination. The boy's pupils were dilated and gave no response to light. His heart was palpitating wildly. His lungs were barely expanding. There was a tight gurgling in his chest. A peculiar odor emanated from his mouth. Dr. Wallace gripped the boy's sensitive Achilles tendon and mashed it between his fingers. The boy did not even flinch.

Wallace looked at the youthful face now gray and gasping for air. "Okay, we've got to try something," he said. "Vicky, start an IV, see if you can get him some blood pressure. Andy, hand me the laryngoscope, and have the tube ready."

He stood behind the boy's head. Andy Tolsma, the medical technician, grabbed a long, thin chrome cylinder from the crash cart and slapped it into his outstretched hand. Wallace held the boy's chin with one hand, pulling it back to form a straight line from the boy's mouth to his trachea. With the pinpoint of light shining from the laryngoscope, he searched the boy's throat for the white-ringed vocal chords.

"Andy, get the tube ready. . . ." He stopped. "Wait a minute, wait a minute. His throat's so swollen I can't even see the damn vocal chords!"

Wallace dropped the laryngoscope. He snatched the plastic tube out of Andy's hand and stuck one end in the boy's mouth. He placed his ear over the other end of the tube and listened for air exchanges. Quickly, smoothly, he manipulated the endotracheal tube through a mass of swollen tissue and farther down the boy's throat. At last it pushed past a triangular flap of skin and slid into the trachea.

Standing up quickly, he said to Andy, "Hook up the bag and start pumping him."

Andy attached a quart-size black bag to the mouth of the tube. A machine filled the bag with oxygen. Andy hand-squeezed the oxygen into the boy's lungs.

The nurse was struggling with a needle in the boy's arm. Dr. Wallace stepped around the table.

"What's wrong, Vicky?"

"His veins have collapsed."

"Let me try it. You get the bottle ready."

Wallace gripped the boy's arm and pressed the needle deep into the flesh. It hit the vein on the first try. Vicky stepped in and attached the tube to a hanging bottle of dextrose. Wallace looked up.

"What the hell is that?"

He stared at the plastic valves of the bag Andy was squeezing. Oozing from the boy's throat was a bloody, pink froth. Wallace could see no explanation for this pulmonary edema unless the boy, in addition to being shot, had also swallowed some sort of caustic.

"Vicky, see if you can suction that stuff out. Andy, you better set up for a trache. Keep pumping and suctioning him. I've got to take a look at the woman."

Across the hall Dr. Allred had also inserted an endotracheal tube in the woman. Chad was bagging her with a similar black oxygen squeeze bag. Ginny Tolsma was trying to X-ray the woman's head when Dr. Wallace hurried in.

"Hon," he said to her, "you're going to have to move a little faster. You've got to finish the woman and do the boy real quick. I might have to do a trache on him. We need those pictures right away."

Ginny nervously realigned a photographic plate beneath the woman's head and maneuvered the bulky machine in closer. She snapped the picture, removed the plate, held another plate to the side of the woman's head, and snapped a second picture. Then she stepped back out of the way and dragged the X-ray machine across the hall.

The two doctors were already examining the woman. She was splotched with blood and vomit. Her breathing was sporadic and only shallow when drawn. Her heart had stopped beating. Her blood pressure was zero.

Wallace said, "Nothing much to save, is there."

"Jess, she doesn't have a chance," said Allred. "I don't even know why we're supporting her."

"I know she's not responding, but I want Hauser to take a look at her before we stop bagging her." He stared at the woman's face. "Boy, she looks familiar."

Dr. James Hauser, the neurosurgeon called in by Dr. Wallace at the time of the alert, appeared in the room and ducked inside the curtain.

"We don't think the woman's got a chance," said Wallace. "Take a quick look at her, then you've got to hurry across the hall and examine the boy."

Dr. Hauser felt the woman's skin, which was cool and clammy. With thumb and forefinger he spread her eyelids and shined a light into her pupils, which were large and unresponsive.

"This doesn't look good at all," he said. "How long has she been here?"

"Not more than four or five minutes," said Wallace.

"What's her blood pressure?"

"I can't get a reading," said Allred.

Dr. Hauser was meticulous but quick with his examination. As he was finishing, Ginny Tolsma brought in the developed X rays. The woman's shadowy skull was marked by two bright metallic spots. The bullet had entered her brain just above her right ear and split in two. One piece of the missile had traveled forward. The other had veered down toward the brain stem. The three doctors only glanced at the X rays.

"I think you should quit," Dr. Hauser said to Chad. "There's nothing more we can do for her."

Chad stopped squeezing the black bag, and the woman made no further attempt to breathe.

Dr. Wallace and Dr. Hauser ran across the hall. Andy was squeezing oxygen into the boy's lungs. At intervals he removed the black bag and Vicky ran a thin, slurping tube down the boy's plastic airway. She was trying to suction out the bubbles. But the bubbles flooded into the airway, faster and faster, redder and redder. Like a machine his lungs were manufacturing copious amounts of reddish foam. It skirted the suction tube, boiled over, and spread across the boy's face. As Dr. Wallace ran into the room, he focused immediately on the boiling pink liquid.

"That stuff won't suction out any faster?"

"No," said Vicky, "and it's getting worse."

Wallace looked quickly at the boy's eyes and thought he saw a slight reaction in the pupils. To Hauser they appeared fixed and dilated.

"Go ahead and take a closer look at him, anyhow," said Wallace, "while I do the trache."

The boy's blood pressure was still zero. His skin was blue and clammy. He was making a hacking attempt to breathe. His left arm had risen from the table slightly, his hand turned to the outside and flexed open. Stiff-armed, it clawed the air.

The blood spurting from the boy's endotracheal tube had begun to splatter, and Andy was hurriedly tying a gown around Wallace as the doctor prepared to open the boy's throat.

"Jess, there's nothing you can do for this boy," Hauser said. "I don't give him more than a few minutes."

"Well, he's not going to die in my emergency room," said Wallace.

"This decerebrate posturing with the hand," continued the neurosurgeon, "and the fixed pupils with this kind of head injury . . . I have never in my life seen this situation in a patient who survived."

Wallace had children of his own not much younger than the boy. When the boy's body had been pulled from the ambulance, Wallace had been struck first by his youth, then by his gasping for air.

"Maybe so," he said to Hauser, "but the kid's still trying to breathe, and we're going to put this trache in and see if we can get him some air. I can't just sit here and watch him die."

"It's your emergency room," said Hauser, "you do what you want. But I'm advising against any heroics."

Andy had prepared the Mayo stand with the tools for the tracheotomy. Wallace took a scalpel from the tray and neatly sliced the boy's throat at the base of his neck. Andy pulled the skin back with hemostats to expose the underlying tissue. Vicky bagged and suctioned the boy through the tube still in his mouth. Dr. Wallace's thick forearms were upraised, his eyes riveted on the slit in the boy's throat. He carefully cut away at the tissue surrounding the trachea. Andy spread the incision wider. The boy's gristly tracheal cartilage emerged. Andy wrenched a hook into it, twisted it slightly, and held it firm as Dr. Wallace cut a dime-size hole in it. Andy spread the cartilage. Wallace reached for the new five-inch plastic tube. As Andy yanked the endotracheal tube from the boy's mouth, Wallace inserted the tracheostomy tube through the cartilage in his throat. Vicky fastened it with cotton ties, reattached the squeeze bag to the new tube, and continued bagging and suctioning the boy. A delicate operation that usually requires fifteen minutes had taken a little under three, and there were no bleeders to tie off. Andy attached a humidifier to the oxygen bag to warm and moisten air for the boy's lungs, while Vicky tried to suction the bubbles flushing out of the new tracheostomy tube.

As soon as he had examined the boy, Dr. Hauser had been paged by the hospital switchboard for another emergency at the McKay-Dee Hospital. Before he left the trauma room, he took up the boy's chart and under Physician's Notes hurriedly wrote the following entry:

> Young white male with gunshot wound of R occipit—has had trache thru which there are copious, pink, frothy secretions. Breathing vigorously but totally unresponsive. Pupils dilated & fixed.
>   Impression: terminal head injury.

Intensive Care had been alerted to prepare for the boy. With his tracheostomy tube now in place he was immediately rushed from the trauma room, down the hall, into the elevator, and up to Intensive Care on the third floor. The IV dangled from his arm as a nurse ran alongside the cart holding the bottle of dextrose. Vicky jogged on the other side, squeezing oxygen into the foam filling his new airway.

Dr. Wallace untied the gown from around his waist and watched the crowd attending to the boy.

"Andy," he said, without turning around, "we're sending that boy up there and he's just going to die." He wadded the bloodstained gown in his fist and threw it into a corner. "What the hell," he said, "maybe Hauser was right."

The cart and the nurses rounded the corner at the end of the hall and disappeared. For a few more seconds Dr. Wallace stared after them. "The whole thing was unreal," he said later, "because I was looking at two people, one who was dead and one who was critically injured for no reason at all. You know, you see people hit in cars and even though it's hard to justify, you can see how it happens. You see a child run into the street and he's hit and killed, it's disturbing and upsetting. There's a certain aspect of Russian roulette to living. But just for somebody deliberately to set out and try, actually try, to kill these people . . . you couldn't understand how anybody's mind could be so depraved. That's what was so unreal about it, to sit there and look and see the straits this kid was in and know that somebody had done it with no more feeling than if they'd crushed a bug."

He turned back and said to Frances Heward, the nursing supervisor, "Fran, why don't you and Andy take the woman on over to the morgue; we'll need to keep her body preserved for the medical examiner."

It had been almost a half hour since the unusual gunshot victims had arrived. Their identities still were unknown. The body of the petite blond-haired woman, listed as Mary Doe, was slipped into the top refrigeration unit in St. Benedict's tiny morgue. Upstairs, in Intensive Care, the teen-age John Doe was spewing blood from his lungs nearly three feet into the air.

No one expected him to live. Even Dr. Wallace, when he sent the boy up to ICU, had listed him as a "no-code," meaning that if the boy's breathing stopped or his heart quit beating, no life-saving measures were to be taken. If the boy's brain shut down to where it no longer was capable of the primitive function of asking for oxygen, there was nothing left of him to save anyhow.

His body remained on the gurney, not enough life in it to warrant transfer to a more permanent bed. They wheeled the gurney into ICU and straight ahead into unit #1, a cubicle with a broad glass front. The boy lay behind the glass, appearing to be a man, much older. His body was mottled gray and white. His cheeks were sunken, and his eyes were dark and hollow-looking. His fingernails were blue-gray. The bloody foam gathered in his lungs, inched its way up the tube in his throat, rising and rising, until his gasping attempt to get oxygen would explode the foam like a small, pink geyser out the end of the tube. The watery pink foam splattered on the nurses and the technicians, until even the walls of the small room were stained with splashes of pink.

Chad Nielsen and John Smith, the respiratory technicians, set up a small pressure ventilator in the cubicle. Dr. Hauser also had left instructions for them to do nothing life-saving.

"Suction him if you want to," he had said, "but if he stops breathing, don't resuscitate him. I don't want you pumping air into a body that's not asking for it."

They dialed the ventilator to Demand, so that it pumped air into the boy's lungs, but only if he initiated each breath. Since the bubbles to be suctioned out would pop and merely reform around the suction tube, they nebulized ethyl alcohol and sprayed the mist into the boy's trache. The mist was designed to break down the surface tension of the bubbles, reducing them to a liquid which then could be easily suctioned out.

As they were spraying the alcohol mist down the boy's airway, John saw two police officers walk into the ICU and stand next to the nurses' desk. He handed the suction tube to Chad and walked out of the cubicle to where the officers were standing. They were still calling the boy John Doe.

"You haven't identified these people yet?" said John.

One of the officers said no, and John said that maybe he could help them eliminate some possibilities.

"A friend of mine in this respiratory therapy program is studying downstairs," he said. "He used to date a girl whose cousin owns the Hi-Fi Shop."

The police knew only that the bodies had been found in the basement of the popular stereo store in downtown Ogden; as yet they had no leads on the victims' identification. They asked John to have his friend come up and take a look at the boy.

John stepped behind the desk and phoned Ray Moser.

"Ray, the police are up here in ICU. I told them about you dating

Claire. They want you to come up and take a look at this boy."

"I don't think I'd be much help," said Ray. "I was standing in the hall when you guys wheeled them by and I didn't recognize either one of them."

"Come on up anyway and tell them yourself," said John. "They're just trying to eliminate possibilities."

Ray left his studies and ran up the stairs to the third floor. He entered Intensive Care, and through the broad plate-glass window he saw John and Chad nebulizing alcohol into the boy's airway. The police stood just to the right of the entrance. Ray glanced at them and walked into the cubicle.

Dr. Wallace had treated a few more patients, then left Dr. Allred in charge of the emergency room. He hurried upstairs to see if the boy was still alive. As he walked in the door, Ray Moser was sliding in among John, Chad, and a covey of nurses to take a look at the boy. Wallace waited by the entrance with the officers. Ray was inside for only a few seconds. When he stepped out again, the casual expression on his face had turned to disbelief.

"It's Cortney," he mumbled, "Cortney Naisbitt."

Wallace was incredulous. "You mean By Naisbitt's boy?"

"Yes, sir. I used to date his sister, Claire."

"Are you sure?"

"Yeah, I saw him go by a few minutes ago and I just thought, 'Well, whoever he is, he won't make it.' But that's Cortney."

One of the officers pulled a small note pad from his pocket and jotted down the victim's name. "Would you mind going downstairs with us to take a look at the woman?"

"No," said Ray, "course not."

Dr. Wallace had already rushed into the cubicle. John and Chad were still spraying a fine mist of ethyl alcohol into the boy's airway, but the alcohol was being overpowered by the edema. The bloody foam gurgled out of the boy's lungs, surged through the mist, and poured into the lines of the ventilator.

Wallace saw the pink froth oozing up the tubes. "What the hell are you doing!" he yelled. "He's trying to breathe! Can't you clear that stuff out?"

"Dr. Hauser told us just to maintain," said John, "not to do anything but nebulize him and suction out what we could."

"I'll be damned! We're not going to sit here and watch the kid die!"

"You want us to shoot straight alcohol down the tube?"

"Anything!" said Wallace. "Just get him more air with that ventilator. I'm going to call Rees, then see if I can get hold of Hauser again. If this kid has hung in here this long, he might have a chance."

Chad and John began a rapid-fire routine. John squirted 20 cc of ethyl alcohol down the boy's airway. Chad capped the ventilator hose back over the mouth of the tube. The alcohol worked on the bubbles. Chad removed the ventilator hose. John suctioned out a small amount of the fluid. Then they started over again.

While the effort to break up the boy's edema continued in the cubicle, Dr. Wallace phoned Dr. Richard Rees, a thoracic surgeon skilled in the use of complicated life-support systems.

"Dick? Jess Wallace. Look, I've got By Naisbitt's boy in ICU. He's been shot in the head, his lungs are full, he may have suffered actual brain death. But he's still alive. I stuck a tube in the kid. I need you to help resuscitate him."

Next he called Dr. Hauser's home, but Hauser had not yet returned from the emergency at McKay-Dee. Wallace left a message with Hauser's wife.

"Tell Jim the kid he looked at before is still alive and trying to breathe. Rees is on his way, and I'd like Jim to come back and take another look at him too. And tell him we just found out it's By Naisbitt's boy."

A quick call to the home of Byron Naisbitt was not answered. As Wallace hung up the phone, the nursing supervisor walked into ICU.

"Fran," said Wallace, "that kid in there is By Naisbitt's boy!"

"You're kidding," she said, "it can't be."

"A friend just identified him. I've tried to get in touch with By, but he's not home. See if you can get hold of his brother Paul, or any of the rest of the family. I don't know what the hell's going on, but somebody ought to be down here with this kid!"

THE MURDERS

That afternoon, Cortney Naisbitt had hurried along the sidewalk in downtown Ogden, his reflection darting in and out of storefront windows. At sixteen Cortney was developing in the mold of his father and two older brothers, all exceedingly handsome men. Nearly six feet tall, he was thin and well-muscled. His hair was blond and hung in bangs angled across the forehead of his rather elfish face: a face with a slightly pointed chin, gray-green eyes, freckle-dotted nose, and an impish grin of straight, white teeth. As he moved, he seemed to bounce, his blond hair lifting and settling smoothly across his forehead, his face hardly concealing a rush of joy. As afternoons go, it had been the most exciting of his life.

A late-April sun cast square shadows of buildings across the city streets and blazed down on rush hour traffic entering the intersections along busy Washington Boulevard. As Cortney came abreast of Inkley's, a variety store selling cameras and film, a tall, pretty girl with glossy lips and auburn hair crossed at the light and hurried toward him on the sidewalk. The girl was smiling and waving, and when she got closer she yelled, "Cortney!"

At first Cortney seemed not to recognize his old neighborhood playmate, Cora Beth Baggs. Cora was also sixteen, and Cortney hadn't seen her since she had moved from the neighborhood in third grade. Now she stood in front of him only vaguely resembling the little girl he had known as a child.

Cortney's forehead wrinkled. "Cora Beth?"

"Yes!" she beamed. "Gosh, Cort, how are things?" And before he could answer, she said: "Are you still living up on Mitchell Drive? I really miss that old neighborhood. I really liked it up there."

"That's right," said Cortney, "you moved like in the third or fourth grade."

"Third," she said. Then she grabbed hold of his arm and laughed. "Remember the old Easter egg hunts?"

Celebrating Easter on Mitchell Drive had been a neighborhood occasion with hundreds of brightly colored eggs and dozens of children looking for them. Cora and Cortney reminisced about the egg hunts and argued over who had found the most eggs. Cora did most of the talking. She felt that she could have talked to Cortney about anything and he would have listened. "He was light and very pleasant that day. Very happy," she later remembered.

Finally, she said to him, "Well, what have you been up to?"

"I just soloed," said Cortney.

"In a plane?"

"Yeah, first time."

"Cortney," she said, "that is so exciting!"

But before Cortney could tell her how it felt to be alone at the controls of an airplane, Cora interrupted to ask him if he knew a friend of hers who was also taking flying lessons. When Cortney said no, Cora dropped the subject of flying.

"Are you going into Inkley's?" she asked. "I've got to pick up some pictures."

"I do, too," said Cortney. "My mom and dad just got back from Hong Kong."

In Inkley's, Cortney charged the pictures to his parents' account, and the clerk handed him a large sack of colored slides. With the sack in his hand Cortney then browsed along the camera counter until Cora came up behind him and poked him in the ribs. "Which way are you going now?"

"To the Hi-Fi Shop," said Cortney. "Why don't you walk down there with me?"

Cora had a schoolgirl crush on Cortney's cousin, Brent Richardson, who owned the Hi-Fi Shop. She said, "Okay."

They strolled toward the shop, Cora telling Cortney how her parents had been "getting on her case" the past few weeks about being home early with the car on weeknights. She said she shouldn't really even be walking down to the Hi-Fi Shop with him. But when they arrived in front of the shop, she asked Cortney, "Do you know if Brent's in there?"

"He's out of town," said Cortney. "I think Stan's working."

"Yeah. Well," said Cora, "I guess I really should be getting home then. I've got Mom's car, and she said, you know, 'Be home at six!' " She looked at her watch. "I'm already going to be a little late, it's ten to six now." Then she added: "You know where I live now, don't you? I live right across from your grandmother."

"That's right," said Cortney.

"Okay, now you know where I live, come on over anytime and visit me."

"Yeah, I'd like that," said Cortney, "I haven't seen you for so long."

"I'm going to hold you to it. I've got to go. Good seeing you, Cortney."

"Good seeing you, Cora Beth. Bye," said Cortney.

Cora had left her mother's car in the parking alcove just behind House of Fabrics, a few doors down from the Hi-Fi Shop. She turned and waved good-bye again to Cortney, then disappeared into the store.

Cortney turned and strode between the stereo-filled display windows of the Hi-Fi Shop, stopping to reach for the door handle and swing it open. The glass door closed behind him with a metallic clack, and the quiet, cozy atmosphere of the shop suddenly muffled the noise from the street. The Hi-Fi Shop was a narrow store, stretching to the alley where Cortney had parked his car. As Cortney walked toward the back, the soft, speckled carpet hushed his quick footsteps. He was in a hurry, bouncing with his long stride past the record racks and glass counters, past shadowed alcoves of receivers and amplifiers spotlighted by small ceiling lamps. Save for the crinkling of the package in his hand, the store was silent.

Closing time on Mondays was six. The store clerks, Stan Walker and Michelle Ansley, should have been turning off the equipment, placing the records back in their jackets, ringing up the day's receipts on the cash register. No one was even in the front of the store. The cash register sat quietly. Halfway through the shop, Cortney could see Stan in the sound room, the last room before the door to the alley. In the sound room, sets of speakers on the floor and mounted on the walls were wired to a master control panel so sound could be switched from one set to another for comparison. Stan was up against the wall on the right. He was still. Two steps beyond him was the landing for the steps leading around to the right and down into the basement. At the back edge of the landing was the door leading to the alley.

As Cortney entered the room, a burnished shaft of light from the late afternoon sun shot through a rear window of thick glass tile and dispersed across the huge speakers squatting on the floor. Cortney walked into the smoky play of light.

"Thanks for letting me park behind the store, Stan."

"Stop, Cortney," Stan said.

Cortney already was past him, reaching for the doorknob.

"Stop, Cortney! He's going to shoot you!"

But Cortney, in his hurry to get home, had turned the doorknob and was starting out the door.

To his left he suddenly heard another voice.

"Take another step, and I'll put a bullet in you."

Cortney stopped and turned, and there on the other side of the broad shaft of light was a tall black man. He was aiming a gun at Cortney's face.

Cortney slammed the door and threw his hands up, the package of slides falling to the floor.

"Geez, if you hadn't said anything," mumbled Cortney, "I never would've even known you had a gun."

Then Cortney was tumbling down the stairs. He was being kicked and punched in the stomach. Someone's knee connected with his balls. He fell into the basement and lay upon the shag carpet, sweaty, frightened, trying to catch his breath. Another man was waiting in the basement shadows.

He was a short black man, not more than five and a half feet tall. When he walked around the room, his ass cocked in such a way that he appeared to be strutting. It made him seem almost portly, but his body was hard. Thick ropes of muscle spread upward from his arms and chest, over his shoulders, and climbed his neck to support a swollen and misshapen head. His tall forehead sloped to meet the back of it. Though his head swelled large for his body, his eyes seemed too small and defined for his head, too sharp and glinty for the high smooth forehead, the broad nose, the bulbous lips. He pulled Cortney's hands behind him and tied them together with plastic speaker wire, then bound his feet.

Cortney lay parallel to the wall at the right of the stairs, his head toward the far corner. He had been in the room many times. It was decorated to resemble a den. Green shag carpeting covered the fourteen-foot-square floor. Three walls were painted eggshell and the fourth, opposite the stairs, was a sliding wood panel, behind which were the workshop and storage. Perpendicular to him ran a display rack filled with new quadraphonic amplifiers hooked to a console for demonstration. That afternoon the room was littered with boxes and with amplifiers waiting for repair.

Stan too had been tied up on the floor of the basement and now lay with his head toward the wall opposite Cortney. A tall, husky boy of twenty, Stan had been left in charge of the shop while Brent Richardson was in San Francisco for a one-day trade show. Stan had thick brown hair and a broad smile of white, slightly imperfect teeth. He liked to wear heavy hiking boots and plaid shirts with the sleeves rolled up, reminding Brent of a jolly lumberjack. But Stan had a genius for electronics and sound systems and an easy way with customers.

The previous Friday night the Hi-Fi Shop had sponsored a dance at Ben Lomond High and Stan had been the disc jockey. Brent had helped him set up the sound equipment, and Michelle, who had worked at the shop for only a week, accompanied them. When the equipment was in place and Stan was testing it with his favorite Jethro Tull sounds, Michelle had dragged Brent onto the dance floor. Michelle's brunette hair cascaded in loose curls about her shoulders, framing a face of exquisite, porcelain features. At nineteen she was a curvaceous five feet five inches tall. Though she was engaged, she loved to flirt, and Brent found her warm and fun; it was a side of his employees he rarely saw. Brent had hired Michelle because he liked to keep bright, pretty girls working in the store. They were good for business.

Now, Michelle lay next to Stan, both stretched in front of the wall of amplifiers, their hands and feet tightly bound with speaker wire.

The black man who had called Cortney back into the shop was now in the basement, watching over them. Physically, he bore little resemblance to the man who had tied up Cortney. He was tall and athletic. Above his thin upper lip was a distinct, neatly trimmed mustache. As he stood in the basement near the foot of the stairs, he held a .38 in his hand.

Upstairs, Cortney could hear the short man and another man in the parking alley behind the shop, one shifting Stan's old utility jeep from near the rear entrance, the other backing up a truck or a van in its place. Noise from the muffler came up tightly against the outside wall, the exhaust echoing loudly off the back door. When the engine shut down, the footsteps began: quick, heavy footsteps out, a pause at the back door, long strides back in. Some of the footsteps popped or squeaked, the men stepping on spilled flakes of packing material. Occasionally came a muffled *clank!* as one of them hit the metal fire grating just above Cortney's head.

Cortney, Stan, and Michelle remained tied and lying on the floor among the boxes and amplifiers, not knowing what their captors had planned for them once the movement upstairs had finally stopped. They lay there while an hour passed, an hour of squeaking and popping and shuffling and clanking upstairs, and stillness in the basement. Earlier, one of the men had threatened to shoot all of them if anything went wrong. Lying in the basement, Stan and Courtney tried talking to the man now holding the gun on them. They pleaded with him to leave them alone, to take the equipment and then be gone. Stan did most of the talking. He was good at reasoning with people. But then Cortney said something about the stereo equipment the men were hauling out of the shop, something that just slipped out of his mouth and that Stan thought would anger the man.

"Shut up," he whispered to Cortney, "do you want them to shoot us?"

"They're going to, anyhow," said Cortney. "Aren't they?"

After school that afternoon Cortney had gone to his flying lesson at the Ogden Municipal Airport, early as always, and walked among the rows of light private airplanes, their wings and tails anchored by drooping chains. He could hear the high-pitched engines of small planes taxiing down the runway, then the receding drone as they lifted off, gained altitude, and shrank in the distance. In moments the planes would become silent white specks against the mountains.

Flying had grown to be an obsession with Cortney. As far back as kindergarten he had brought model airplanes to school and assembled them with puddles of glue. Then he had advanced to the sophisticated radio-control planes with the broad wingspans and the light balsa wings stretched over with thin fabric and painted with shiny wood dope. He was fascinated with the physics of it all, the way vortex and vacuum and the speed of air molecules all came together to lift a wing so simply and effortlessly. Cortney's dreams were filled with wings and clouds and sky the way homecoming queens and the winning run melted into the wishes of most boys.

Cortney's flight instructor was Wolfgang Lange, a round-faced, stocky German of thirty-six with bright blue, jocular eyes. When Wolfgang talked about flying, his hands fluttered and arced as though they were little planes.

"Cort was a happy kid and a little bit of a wise guy like all sixteen-year-olds," recalled Wolfgang. "But he was an easy student to teach. I mean very, very easy. I called him an airport bum, because he came out here even when he wasn't flying. I asked him once, 'What're you gonna do after you graduate from school? You gonna be a doctor?' And he says: 'Oh, no. I want to be an aeronautical engineer.' He had the stuff for it, too. I'd show him a maneuver once and he'd have it mastered. There was a few times I even had to hold him back just a little to put him in his place. I try to teach 'em judgment, too. But it was a joy to fly with him. When I knew he was coming out, I knew it was gonna be easy for me. Cortney just loved to fly."

It was a warm day in early spring. The snow had disappeared from the ground and from halfway up the awesome rock wall known as the Wasatch mountain front. The jagged peaks would remain white even into summer. Just prior to 4:30 Cortney wandered over to the small Cessna building, where Wolfgang had his office. Wolf was waiting for him.

"Hello, Cort," he said.

"Hi, Wolf."

"Have you done your homework?"

"Sure," said Cortney. "I know what we're going to do. I'm pretty sure I know how to do it."

"Any questions," asked Wolf, "anything you don't understand?"

Cortney said what he always said. "Nope. Let's go fly."

They left the office and walked down a row of parked planes until they came to a red and white Cessna 150 Skyhawk. After removing the tie-down chains and inspecting the outside of the plane, Cortney climbed into the left seat and Wolfgang into the right.

"Okay," said Wolf, "it's your airplane. I'm just watching."

Cortney flew the Cessna in wide arcs around the airfield, landing and then gaining speed to take off again. Wolfgang had a policy never to tell a student when he would be soloing for the first time. Otherwise, it made the student nervous and he didn't sleep the night before. Somewhere between ten and fourteen hours in the air, the student would begin naturally to reckon with his own mistakes before the instructor had to. At that point, Wolfgang would get out of the plane. As he appraised Cortney's performance that afternoon, he knew that Cortney was ready to fly on his own.

When they landed after the third touch-and-go, Wolfgang reached for the radio mike next to Cortney's right knee.

"Ogden Control, this is Wolf. I've got a first solo here, so give him a little room, okay?"

Wolfgang replaced the mike and looked at Cortney. "Now, I want you to go back up. I'm going to get out of the plane. Remember, I weigh about one hundred seventy-five pounds. When I get out, the plane will be flying faster because it's just you in here. And it will glide farther. So you have to make the proper corrections. Keep your nose down when you climb out."

"Gotcha," said Cortney.

"Now hold on a minute. When you come down and you start to glide, you gotta close your throttle a little bit sooner, because it's going to glide farther on you. You got that?"

"Yeah."

"Any questions about anything?"

"Nope."

"Okay, I want you to go back out and make three touch-and-gos, like we just did, and then on the fourth time around make a full stop landing. You nervous? You don't look nervous."

Cortney shook his head.

"And, Cortney, don't go buzzin' around ten feet off the deck like you like to do. Remember, judgment."

Wolf stepped out of the plane and signaled to Cortney that he was a safe distance from the propeller. Cortney mentally checked off the oil level, the gas drain to rid the fuel of water, the primer to pump the fuel directly to the cylinders.

"Clear!" he yelled out the window.

The propeller turned slowly, caught, and whirred into invisibility. The plane vibrated, and the loud thrum of the prop filled the cockpit. Cortney checked the oil pressure and called the tower for clearance.

"Ogden Control, this is Cessna one-one-zero-niner-two at Cessna building to taxi to takeoff."

"Roger, Cessna zero-niner-two, you're cleared to taxi to runway three-four. Wind is two-seven-zero at six, altimeter niner-niner-eight."

The propeller pulled the light plane slowly along the taxiway. Cortney brought the plane up to the stop line, adjacent to the runway, where he ran the engine up to 1,700 rpm to check the magnetos. He scanned his instrument panel. Everything was functioning properly. He swung his rudder in each direction and switched his radio to Tower frequency.

"Ogden Tower, this is Cessna zero-niner-two, ready for takeoff."

"Roger, zero-niner-two, cleared for immediate takeoff."

With the rudder pedals on the floor Cortney swung the plane in a tight turn to the right and onto the runway, which disappeared into a dot, seemingly at the base of the mountains miles away. Cortney eased open the throttle. The plane moved forward, all noise and vibration, gaining speed until it was hurtling toward the dot at sixty miles an hour. Cortney reached down by his right knee and spun the trim wheel to raise the nose, but only slightly, as Wolfgang had warned him. Then the wheels sprang from the runway and he was climbing, angled toward the sky.

Cortney gained altitude, rising over the freeway, over the city, aimed at the undulating, white-capped wall of the Wasatch Range.

In a long, wide arc he banked the plane to the left, heading west toward Antelope Island, the big mountain rising amidst the afternoon shimmers of the Great Salt Lake. He looked down upon the green and brown farming squares on the plain below, the orderly roofs of housing tracts and trailer courts, the drying puddles of white crust left behind by the receding salt lake. The view had been his many times before, but now he was flying above it all for the first time alone.

He circled back toward the south and reached for the radio mike at his knee.

"Ogden Tower, this is Cessna one-one-zero-niner-two ready to land."

"Roger, Cessna zero-niner-two, you're cleared to land."

The red and white Cessna approached the runway from the southwest. Cortney remembered at the last minute to ease up on his throttle. The plane floated down toward the runway. The concrete came up quickly in sharp focus and moved swiftly beneath him. The plane listed slightly to the left, the left wheel hit, then immediately the right. The plane bounced. Cortney picked up speed again, hit sixty miles an hour, rolled the trim wheel, and lifted off for his second loop around the airport.

When he had landed for the fourth time, Cortney taxied to the end of the runway, switching frequencies on his radio.

"Ogden Control, this is Cessna one-one-zero-niner-two, off the active, would like to taxi to the Cessna building."

"Roger, Cessna zero-niner-two, cleared to taxi to Cessna building."

Cortney steered the plane along the taxiway, maneuvered it into the empty tie-down slot near the building, and cut the engine. Wolfgang had been watching from the time Cortney had first taxied out to the runway until he had landed for the last time. He opened Cortney's door.

"See," he said, "it flies without the instructor."

Cortney jumped out of the cockpit. "That was easier than I thought it was going to be!"

"That first landing you made was a little rough, but not bad."

"I know, I almost forgot to close the throttle like you told me."

"You'll learn. When you come out next time, we'll go around together first, then I'll let you solo again."

"Okay!"

"In the meantime, you better get your butt up to that ground school tonight."

"Yes, Master Instructor."

"I mean it."

"Okay, I'll go, I'll go. I just think I'm wasting my time up at that college."

"I know, but you gotta get that written examination passed, or you can't get a license. So get your rear end in gear, you haven't got a lot of time till that class starts at seven. Come on in the office now and we'll fill out your logbook."

When they walked into the office, Wolf said to the secretary, "Get the scissors out, we're going to cut his shirttail!"

For months Cortney had waited for this moment. It was a ceremony of sorts, informal but meaningful, like a pilot getting his wings. Cortney pulled his shirt out and the secretary snipped the tail off and pinned it to the wall with the other shirttails. While Cortney and Wolfgang filled out Cortney's logbook, she typed a card and placed it just above the shirttail. The card read:

CORTNEY NAISBITT—MONDAY, APRIL 22, 1974—WOLFGANG LANGE

Wolfgang signed Cortney's logbook and Cortney went over to the wall and looked at the shirttail with his name above it. "I can't wait to tell my mom and dad," he said to the secretary.

"Cort!" said Wolfgang. "Ground school."

"I know, I'll be there."

Cortney was walking out the door when the office phone rang. It was for him.

Another hour in the basement had passed. It was now just after eight o'clock. The vehicle parked at the back door had started up and pulled away across the cinder alley, and another had been backed up in its place. The tall man who had stood over Cortney and the others in the basement had gone back upstairs, and the footsteps overhead had begun again. Back and forth they traveled through the sound room to the rear door of the shop. They had been traversing the sound room but a short while when suddenly above his head Cortney heard two men running. The men ran to the back door and raced down the stairs in quick, indistinguishable footsteps. They stood in the shadows at Cortney's feet, away from the shaft of light still beaming down the stairs. One was the taller man who earlier had held the .38 on Cortney, Stan, and Michelle. The other was the short man with the high forehead. Cortney could hear them both panting.

In the alley a car door slammed. Cortney heard footsteps crunching on the gravel. They paused near the back door; for seconds they shuffled. Then he heard the crunching again. It moved toward the door.

The Hi-Fi Shop was silent as the door opened.

Gary Naisbitt hadn't thought about it for six weeks. When he awoke that morning, he suddenly recalled: "It's Monday, the twenty-second! I'm supposed to have a tooth filled today!"

At twenty-nine Gary Naisbitt was a handsome man: five eleven, slim, muscular, with light brown, very straight hair. He was the Naisbitt's eldest son, the loner in the family, intense, articulate, introspective. Although he held college degrees in chemistry and German, he was now involved in real estate, but was becoming increasingly unhappy with the profession. His unhappiness had deepened recently when his Danish wife, Eva, had left him to return to Denmark.

The dentist's office was in Ogden, twenty-five miles from Gary's apartment in Centerville. He arrived a few minutes late, had his tooth filled, and departed with a rubbery jaw. It was too late to return to his office, and as long as he was in town, it seemed a good time to look for a house he had promised to find for a friend.

Gary talked with one owner till late in the afternoon. When he left, he realized he hadn't eaten anything since breakfast. The Novocain had worn off long ago and he was getting hungry. He thought, Maybe I'll just drop by Mom and Dad's and see what's for dinner.

He was driving to his parents' house when he had second thoughts about seeing them again so soon. On Friday they had returned from two weeks in Hong Kong, and he had spent the entire weekend with them and Cortney. His father had shot every roll of film on the trip at the wrong film speed, but Gary and Cortney had taken the film to Inkley's for special processing. The pictures would be ready on Monday or Tuesday. It had been an enjoyable weekend, but Gary didn't want to return to their house so soon.

No, I was just home all weekend, he reasoned, and if I show up again today, they'll wonder why I'm here, and they're always interested in whether I'm working and making money, and I haven't done anything for a while, so what have I got to report?

Then he remembered the TV set he was to pick up at his uncle's house just two blocks away. Oh, well, he decided, I'll just stop for a minute, say hi and be friendly, maybe stay for dinner.

His mother was lying on the couch in the den. Carol Naisbitt was a diminutive woman. Her fine-spun blond hair was short and puffed in a medium coiffure, wispy bangs hanging across her forehead. Perhaps because of her vivacity, Carol's figure was still trim and petite at fifty-two. She was not a beautiful woman, not to the extent that her husband was a strikingly handsome man. But Carol was possessed of two lasting qualities that made her unusually appealing: exquisite taste and a high-energy charm that had drawn people to her since she was a little girl.

Gary opened with his standard "What's going on?"

"Hi," his mother responded. "Not much, just doing a little reading."

"A little reading," Gary repeated. "How are you feeling now?"

"Better," said his mother. "I've got this same headache I've had all weekend, but other than that not too bad."

"Probably just jet lag," said Gary. He couldn't think of anything else to say, until he remembered the pictures. "Hey, are the pictures back from Inkley's yet?"

His mother said no, but that Cortney was still out at the airport. "Why don't you call and see if they're ready," she suggested. "Then have Cortney pick them up on his way home."

Gary called Inkley's. The pictures had been successfully processed and were ready to be picked up, so he dialed Cortney at the airport.

"Hold on a minute," said the secretary who answered. "He's just heading out the door." Gary could hear her in the background. "Cortney, you've got a telephone call."

Cortney picked up the phone.

"Hello?"

"Cort? I'm glad I caught you before you left."

"Oh, hi, Gary."

"How was your flight lesson today?"

"Well, I . . . uh, it was good, yeah, it was good."

"You sound funny."

"Funny ha-ha, or funny weird?"

"Okay, never mind," said Gary. "How about doing me a favor on your way home? It'll only take a minute." Cortney said nothing. "I want you to stop by Inkley's and pick up those pictures of Mom and Dad's trip."

"Gary, I . . . well, I kinda wanted to get home, you know. I've got ground school at seven, I've got to eat dinner and get ready."

Gary asked him again, and Cortney said, "Oh, all right, I guess it'll only take a few minutes."

"Thanks," said Gary, "save me a trip. You can park either behind the bank and they'll validate the parking ticket for you in Inkley's, or you can park behind the Hi-Fi Shop, but if you do that, don't stand around talking to Brent all day, come on home. I'm anxious to see if those pictures came out all right."

"Okay, okay, no problem. Are you staying for dinner, again?"

"Yeah, I think so."

"Okay, I'll see you then, I've got to get going."

"Thanks, Cort."

Cortney hung up before Gary could say good-bye.

Gary said to his mother, "Boy, Cort sure was antsy over the phone, what's his problem?"

"I don't know," said his mother, "maybe he soloed today. Wolfgang won't ever tell them, but Cortney said he had it all figured out." She chuckled softly. "Maybe he wants to surprise us."

Cortney's aeronautics ground school was at Weber State College, only a few blocks from the Naisbitt home. His mother had dinner

ready for him at six. At six thirty he still had not shown up. She
had put his food back in the oven to keep it warm.

"I wonder where Cortney is," she said to Gary. "He's going to be
late for class."

Gary was glancing through the evening paper.

"He's probably in the shop talking to Brent. I told him not to stop
and talk, but if he soloed today he's probably telling Brent about it."

As Gary and his mother were discussing Cortney, Byron Naisbitt
arrived home from the hospital. In Ogden medical circles the
swarthy, hazel-eyed obstetrician was known as the Silver Fox. At
fifty-one, his gleaming hair was the crowning touch to a rugged,
almost Latin countenance. His voice was low and raspy, and though
he sang off-key, he seemed always to be singing. When he wasn't
singing, he puckered his lips and whistled. When he was neither
singing nor whistling, he hummed. He was a thick-chested, robust
man, and though he was reputed to be aloof outside of his office, he
was charming to his patients and they adored him. He delivered
nearly four hundred babies a year. Into his hands and those of his
younger brother, Paul, a large part of the population of Ogden under
twenty-one had been born.

The back door snapped shut, and he walked into the den adjacent
to the kitchen.

"Howdy! Hey, Garrr! Where's Cort?"

"I don't know, By," said Carol walking over to him. "I've had his
dinner ready for him for half an hour so he could get right to class,
but he hasn't come home yet."

"Do you think the little bugger soloed today?"

"We're not sure. Gary talked to him on the phone about an hour
ago and he sounded excited about something, but he wouldn't say
anything else."

"Wellll, for hell's sakes, if you're worried about him that's your
answer right there. That little clinker's still out at the airport celebrating with his friends."

"By, it's not like him to stay out there without at least calling. You
know that."

"Well now, calm down, Shorty," he said, using her nickname.
"It's only been a half hour." He gave his wife a quick, playful hug.
"If we got upset every time one of the kids was a half hour late,

we'd both be frittering around the funny farm. Right, Gar?" He winked at Gary and let go of his wife. "Let's eat! All this talking's got me hungry."

At dinner Byron and Gary discussed a recent real estate transaction that was beginning to turn sour on them. Carol half listened while she dragged her fork around her plate, picking at her food. Each time a car passed by the house, her eyes snapped to the ceiling and darted back and forth while she listened. As each sound faded, her head lowered and she went back to pushing her food around her plate.

Byron watched her out of the corner of his eye. Finally, he put down his fork.

"Okay. Gary, what did Cortney tell you when you talked to him on the phone?"

Carol turned and looked at Gary.

"I just called him out at the airport, and he hemmed and hawed a little bit and said he'd had a good lesson, and I asked him to stop by Inkley's on his way home and pick up the pictures of your trip, the ones you blew. . . ."

"Ricky-tick cameras," said Byron.

Gary chuckled and glanced at his mother. Her expression hadn't changed. She was still staring at him, waiting for him to tell the rest of his story.

"Anyhow," Gary continued, "I told him he could probably park behind Brent's store, but not to stop and talk to Brent all day. Then he asked me if I was staying for dinner, I said I probably was, and he said, 'Okay, I'll see you when I get home.' He's probably still down there talking to Brent."

"The Hi-Fi Shop closes at six o'clock," Carol reminded them both. "It's now after seven."

Byron thought about this for a second.

"I imagine he got to talking with Brent and hung around for a while after the shop closed and then realized how late it was and decided to go straight to class without coming home. That makes sense, doesn't it?"

Carol jerked her head to look at her husband. "Does it make sense that he wouldn't call home and let us know what he's doing?"

"In all the excitement," said Byron, "he probably forgot. It's not like he's never forgotten to call home before."

Carol stood up and began grabbing the empty dishes from the table. "I don't care what you two say, I know something's wrong and you're not going to talk me out of it!"

Byron looked at Gary, and motioned with his head that the two of them should retire to the den.

In silence Carol rinsed the dishes and loaded the dishwasher. It was now seven thirty. She took Cortney's dry dinner out of the oven and threw it down the disposal. Then she untied her apron, turned off the kitchen lights, and marched past her husband and son without saying a word. They heard the jangle of her car keys and watched her walk back through the den and out the back door, never looking in their direction.

The basement of the Hi-Fi Shop brightened, then quickly turned gray again, as the back door opened and closed. With their backs to Cortney, the two men stood in the shadow to the side of the staircase, their guns drawn. The footsteps paused at the top of the stairs. Then they moved slowly into the sound room. They were not as distinct, not as purposeful, as the footsteps of the two men, but rather contemplative, as though strolling through a museum. They passed above Cortney's head, avoided the fire grating, then stopped where the office would be. From the office one could see all the way to the front of the store.

For a short while the footsteps remained still and the shop was silent. Then suddenly they turned and were coming back, now more forthright, a little quicker. They touched lightly on the grating. The short man crept up the stairs, his body sideways and snug against the banister. The footsteps padded above Cortney's head into the middle of the sound room. The taller man stepped silently to the base of the stairs and aimed his gun upward. The other man crouched at the top. The footsteps neared the back door. They turned the corner to come down the stairs. The short man raised his gun to eye level. Cortney heard someone gasp.

The taller man started. "What are you doin' here, man!" he yelled up the stairs.

There was no answer. The short man flicked his gun toward the basement. The footsteps, now heavier, descended the stairs. The taller man followed them with the barrel of his revolver.

A man appeared at the bottom of the stairs. He was thick through the arms and barrel-chested. He stepped slowly to the middle of the room and stood, his hands at his side, as the two men held their guns on him.

Cortney heard Stan moan, "Why'd you have to come down, Dad?"

His last word was no sooner spoken than the sound of a gunshot exploded against the acoustical walls.

The taller man jumped, whirled to the short man behind him.

"What'd you do that for, man?"

There was another flash, another explosion.

Michelle screamed, "I'm just nineteen, I don't want to die!"

Cortney screamed at the wall. "I'm too young to die!"

The smell of burnt gunpowder drifted about the room.

Then Stan said, "Just take the stuff and go, we can't identify you."

"Take the gear and leave," added his father. "We can't identify you, we won't identify you."

Mr. Walker was still standing in the middle of the room. Cortney could hear Stan and Michelle pleading with the two men. No one was shot. In a sudden frenzy the short man had pumped two bullets into the wall.

The two men stood at the bottom of the steps, holding their guns and arguing. The short man waved his gun angrily toward the south wall.

"What about me being booked?" he said. His speech was peculiar, almost singsong, yet deep and proper-sounding.

"*You* been booked before," said the taller one, "but I ain't got a record, man."

From the middle of the room Mr. Walker said, "If you guys'll just take the stuff and get out of here, we won't identify you."

Cortney still faced the wall. In the alley he heard another car pull in. A car door opened and slammed shut. Footsteps, short and hurried, went into the back of the Kandy Korn shop next door. The short man stopped his arguing and bounded up the steps. He eased the back door open, then slipped into the alley. Light footsteps were shuffling around the car that had just parked.

"Your fodder in dere?" said the man.

"What?" It was the voice of a young girl.

"Your fodder in dere, in dat shop?"

"I'm sorry, sir," she said, "I can't understand you."

"Your fodder, is he in dat shop?"

"Oh. No, my mother's in there, she owns it."

The voices stopped. The taller man stood at the base of the stairs, holding his gun on Mr. Walker. His eyes darted from the basement up to the back door and down again. Cortney heard the short man slip inside the door and start down the stairs. The taller man looked up.

"What're you gonna do now?" he asked.

"What I told you we would do," said the short man. He told the taller man to get out the bottle, that he would find something in the back room to pour it in.

The short man pulled aside the sliding panel door leading to the workshop, reached up on tiptoe and with a flick of his wrist screwed a bare light bulb loosely into its socket. In a few seconds he returned with a green plastic cup. The panel door he left ajar, allowing a sliver of light to fall from the workshop into the front room, which was rapidly growing darker.

Mr. Walker still stood in the middle of the room. The taller man held his gun on him. With his other hand he grasped a container nearly a foot high, wrapped in a brown paper bag. He unscrewed the lid and poured a thick blue liquid into the green cup the short man held out to him.

Cortney heard Michelle say, "What is that?"

"It's a mixture of vodka and a German drug," said the taller man. "It'll make you sleep for a coupla hours."

The short man chuckled deep in his throat but said nothing. He handed the cup to Mr. Walker and motioned for him to administer the liquid to the three young people lying on the floor. Mr. Walker stood still. The man pushed the cup closer to him, but Mr. Walker looked away.

The taller man gave a sharp twist to the cylinder in his revolver. "Man, there is a gun at your head!"

Mr. Walker did not move.

The short man set the cup on a stool. With his gun he motioned for Mr. Walker to step in front of the doorway leading to the workshop. He pulled a length of cord from a pile on the floor and tied Mr. Walker's hands behind his back.

"Lay down," he ordered.

Mr. Walker knelt on a plastic runner reaching from the foot of the stairs to the workshop door. The short man grunted as he pulled tight the last knots around Mr. Walker's ankles, then left him lying on his stomach.

He rose from the floor and picked up his gun. The other man had replaced the cap on the bottle and was holding his revolver on Mr. Walker.

"Now what?" he asked.

The short man pulled him over near the bottom step, where the two men talked in a terse whisper, the short one waving his gun over the room and saying again that he had been booked. But the other man hadn't been booked and he didn't seem to care about being identified. He was beginning to sound less sure of himself.

"I can't go through with this," he said to the short man. "I'm chicken."

Before he could say anything else, another car drove into the alley and parked. A car door slammed. Footsteps started toward the Hi-Fi Shop door. The young girl to whom the short man had spoken only minutes earlier called out.

"Ma'am, you left your lights on."

Carol Naisbitt had screeched out of the driveway from their home on the east bench overlooking Ogden. Then she had slammed the car to a stop, popped it into drive, and punched the accelerator. If her husband and son were not concerned about Cortney, she was not afraid to go looking for him by herself.

She drove the family station wagon to Weber State College and cruised through the parking lots of the small campus looking for Cortney's old brown Buick. When she didn't see the car, she parked and found his classroom. She peered in. Cortney wasn't there. She returned home, ignored her husband and son, proceeded up to her bedroom and called Cortney's friend, Chris Southwick.

"No, Mrs. Naisbitt," said Chris, "I haven't seen Cort since school this afternoon."

She called two more of Cortney's friends, but neither could add to Chris's story.

With this new information she stomped downstairs and confronted Byron and Gary. Neither had a chance to look up before she started in.

"Cortney's car is not anywhere on the campus. Cortney is not in his classroom. Chris has not seen him since school. Neither has Dave, neither has Kelly. The Hi-Fi Shop has been closed for two hours. . . ." She was in tears as she ticked off the facts.

Gary had witnessed this scene before. As far back as he could remember, his mother was constantly worrying about one of her four children.

"Mom, look," he said, "Cortney is sixteen years old now, he can take care of himself. You worried about me, you worried about Brett, you worried about Claire, and did anything ever happen to us? No. All that worrying for nothing. I know Cort's the baby, but you're going to have to let him grow up sometime. Now just settle down, if something was wrong you'd hear from him. He's just gotten sidetracked somewhere."

Her husband said nothing.

Carol's eyes flashed. She turned abruptly and went back upstairs. In a few minutes, her eyes red and swollen, she returned to the den. She was mad, and she was hurt.

"Aren't you two concerned at all?" she yelled. "Something has happened to Cortney! I know it! And you won't even try to help me find him!"

"Carol! This is just foolhardy," said her husband, "and I think it's gone far enough. Cortney told me this morning he's got two papers to write for school tomorrow. I will bet you that his little butt is right now sitting in the library working on those papers. Now I wish you would calm down a little bit. Get hold of yourself. You're overreacting again. There's no reason to be acting like this. . . ."

Her eyes quivered as she glared at her husband. "How can you sit there and keep making excuses? He's at the airport! He's talking to Brent! He's in class! He's at the library!" She mimicked her husband. "How many more excuses are you going to come up with?"

"You know I'm on call all this week," said Byron. "I've got to stay by the phone. Now just what the hell do you want me to do?"

"I want you to sit there and be unconcerned about your youngest son, that's what I want!"

Byron stared at the ceiling, flexing his jaw. Carol grabbed the car keys again and ran out of the house, slamming the door behind her. They heard her screech out of the driveway for the second time and roar down the street.

"You were right," Byron said to Gary. "She always did worry too much about you kids. I like her spunk, but sometimes she gets a little too spunky. I guess she'll be all right."

The back door of the Hi-Fi Shop burst back on its hinges. Carol Naisbitt gazed down the stairs, directly into the barrel of the taller man's revolver.

"What're you doin' here, man!"

"I'm checking on my son," she snapped. "What is going on here?"

When Cortney heard his mother's voice at the top of the stairs, he said to himself, "God damn it!" But he was still tied and helpless, facing the wall, afraid to speak out. He said nothing as his mother stood on the landing above. Then the short man sprinted up the stairs, squeezed in beside her, and waved her down into the basement. When they reached the bottom, he ran up the stairs again, pressed the door shut, and with a sharp click threw the bolt.

The light now was dim. Only the workshop bulb cast a faint glow through the crack left by the sliding panel. The short man tiptoed quickly down the stairs. He grabbed Carol by the arm, pulled her into the corner next to Cortney, and pressed down firmly on her shoulders. She bent awkwardly on her hands and knees, and finally lay flat on the floor. A few inches from her face was the back of Cortney's head. Neither Cortney nor his mother spoke.

As Cortney faced the wall, the man knelt over Carol and tied her hands and feet. When footsteps again were heard in the parking lot, the man stopped to look up. But then a car door opened and slammed shut, an engine turned over and the car backed around, rolled across the gravel toward the exit, and turned right on Kiesel Avenue.

The parking lot was quiet once again. The basement, too, was silent, except for the short man's light footsteps as he walked over to the stool and picked up the green cup with the blue liquid.

The man walked back across the room, the cup in his hand. He knelt next to Carol, propped her into a sitting position, and put the rim of the cup to her lips.

"We're going to have a little cocktail party," he said.

"I don't drink," said Carol.

"You will drink this," said the man. He seized the back of her head. The cup pressed against her teeth.

"What is it?" she asked.

"It's vodka and some kinda German drug," said the taller man. "It'll just put you to sleep."

Cortney heard his mother swallow the liquid in a large gulp. Then she choked and began coughing loudly, spewing the liquid from her mouth and nose. The man lowered her to the carpet again, where she lay, still heaving and spitting.

He strutted to the other side of the room, held out the cup, and the taller man filled it again from the bottle in the brown bag. Cortney heard the man coming toward him. The man stepped over Carol. Cortney was twisted onto his back, then lifted by his neck into a sitting position. The edge of the cup was at his lips, the man's hand gripped the base of his neck. The fumes rising from the cup stung his nostrils as the cup tilted upward. The viscous liquid flowed across his lips, and suddenly they felt scalded. Then Cortney opened his mouth and the liquid poured in until it overflowed onto his chin. His throat flexed, and with a jerk of his head he swallowed. The liquid scorched his throat and oozed into his chest. He gagged, coughed violently, and vomited as the man lowered him onto the carpet. His mouth and esophagus were inflamed, and the burning was beginning to drip into his stomach.

He lay on his side again, sweat beaded across his forehead. His stomach and chest rolled in convulsions. Behind him his mother was moaning softly and spitting. He coughed. His throat puffed out and his lower lip sucked in as he gagged, then vomited more. Light tears wet the rims of his eyes. In his mouth and across his lips sores were beginning to form. Some of the liquid still stuck in droplets to his chin and his cheeks, burning his skin.

Across the room he heard the liquid gurgle from the bottle as the cup was filled again. Light footsteps trekked behind him. The man grunted with the effort of propping up Stan. Stan swallowed from the cup, then coughed explosively and began spitting. The man tip-toed back for more of the liquid and returned to Michelle. She swallowed too, but her coughing and spitting were not as loud as the others'.

The fifth cupful went to Mr. Walker. The man hoisted him up and poured the fluid into his mouth. Acrid fumes knifed up his nose, and the lining of his mouth felt singed. He pretended to swallow. When the man lowered him into the shadow, he parted his lips and let the caustic leak out over his shoulder and onto the carpet. Then he coughed and spit as he had heard the others do. Mr. Walker had worked on electronics projects with Stan and had some knowledge of chemicals, especially those strong enough to etch metal. From the biting fumes and the sizzling in his mouth, he guessed that the liquid dripping onto his shoulder was hydrochloric acid.

When the short man had lowered Mr. Walker to the floor, he filled the cup for the sixth time and returned to Stan, making him drink again from the cup. This time Stan began vomiting violently. Cortney had ceased vomiting, but the caustic burned his throat, forcing him to cough and spit. The low moans and spitting and impulsive coughing had increased with each cupful the man had served, until the room was filled with retching. To keep them from spitting the caustic out, the short man tried to cover their mouths with masking tape, but droplets of the caustic had formed on their lips and chins, and the tape wouldn't stick.

No lights shone in the basement now. Out back a streetlamp lit the parking alley like soft moonlight, the light coming dimly through the glass brick into the sound room above. Only a shaft of gray settled over the two men as they huddled now at the base of the stairs, whispering. Cortney heard their voices raise and lower, but he couldn't understand what they were saying. His wrists were rubbed raw by the cord, the skin beginning to break. His arms and shoulders felt stiff. If he pushed back against the cord, trying to stretch them, his muscles seized up and prickled. But the pain on the outside of his body was merely numbness. Inside, the caustic was burning his throat, down the lining of his esophagus and into his stomach.

The conversation by the stairs stopped.

"What time is it?" Cortney heard the short man ask.

The taller man held his watch up to the dim light.

"Nine o'clock."

By now Cortney could distinguish the two men by their footsteps: the short man stepped lightly, almost daintily, on the stairs, while the bigger man lumbered. As he lay in the darkness, Cortney heard heavy footsteps tramp up the stairs and those of the short man follow. The bolt on the back door clacked open and the taller man slipped through the doorway. As the door closed and the bolt snapped shut, the vehicle parked in back started up and the exhaust reverberated against the door until the tires edged forward and moved slowly across the gravel.

The short man tread lightly down the stairs, crossed the room, and slid open the panel door. He stepped into the workshop and again reached up to twist the naked light bulb into its socket. The yellowish light fell through the doorway, and with it the man's shadow, gliding back and forth across the carpet, looming larger then smaller, sometimes disappearing altogether. At times Cortney could hear him beyond the workshop, shuffling boxes at the rear of the stockroom.

Before long he heard the same vehicle back up against the building. The engine died, then five hard knuckle raps came at the back door. The short man unscrewed the light bulb in the workshop, pulled the panel door shut, and ran up the stairs. The bolt clicked back and the door opened. Cortney heard the heavy footsteps of the taller man as he stepped inside.

The basement was dark. The shaft of light that once beamed down the stairs had turned from gold to gray, and the gray had slowly darkened until only the faint light of the streetlamp found its way through the window of glass brick, and even that now faded into the blackness at the bottom of the stairs. When Cortney opened his eyes, he could see nothing. Behind him he heard his mother's raspy breathing. The coughs from deep within her chest jolted her body and broke the silence, as did the others with their coughing. Cortney burned inside, and bubbles were beginning to form in his throat, making it difficult for him to breathe. He tried to cough the bubbles out, but each time he coughed they quickly formed again.

Upstairs, the two men moved as before, back and forth, stepping on the fire grating. But now there was no pattern of quick heavy footsteps out and long strides back in. They shuffled from one side of the shop to the other, starting near the street entrance and working their way back into the sound room above Cortney's head. He could hear the rustle of cloth or tissue paper, wiping sounds, as though the men were dusting the shelves and equipment. The footsteps and the rustling moved through the sound room and ended at the back door, where one of the men rubbed hard on the doorknob.

The short man tiptoed down the dark stairs, felt his way across the room to the panel door, and again twisted on the light in the workshop. The glow from the bulb spread into the black room where Cortney and the others lay, lighting parts of it, leaving the rest in soft gray shadow. In the dim light the taller man walked heavily down the stairs, and the two of them continued wiping and rubbing in the basement.

When they had finished, the men stood in the shaft of light coming through the panel door from the workshop. Cortney heard the thin, crisp snap of rubber, like surgical gloves being pulled tight. The short man stood over Mr. Walker. He bent down and removed Mr. Walker's watch from his wrist. Then he slid his hand into Mr. Walker's back pocket and pulled out his wallet. He unfolded the wallet and flipped through its contents.

The taller man was watching.

"How much's he got in there?" he asked.

"Five bucks," said the short man. He ripped it out of the wallet.

"No," said the taller man, "take the whole thing."

The short man stood up and stuffed the wallet into his pants. Cortney heard light footsteps coming toward him, then felt a hand slide into his back pocket and take out his wallet. He had on no watch or rings, but lying behind him, his mother was wearing expensive jewelry: a gold Rolex wristwatch, a large diamond ring, and an ornate ring of gold and jade. Michelle too was wearing a watch, a diamond engagement ring on her left hand, and another gold ring set with a ruby on her right. Around her neck was a gold necklace. The man took Carol's purse and that of Michelle, and removed the wallets of the men, but when he had finished, the jewelry on both women was left untouched.

At the base of the stairs now, the two men again were arguing. Their voices were low and the words hard to distinguish, but it was clear the argument was over what to do with their captives. The talk went back and forth, and got louder and louder, until finally Cortney heard the taller one say: "No, I can't do it, man! I'm scared!"

The short man snapped something back, then said, "Give me about thirty minutes."

The taller man ran up the stairs. The bolt clicked open. The door swung wide and quickly closed again.

After Carol had stomped out of the house, Byron and Gary had continued talking in the den.

Gary said, "Mother sure is hyper about Cort not being home on time."

"That's just the way your mother is," said Byron.

"But I think she carries it a little too far sometimes."

"She's more agitated than usual," admitted Byron. "But maybe something is wrong."

"You don't think he stopped to talk to Brent?" asked Gary.

"Oh, he probably did. Then I suspect he decided to try and dig himself out in English with those two papers he told me about." Byron stretched back on the couch and placed the phone on the floor where he could easily reach it. "You said you wanted to talk about Eva?"

The conversation turned to Gary's recent divorce. Gary had met Eva in the Sistine Chapel in Rome. They had been married in Utah. For a year Gary had tried for his Ph.D. in toxicology and Eva had worked as a ward clerk in a hospital. Then her unhappiness at being away from family and friends had turned to depression, and finally, she had left Gary and returned to Denmark. The problem had been predictable from the beginning, but Gary still felt guilty about the relationship. It was good therapy for him to explore its failure with his father.

About nine o'clock the phone rang.

"Dr. Naisbitt?" said the caller. "This is Dave. Mrs. Naisbitt called a while ago about Cort. Has he gotten back yet?"

"Hello, Big D! No. I think he's at the library doing some reports for school tomorrow."

Dave Whiteley was a high school friend of Cortney's. While Cortney took flying lessons from Wolfgang at the Cessna school, Dave was learning to fly in the Piper program.

"I heard Wolf let him solo today," he said.

"I haven't talked to him," said Byron, "but we think he did."

"Well, just tell him I called to find out how it went. I'll see him tomorrow when I pick him up for school."

"Okay, Dave, I'll tell him. We'll see ya later."

In a while the phone rang again. Byron answered on the first ring.

"Well, good for you, grabbing the phone so quick like that," said the voice on the other end. It was his brother, Paul. "What are you doing?"

"Oh, just sittin' bulltickin' with Gary."

"Any calls from my patients?"

"No, it's been quiet so far."

Paul took the opportunity to razz his brother about being "a pain in the butt to stick around" when he was supposed to be on call, and told him, by hell, he expected him to be right by that phone every minute. "We're going to bed here pretty soon," he said. "I'll sleep better knowing you're right there."

"You do that, little brother," Byron laughed.

They hung up, and Byron settled back on the couch, his hands clasped behind his head. "Now, where were we?"

The two men talked until almost ten. When Gary left the house, his father was lying on the couch, reading, the same as his mother had been when he had stopped by to see them nearly five hours before. He hadn't planned on staying so long, but it had delayed his having to go home alone. Even now, still disturbed by his personal problems, Gary avoided returning to his apartment and went instead to a drive-in movie.

Gazing through his reading spectacles at the day's paper, Byron was now alone in the house. Once a month, from Wednesday to Wednesday, he went on call at the two Ogden hospitals. Soon, his medical group would be getting the small portable pagers, which would give him more freedom when he was on call. But for now, he had to stay near a phone. Typically, it rang frequently and he would answer, "Well, howdy!" or "Hello, senorita!" or "Lorda mercy, what's happening up there?" But tonight things were quiet. The stillness, broken only by his crinkling of the paper, was a subtle reminder to him: *I wonder where Carol and Cortney are?*

When Carol hadn't returned after her stormy departure, he assumed she had found Cortney at the library and was there helping him with the two papers he had to write. It was now after ten o'clock, and Byron was concerned that they were not home. *Doesn't the library close at ten? Or is it nine? They should be home pretty soon. Byron, for hell's sakes, you're thinking just like Carol. Stop worrying.* He continued reading the newspaper.

Secretly, Byron Naisbitt worried about his children almost as much as Carol did. But he had learned to be more discreet, which was a relief when, as things always turned out, there had been no cause for worry in the first place. Still, it *was* unusual that Cortney hadn't called.

Byron let the paper collapse in his hands, and reflected on Carol's mockery of his excuses. *He's at the airport! He's talking to Brent! He's in class! He's at the library!* She was right, Cortney didn't appear to be in any of the places he was supposed to be. *I wonder what the little bugger did! And where's Carol? Byron! Stop worrying.* He returned to his paper.

As the taller man ran from the shop, the door crashed closed at the top of the stairs. The noise dispersed quickly through the basement and died. In the silence that followed, the short man began creeping across the room. From the workshop a sliver of light fell across the carpet, beaming on the man for an instant as he drifted through the light and into darkness again. He probed with each step, moving steadily toward the corner where Cortney lay. Cortney heard his mother breathing behind him, quicker now and rough. The man came closer and knelt next to her. In the darkness he held out a gun, searching with the barrel until he had found the back of her head. Then the corner of the room exploded. Cortney heard the slug enter his mother's head and a moment later her blood spurt out and spatter on the carpet inches away from him.

The man straightened his knees and stepped over Carol's body. He was now standing above Cortney, the gun still in his hand. He bent down and Cortney could feel the hot muzzle of the gun probing through his hair at the back of his head. Then the gun stopped, and the man pulled the trigger, and the air around Cortney's head exploded, a bullet burrowing into his skull. Cortney's body went limp and he crumpled forward.

The man rose. The reports from his gun died among the walls, and the smell of gunpowder drifted about the room. For the next few minutes he stalked the shadows, only the measured fall of his footsteps breaking the silence. His head toward the stairs, Mr. Walker lay at the edge of light cast from the workshop into the room. The man crossed back through the light and stood with his feet at Mr. Walker's head. He straightened his gun arm toward the form lying at his feet and jerked the trigger. The bullet ripped through the carpet next to Mr. Walker's head and ricocheted into a wall. The man stepped to his right, over Michelle, bent low behind Stan and fired a bullet into the back of Stan's head. Before the noise had abated, the man spun, walked across the room and ran up the stairs.

Michelle whispered into the shadows in front of her: "Stan? Are you okay?"

Stan was still alive. His voice was low but clear. "I've been shot," he said.

A moment later the man's tiptoe hurried down the steps into the basement, crossed the room and stopped at Mr. Walker's head. This time the man leaned close and took aim, and this time he didn't miss.

Mr. Walker's head was jolted and a hot sting spread across the back of it. He fought to stay lucid. Two times two is four, he thought, two times three is six. He twitched his fingers and within his shoes wiggled his toes.

Only Michelle was left. The man now stood over her with the gun in his hand, and Michelle pleaded with him not to kill her. He said nothing as he untied her feet, then her hands, then pulled her to a standing position. With his gun in one hand he led her past Mr. Walker's body and through the sliding panel door. Despite the clamor in his head Mr. Walker heard them pass the workshop area and proceed to the far end of the basement. There the man made Michelle remove her clothes: a pair of jeans, a blouse, bra, and panties. She stacked them neatly on a table. For the next twenty minutes, as the four bodies lay motionless in the front room, the man raped Michelle.

When the man and Michelle first left the room, Mr. Walker could hear the rustling of paper at the back of the basement, but then he heard nothing. The clanging in his ears reminded him of being in a duck blind, too close to the accidental blast of a shotgun. His shoulder ached so badly from where the caustic had dripped and burned his skin that he was about to lose consciousness. He rolled halfway onto his chest and lay still, pretending to be dead. Across the room, still tightly bound, Cortney and his mother lay side by side, sweat drying on their bodies, blood congealing around the jagged, finger-size holes blown in the backs of their heads. The skin around their mouths festered and the caustic ate holes where it had splattered on their clothes. Mr. Walker heard Stan in the other corner still breathing.

The light from the workshop still shone through the sliding panel. Michelle's footsteps, now only sock-clad padding on the concrete floor, dragged from the far end of the basement to the workshop. They were followed by the more distinct, gritty footfall of the short man. The bare light bulb cast their shadows ahead of them into the room.

Michelle hesitated at the panel door. The man preceded her across the room, stepped lightly around Cortney's feet, and opened the door to an employee bathroom adjacent to the stairs. Mr. Walker opened one eye and saw the man's shoes and the bottom of his pants as he glided by. Michelle, now wearing only white cotton socks, followed him into the bathroom, where the man had switched on the light. Through the subsiding ring in his ears Mr. Walker heard Michelle in the bathroom urinating.

"I sure had to go a lot, didn't I?" she joked with the man. But her voice was strained and she was coughing.

The toilet flushed. As it swirled, Michelle walked from the bathroom, pleading with the man to take her with him. Her forced light manner had cracked. The man motioned for her to return to her place on the floor. She edged across the room and stood where she had lain between Mr. Walker and Stan, unclothed, frightened, begging. He forced her to lie down again, her head next to Mr. Walker's, where he left her untied, lying on her stomach, and ran up the stairs.

When his footsteps had cleared the top and she could hear them above in the sound room, Michelle raised up and nudged Mr. Walker with her elbow.

"Are you okay?" she said softly.

Mr. Walker said nothing. Slowly, he opened one eye to signal that he was still alive. In the dim light he could see her bare shoulder and her bare right breast. He didn't know if she saw his single open eye. In a moment he closed the eye again and continued playing dead.

Seconds later the man's shoes were heard again, tapping rapidly on the wooden stairs. He came off the bottom step, marched across the carpet, and knelt beside Mr. Walker. His thick fingers cupped Mr. Walker's throat, searching, squeezing against the blood vessels in his neck, feeling for a pulse. Mr. Walker lay still, as the fingers crabbed about his neck.

The fingers lifted away, and for a moment there was silence and darkness. Then a click broke the silence and a harsh beam of light glared into Mr. Walker's eyes. His face remained limp. As suddenly as the light had shot down upon his face, it jerked away. A tube of illuminated dust particles angled now toward the ceiling, now against a wall. Then back into Mr. Walker's eyes. And away again. And back again. Then the man whirled and the beam of light swept across Michelle's hair, and a gunshot again shattered the silence, and before the full force of the explosion had hit, another thundered from the corner above Stan. The explosions cracked louder, more powerful than before, and as they died away, Mr. Walker heard Michelle moan lightly, and then everything was silent again. In the silence the short man tiptoed away. When the man returned moments later, Mr. Walker felt himself being raised up and a cord being slipped around his neck.

Mr. Walker's body hung limp, weighing heavily against the man's efforts to lift him. As the loop closed about his throat, he carefully expanded only the muscles in his neck until he felt his skin tight.

The man cinched the cord hard, then cinched it again and again, until it dug into Mr. Walker's bulging flesh and squeezed against his windpipe. But when the man had yanked the cord tighter for the last time and finally lowered him back onto the carpet, Mr. Walker slowly relaxed his neck and found that within the tight clasp of the cord he could still eke enough air to stay alive.

He continued to play dead, breathing shallowly, as he heard the man's footsteps once again ascend the stairs. The basement was silent. Above in the sound room the same soft steps padded about. Soon they hurried to the back door and down the stairs again.

Mr. Walker still lay on his side, collapsed partly forward. As he lay, not moving, he felt something brush his left earlobe. Then a ball-point pen was wedged in his ear and jammed into his head. The man's feet shuffled slightly. One foot shot up and stomped the end of the pen, driving it deeper into Mr. Walker's head. Again the foot raised up and pounded the pen. The third time the pen was kicked, Mr. Walker felt the point enter his throat. It tickled there and made him swallow for the first time since before the green cup had been passed. When he swallowed, the pen rose through his ear just slightly. And then the man was gone.

The light, quick footsteps tapped up the stairs. The naked bulb in the workshop was off. The rays of sun that once flooded down the stairway had long ago vanished, and the basement was black. Footsteps no longer clomped or tiptoed on the stairs, or moved back and forth overhead. Everything was black, everything still. Mr. Walker lay tilted on his side. Stan and Michelle faced into the carpet. Sometime in the night Carol Naisbitt had rolled onto her back.

In the darkness of his corner Cortney moved. He twisted his body until his head was pointed toward the stairs, and began crawling. As he crawled, his eyes were open, and from his throat gurgled the growl of an animal. His hands and feet still bound, he slid his body inch by inch across the carpet toward the bottom of the stairs.

DISCOVERY

It was nearing ten thirty when police officers Kevin Youngberg and Gale Bowcutt cruised down Kiesel Avenue, past the Hi-Fi Shop alley, and turned west on Twenty-third. A taciturn man, square-built with thick, hairy arms, Bowcutt had been with the Ogden Police two and a half years. That night he was training the rookie Youngberg, who had been in uniform for thirty-two days. Youngberg was twenty-two, a tall, hefty man with coal-black hair and a creamy, boyish face. They were approaching the intersection at Seventeenth and Wall, when the dispatcher radioed them to investigate "unknown trouble" at 2323 Washington Boulevard.

Bowcutt spun the car south to Twenty-fourth, raced without siren to Kiesel Avenue, and turned north. The patrol car crept into the gravel alleyway, its headlights off. A heavy-set boy was standing near the back door. Youngberg stepped out of the car as the boy yelled, "They're inside!"

The young officer hurried across the gravel and entered the rear door of the shop. The doorjamb and the molding around the door were splintered. The stairs before him led down to a seeming black void, but upstairs the lights were on. Youngberg veered to his right, into a room lined with empty shelves and bare wires jutting from the walls. He saw a man and a woman walking back and forth near the front of the shop. The man's hair was matted with blood, and Youngberg noticed what he thought was a pen on top of the man's ear.

"What's going on?" he yelled.

"They're downstairs," said the man.

"Who?" yelled Youngberg.

"Four of 'em," said the man. "They're all shot."

Before he took time to consider that the perpetrators might still be in the building, Youngberg turned and ran to the back of the shop. As he hit the landing at the top of the stairs, Bowcutt slipped in the back door next to him. Shoulder to shoulder they descended the stairs into the blackness. Halfway down, Youngberg flicked on his flashlight. Dark shadows jumped and realigned. In the circular pool of light by the bottom step lay a blond-haired boy, his green eyes open and staring at the ceiling. Bright red scars trailed across his face. His mouth gaped open and from it emanated a sound like nothing the two men had ever heard. At the edge of light lay another pair of feet. Youngberg jerked the flashlight. The boy faded to the shadows, and in the spotlight now was the body of a woman. Eyes open, she stared glassily at the ceiling, and the same red burns surrounded her mouth. Like a horror slide show, the beam flicked to another pile of flesh, the nude body of a girl, a bullet hole in the back of her head. The beam jumped again to encircle still another body lying in the far corner, a young man with a large hole in the back of his head and bruised, purple hands tied behind his back.

Bowcutt thought it was a joke. He was waiting for the lights to come on and the actors to jump up and start laughing and the wounded man behind them on the stairwell to clap them on the back and say something like, "We was just checking to see how fast you boys'd get here!"

But there was an atmosphere in the basement that no staged drama could reproduce. The stench of blood and vomit suffused the plastic-metallic smell of new stereos wafting toward the stairs. The flashlight swept across the room, shadows leaping and hiding in the beam, flesh seemingly in puddles on the floor. In the darkness at their feet a death rattle gurgled in the boy's throat. It was almost like the growl of a dog.

Youngberg froze on the bottom step, his hands hanging at his side, saying to himself: "What the hell is happening? What the hell is happening? What the hell is happening?"

He felt his guts tighten and his mind begin to fuzz. He heard himself saying to Bowcutt, "We're gonna need an ambulance."

The wounded man was on the stairs behind them. Youngberg saw the man's mouth moving.

"We've already called the ambulance."

Youngberg looked back to the basement. Seconds passed as he stood still trying to blink away the smell and the sound and the people with the holes in their heads. He turned toward the wounded man and felt his own mouth moving again. "Who did this?"

"Two Negroes," said the man.

A thick hand reached out and clasped the back of Youngberg's neck.

"See if those two are alive, then look after him." Bowcutt was pointing to the boy at Youngberg's feet.

A third officer pulled his motorcycle up to the back door and started down the stairs. Bowcutt ran up and stopped him.

"Call for assistance," he yelled. "There's a bunch of people dead in here!"

The wounded man was moving past Youngberg and into the darkness. Youngberg heard the sliding panel door roll back and felt himself drifting toward it over the bodies. In the middle of the room he stopped. The girl and the boy lying side by side were still. Youngberg combed the two bodies for life signs. As he did so, his eyes focused on the girl's right hand. On her ring finger was a tiny gold ring set with a red stone. Youngberg's wife had once worn an identical ring. For years Youngberg would have nightmares over the image of the girl's right hand. He rose slowly and left the cold bodies exactly as he had found them.

In the dark the wounded man was rummaging through the tools on the workbench. Youngberg heard the clanking of metal, and then the man was talking to him, asking for his flashlight.

Youngberg's hand stretched toward him with the light. "What are you doing?" he heard himself say.

"This is my boy Stanley," said the man. "I've got to save him. I need a pair of dykes or a knife or something to cut him loose."

"Which one is your son?" asked Youngberg.

The man pointed into the darkness with the flashlight, illuminating the body lying facedown in the corner.

"Your son is dead," said Youngberg, his own voice sounding like someone else talking. "There's nothing you can do for him. Why don't you help me with these other two?" Youngberg looked again at the man's face. "I'm sorry, sir. Why don't you just go outside and we'll take care of things down here."

The man trudged up the steps. Youngberg crossed the room again and sank to his knees next to the boy gurgling at the foot of the stairs. Bowcutt glided down the stairs past the man going up.

Youngberg looked up and saw him settle on the other side of the boy.

"I think he's been shot in the lungs," said Youngberg. "It sounds like a sucking chest wound."

"Take his shirt off," came Bowcutt's voice, "and see if you can find something to cover the lung with, a piece of plastic or something."

Youngberg fumbled with the buttons on the boy's shirt, but he couldn't coax them through the buttonholes. Suddenly he saw his hands grab two handfuls of shirt on each side and rip the buttons off from bottom to top.

The boy's chest was collapsed, but clean.

"I can't find anything, Bowcutt!"

"Okay, let's turn him over. It sounds like he's drowning in his own blood."

The boy stared up at them, his eyes fixed. As they rolled him onto his stomach, the bullet hole in back of his head rotated into the beam of Youngberg's flashlight. It had stopped bleeding, and the blood was turning to jelly in his blond hair. Youngberg closed his eyes for a moment, then reached down and carefully turned the boy's head sideways to let the blood drain from his throat.

"Youngberg," said Bowcutt, "roll the woman over, and see if you can find something to cut them loose."

As Bowcutt and the motorcycle officer checked the boy for other wounds, Youngberg stepped further into the darkness, the beam from his flashlight jiggling across the woman. The rattle in her chest was quieter than the boy's, but she was trying to breathe and her flesh was still warm. He rolled her onto her stomach and tilted her head to the side. Then he found his way to the tool room.

Sergeant Dave White, a gruff, long-faced police veteran of seventeen years, was the fourth officer to arrive at the Hi-Fi Shop. He hit the last step in the basement and stopped. "My God! It's wall-to-wall bodies!"

Bowcutt looked up, but before he could say anything, White ran back up the stairs and out to his patrol car. He ripped the microphone off his radio and yelled: "This is a major homicide! Get people down here! Call the Tac Squad! Call Tech Services! And tell them to hurry the hell up!"

Youngberg spotted a pair of wire cutters and plucked them from a pile of tools. Then he drifted back into the main room where he heard White and Bowcutt yelling at the ambulance attendants stopped halfway down the stairs.

"Get the stretcher! Get two stretchers!"

Two of the attendants ran back for stretchers. Another hurried into the basement with a first-aid kit in his hands. Youngberg was kneeling next to the boy, trying to cut through the cord binding his wrists. He heard the attendant clomping down the wooden stairs, then saw his vague outline drop down next to him on the floor. He handed Youngberg a pair of tape scissors. Youngberg snipped the cord in two. The boy's arms slid limply across the small of his back and onto the carpet.

Youngberg stood up slowly and surveyed the blur in the basement. Stretchers were poking down the stairwell. The room was filling with people. Short, plastic airways and rolls of gauze had popped out of the first-aid kit, and the attendants were trying to wrap the dry bullet wounds of the woman and the boy. Through the haze of flashlight beams, Youngberg saw White wave his arm and heard him yell.

"Quit screwing around with that goddamn bandage and get them the hell outta here!"

"This is the way we've been trained," said one of the attendants.

"Their heads aren't bleeding!" yelled White. "They're gonna die before you can get them to the hospital!"

The attendant ignored White and kept bandaging the boy's head.

"All we can do is what we've been told to do in situations like this, and that's stop the bleeding and try to establish an airway."

"And he's telling you you're wasting your time," said Bowcutt. "There ain't no more bleeding and the kid's choking down in his chest. That little piece of plastic you're sticking in his mouth won't reach his lungs!"

None of the attendants seemed to hear.

"What the hell," said White, "they're gonna die anyway." He waved his flashlight over the woman and the boy, then in the corner behind. His own daughter was the same age and even looked similar to the girl lying on the floor. "I wish we could take some of these sob sister do-gooders by the scruff a the neck and drag them down here and show them just what the hell these animals did."

Youngberg floundered through the bodies on the floor. The smell of the basement was choking him. His eyes were bleary, and he felt sick, like he was about to vomit. He wobbled up the stairs. When he got to the top step, his eye was drawn to the edge of the carpet by a glimmer of brass. A crime-scene expert from Tech Services was walking in the back door. Youngberg stopped him with a hand on his shoulder and without speaking pointed to the glimmer. It was a .25 caliber bullet, still jacketed. The officer photographed the bullet, then stooped to pick it up. Youngberg stumbled out the back door.

Red lights from the ambulance and a knot of police cars whirled around the buildings and flashed across his face. Sergeant White had run up the stairs ahead of him and was leaning against a wall in the alley. His face was enshrouded in white smoke, and a pile of cigarette butts at his feet was already beginning to build. Youngberg walked past him gagging, his hand cupped across his mouth.

"Youngberg!" yelled White. "You're a police officer, it's time you started acting like one!"

"Yessir," said Youngberg. He gagged again.

"Youngberg!"

"Yessir?"

"Come here, Youngberg. I've been a police officer almost seventeen years, and that's the most shocking thing I've ever seen in my life. Any other rookie would've flat gone to pieces in there." He flicked his wrist and a cigarette rose in the package. "Have a cigarette and go lean against the building for a few minutes. Try to relax."

"Thanks, Sergeant," said Youngberg, as White snapped his lighter on. Youngberg walked away puffing on the cigarette, then stopped and turned around.

"I don't know why I did that," he said to White. "I don't even smoke."

The three people who had been upstairs when Youngberg and Bowcutt arrived were standing in the parking alley, away from the back door. When Youngberg had had a few moments alone, he got out his notebook and began questioning them. The man's name was Orren Walker. The woman and the boy were his wife and younger son. When Stan had not shown up for dinner, Mr. Walker had driven to the shop to see if he had had trouble with the utility jeep they had just bought. Mrs. Walker began to worry when two hours had passed and neither had returned home. A little after ten she and the younger boy had gone to the shop. The boy, a strapping sixteen-year-old, had rung the buzzer in back. When he heard his father yelling for them to call the police and an ambulance, he had reared back and kicked in the locked door.

While talking to Mr. Walker, Youngberg thought the man had a pen sitting on top of his ear. Now he looked closer. By the light cast from the streetlamp and splashes of red from the ambulance and police cars, he saw Mr. Walker swallow and the pen rise half an inch. Youngberg looked away, easing off his hat and setting it on the hood of the ambulance.

Within minutes police officers and ambulance attendants rushed the bodies out the back door into the ambulance, and the ambulance raced out of the parking lot, lights flashing and siren beginning to scream. Another backed up in its place, and Youngberg put Mr. Walker into the second ambulance, assuring him that his wife would be escorted to the hospital right behind him.

Youngberg was then standing near the back door trying to record the license plate numbers of all vehicles in the parking lot, when the first of the press arrived. Television news stations opened up with their bright lights. Youngberg was trapped before the cameras. He was trying to appear smooth and professional, though he still felt dizzy and sick to his stomach. From back in the dark he heard a colleague's voice.

"You're gonna get your ass chewed out, Youngberg, when the chief sees you on TV with no hat!"

* * *

"Byron, what the hell's going on in Ogden?"

It was a friend calling from Salt Lake City on the Naisbitt's private phone. Byron was still reclining on the couch.

"Not much," he said.

"Didn't you just hear the news?" said the caller. "Five people were found shot in your nephew's store."

"At the Hi-Fi Shop!" He sat up. "Who was it?"

"They didn't say, just five people. I figured you might know something."

"No. No, I don't. Thanks for calling."

He dropped the phone and lay still for a moment, remembering Carol's words. *Something's happened to Cortney! I know it! And you won't even try to help me find him!*

That old feeling of fear and anxiety kind of struck like it would, and I figured that that was a good explanation for where they were, but I wasn't sure, and I was hoping that wasn't it, but I knew it might be. And so I hurried and threw some clothes on and grabbed the keys, and jumped in the car and went down there.

I got down to the Hi-Fi Shop and went to the front door. I didn't see any cars there and I started pounding on the door, but I couldn't get anybody, and then I started getting angry and anxious and I beat on the damn door and no one answered, and it just takes more time to drive around the block. And then I got around back and a cop stopped me at the curb, and I told him I was going on in, that I thought my wife and son might be down there, and then I saw the wife's station wagon and I knew I was in bad trouble. That wave of fear and despair and anxiety and the whole damn thing hit me. Then I saw Cort's old Buick and I knew they were both in trouble.

Robert Newey, the county prosecutor, had been called to the scene of the crime to witness firsthand the gathering of evidence and to determine whether autopsies would be performed on the bodies. During twenty years as a prosecutor Newey had tried nearly fifty first-degree murder cases. His style in the courtroom was imperturbable, dogged, meticulous. To match his relentless trial demeanor, he had a serious, square-jawed face, silver hair, and steady, sky-blue eyes.

As young boys, Bob Newey and Byron Naisbitt had gone to school together in Ogden, and Cortney had swum competitively with Newey's children at the Ogden Golf and Country Club. Newey was aware that Byron's nephew owned the Hi-Fi Shop. When the victims who had just been rushed to the hospital were described to him by one of the officers, he had immediately pictured Carol and Cortney Naisbitt.

Newey was at the back door of the Hi-Fi Shop, talking with a police captain, when Byron Naisbitt came running from the parking alley toward the rear entrance of the shop. The captain stepped in front of Byron.

"You can't go in there!"

"I've gotta go in there," said Byron. "I've got to go in!"

Newey stepped up calmly beside the police captain. "Hello, By," he said. "By, you can't go in there."

"How many people are down there?" asked Byron angrily.

Neither the captain nor Newey responded.

"How many people are down there!" he repeated.

"Well," said Newey, "there are just two down there now."

Byron locked eyes with the prosecutor. "I don't believe you," he said. "My wife's car's parked right over there." He pointed without looking. "My son's car's parked right next to it. They're down there. I know they're down there!"

"By," said Newey, speaking in his steady, courtroom voice, "they're not down there. I've been down there, and they're not there."

Byron said again, "I don't believe you."

The basement was like no crime scene Newey had ever experienced. He was sickened by it. In his own mind he assumed that Carol and Cortney had been trapped and tortured in the basement by the perpetrators. But since he had not seen the bodies himself for a positive identification, he did not want to tell Byron that, yes, his wife and son had been down there. He had seen immediately how the situation could get out of hand, and pictured Byron killing himself or someone else in a desperate drive to the hospital. Yet he didn't know how to appease Byron's anger and frustration. He chose his words carefully, hoping to calm him down.

"They've taken a woman and a boy, a young boy," he said, "up to Benedict's."

"Is it Carol and Cortney?"

"We don't know," said Newey. "We have no idea who they are."

"Is it my wife and son?"

"We don't know, we don't know who it is."

"God damn it! I know they're in there," said Byron. "I've got to go down and see!"

"They're not down there, By," said Newey. He looked at Byron's anxious face and knew he was losing ground. "But I guess the only way I can convince you is for you to see." He turned to the officer guarding the door. "This is Dr. Byron Naisbitt. He believes that his wife and son are down there. I told him they're not, but he wants to see for himself. He's not to disturb anything." He looked back at Byron. "By, you can go down to the fourth step from the bottom. You can look for a second, and then you have to come out."

Byron hurriedly followed the officer down to the fourth step. The lighting in the basement was dim, broken only by the erratic pop of flashbulbs as Tech Services photographed the scene. On the floor in front of the master panel lay the body of a young man, blood soaking the green carpet brown beneath his head. Straight ahead, in front of a dark-paneled sliding door, a girl in her late teens was clad only in a pair of socks, a red hole in the back of her head.

When I got downstairs, I saw the girl and I saw this other fellow both laying there dead. I didn't know the circumstances and the cops weren't anxious to say. They just said the other parties had gone to the hospital, the younger fellow and the lady down to Benedict's, and the man had gone to the McKay. They described the lady and the boy, and then I knew for sure that the wife and Cort were there, that they'd been victims. Then I got a little ray of hope, because both were alive when they took them out.

Within a few seconds Newey heard heavy footsteps running up the stairs toward him. He turned around as Byron hit the landing.

"By," he said, "let's check this out. We'll call the hospitals and find out if it's Carol and Cortney, and if it is I'll send one of the officers up there with you."

Byron looked at Newey, mumbled something Newey couldn't hear, and pushed past him. He ran toward his car.

Newey hollered: "Hold it, By! Hold it! I'll get a police officer to drive you. By, stop!"

The Mercedes leaped across the alley in reverse, spraying gravel. The tires grabbed, spun forward, and the car fishtailed out of the parking lot onto Kiesel. Newey turned to the captain.

"That's exactly what I was trying to avoid."

They heard the squeal of rubber as Byron took the first turn, racing toward the hospital.

All the way to the hospital I didn't know what to think. What can you think? You know you're in trouble, but you don't know how bad; you're trying to get there as fast as you can and everything keeps getting in your way. I was angry and upset and speeding. I was thinking of all the possibilities, everything going through my mind all at once, one right after the other, but the one thing I knew for a fact was that they'd both been shot, my wife and my son had both been in a disaster, and there was no way I could do anything about it, but I wanted to get there to see if I could help, and I had a feeling that nothing could go fast enough, like I was coming to a deadline I couldn't beat. I had a hollow feeling inside, I felt emptiness, I felt fear, I felt anxiety. I wanted to get there, get there, get there, and nothing could get me there fast enough. I guess it could have been dangerous for anyone around because I was going like hell. I had it floored all the way to the hospital.

Dr. Allred was standing in the hallway, his back to the doors, when Byron Naisbitt swept into the emergency room. "My family!" he shouted, out of breath. "Are they here?"

Allred turned and recognized the silver-haired obstetrician who was already abreast of him, still striding.

"They brought some people in and took them up to ICU, but I don't think they know their identification yet."

"Where the hell's ICU?" He was down the hall now.

"Third floor!" yelled Dr. Allred.

Andy Tolsma, the medical technician, had heard the exchange and stepped into the hall as Dr. Naisbitt rushed past. "I'll take you there," he said, falling in next to the doctor who was now almost sprinting.

They hurried around the corner in front of the Coke machines, and Andy reached out and slapped the elevator button. The doors rocked hesitantly open, and the two men stepped in. Neither had spoken. As the elevator shimmied to the third floor, Dr. Naisbitt glared up at the lighted floor numbers moving slowly by.

"My wife," he said, "is she serious?"

The question startled Andy. He felt it wasn't his place to tell Dr. Naisbitt that his wife was dead. But then what could he say, she's fine, she's fine, don't worry about her?

"I'm sorry, sir, she's dead."

There was not even a ripple in his anxious demeanor. "Why didn't somebody call me?" he blurted.

"We tried," said Andy.

The doors spread and Dr. Wallace was standing in front of the elevator. Dr. Naisbitt bounded through the doors before they were fully opened and grabbed him by the arm.

"Jess, what's going on with my family?"

"By, I've been trying to call you. Come with me."

They rushed down the hall.

As the ICU door swung slowly open, Byron Naisbitt beheld his son in the glass cubicle. The boy's body was blue-gray like a cadaver, and the tracheostomy tube protruding from the base of his neck was filling with a bloody foam. Four people hovered over him, trying to clear the airway and pump oxygen to his lungs.

Cortney looked dead. Byron ran into the small room, stopped abruptly, staring at his son, then turned away in complete detachment. He grabbed hold of Dr. Wallace again.

"What the hell is going on?" he cursed.

But before Wallace could explain, Byron began running from cubicle to cubicle, staring wildly into each one and mumbling: "Where's my wife? Where's my wife?" He ran the length of the ward, and when he got to the end, he just stood there, looking frantic and bewildered.

Dr. Wallace grabbed his arm and pulled him into an alcove stacked with towels and linen.

"By, will you listen to me, settle down. I'm going to try to explain what has happened . . . listen to me. I'll do the best I can, but I don't know much. . . . Cortney's got a bullet in his head, and—"

"They shot him in the head!"

"—it looks like he drank some sort of acid."

"Acid! ACID! Jess, what in the hell's going on? What kind of nightmare is this! My God!"

Wallace gripped him by the shoulders. "I don't know. We've heard all kinds of rumors, from the ambulance drivers, the police . . . nobody knows what's going on. Cortney's got some burns around his mouth and he's been in severe pulmonary edema ever since he got here. We've established an airway in him and they're shooting straight alcohol down his tube now, and it looks like we're getting a little oxygen through, but that stuff's tough to break up. His pupils are starting to react . . ."

"Jess, is Cortney going to live?"

"I don't know, By. He's showing a few primitive signs of life, but I don't know if it's enough. Jim Hauser's seen him and said he would probably die within a few minutes, that was about forty-five minutes ago, and he's still hanging in there. I called Rees and he should be here any minute to see if he can get these life-support systems plugged into him."

"What about my wife?" said Byron. "Where's my wife?"

"Carol? I don't know," said Wallace. "I haven't seen her."

"She's supposed to be here! Where the hell is she?"

Although Byron had already been told that Carol was dead, he either refused to believe it or was asking to see her body to confirm it. Perhaps, in his emotional state on the elevator, he misunderstood what Andy had said.

Curiously, in the confusion, Jess Wallace had not connected the woman with the boy. He knew Carol. He had examined the patient. He had thought she looked familiar. He was in the room when Cortney was identified. But he had failed to ascertain any relationship between the two. As he tried to explain to Byron that he knew nothing about Carol, a nurse began tugging at his sleeve, trying to whisper something to him. Finally, she dragged him aside.

"Dr. Wallace!" she said impatiently. "That's probably Mrs. Naisbitt down in the morgue!"

Wallace was stunned and annoyed that he had not recognized Carol or thought of her when Cortney was identified. "Damn!" he cursed. He put his arm on Byron's shoulder.

"Let's go outside, By."

Dr. Rees passed them in the ICU doorway. Byron turned to Rees

and with no emotion said, "Get your ass in there and save my son."
Then he and Dr. Wallace proceeded down the hall to the nurses'
station.

"By, I don't know why this didn't hit me before," said Wallace.
"They brought a woman in with Cortney. She was shot in the head,
too." He hesitated for a moment, searching for words. Then finally
he said, "Does Carol wear a jade ring on her right hand?"

Byron had bought the ring for Carol in Hawaii. She hardly ever
took it off. "Yeah," he answered slowly. "Yeah, she does."

"I'm sorry, By, she's dead. They took her down to the morgue a
little while ago."

They had reached the nurses' station.

Byron leaned heavily against the counter, his hand covering his
eyes. Dr. Wallace phoned Frances Heward, the nursing supervisor,
and told her to meet them downstairs with the key to the morgue.

The St. Benedict's morgue is in the basement, a full seventy-five
yards from the elevator. For those who must travel that distance to
identify a loved one, it is a seemingly endless journey. The first half
is a beige corridor rigidly lined with floor-length lockers and tiled
with linoleum squares. Abruptly, the ceiling lowers, the floor turns
to colorless concrete, the walls change to ice white, and the air becomes chill. It is a tunnel, and every twenty feet a short, austere
fluorescent tube dimly lights the way. But what attacks the senses
is the dull moan of the generators emanating from behind the walls.
The sound is like the hum of a choir.

In silence the trio entered the tunnel, feeling the cooler air and
hearing the choir-like sound around them. Dr. Naisbitt walked lan-
guidly between the other two. *I knew that we were going to the
morgue, and I knew what we were going to see, and I had a feeling
of deep loneliness. My thoughts would flash back to Cortney upstairs, and I wondered what was going on up there, because that
was the only hope I had left.*

The two doctors stood aside as Fran Heward unlocked the door to
the morgue. Air, stale and refrigerated, settled like dust about the
dreary room, covering the grim tools of the pathologist. Fran Heward slid open the top metal drawer, but before she could draw

back the white drape covering the body, Dr. Naisbitt had already glimpsed a tag of red material showing from beneath it.

"I think that's the dress she was wearing tonight," he mumbled.

The supervisor drew back the drape.

That's a shock. That's a shock no one can describe. Here's your wife that you've known and loved and lived with and raised your family with and shared experiences with nearly all your life. . . . And here she is, she looks grotesque, she hasn't been cleaned up. I don't know how you describe the feeling. I don't know how in the hell you can describe feelings that rip your guts. It's remorse and despair and agony in your heart, and you get real pain in your chest. When you hear someone say they've got a heartache, they've got a heartache, a heartache. It aches. It hurts, it pains, it throbs. When I looked at my wife, I had real pain in my heart.

They left the morgue and journeyed back through the tunnel. The generators droned behind the walls. The fluorescent lights clipped slowly by. Byron Naisbitt's mind was as numb as during those moments just before waking when the clamor of thoughts cannot be grasped as fact or the fantasy of a fresh dream. Or rather a nightmare. As he walked silently through the tunnel, he kept waking up to it.

That's where the feelings and thoughts were, down in that basement. My wife and son, the victims. What was going through their minds? Lord, the fear and the terror and the torture. They didn't care what happened to my wife and son. Pouring acid down their throats and then shooting them! God Almighty! You can face a lot of things, but when somebody's abusing you at their own whim and in their own fashion, that's terror and that's torture and no one should have to experience it in a lifetime, no one should! I can't believe that! It's out of my realm of thinking! Someone takes you and ties you up and makes you helpless and then terrorizes you and you're completely at their mercy and they have no feelings for you, they don't care, they've already decided what they're going to do with you, and then they take their own sweet time and torment you! No one should have that right over another person! No one! I don't . . . I don't . . . I can't believe. . .

They were through the tunnel and abreast of the nurses' lounge when suddenly his knees buckled, and he crumpled onto the shoul-

ders of the nursing supervisor. Dr. Wallace caught him from behind.

"Fran, let's take him in here."

There was no emotional outbreak, only tears welling up in his
eyes as he sat, hunched forward on an old sofa with his head cradled in his hands.

*I was devastated. I've got a family of six and two of them, a third
of my family, are wiped out. My wife is dead and my son is not
expected to live. I don't know, what do you do with something like
that? Grief is bad. Grief is a terrible thing to have to confront. I
shed a tear or two and some of the things of the afternoon, of her
wanting to go, went through my mind, and I wondered why I hadn't
gone myself. I had a real feeling of loss and despair. You lose your
wife of thirty-something years and it's a little tragic, I think. But
from then on I had to put her out of my mind, I couldn't keep thinking about her because I couldn't get functioning if I did. I had to
put her out of my mind because I knew there was nothing I could
do for her. But flashes of the pain and discomfort and anxiety and
loss kept coming back, and I just had to keep squelching them down
and get done what I had to get done. Because there was one fact
that was an absolute fact and that was never going to change, and
that's the fact you've got to look at right off the bat: She was out of
my life; forever.*

*Suddenly I realized that my son was alive upstairs and that
brought some hope, and I was anxious to see how he was doing and
if there was anything that I could do. He had looked dead and nobody would tell me he would be alive by morning, but it gave me
something to hold on to, something to hope for. I had terrible feelings
about how a kid could be put through that kind of stuff, but at least
he was alive.*

DILEMMA

It was after midnight. Don Moore, a former homicide investigator and now a member of Ogden's new Tactical Squad, knelt in the middle of the Hi-Fi Shop basement, thinking. The beam of his flashlight crisscrossed each wall methodically, rippled over the boxes and stereo components on the floor, then slowly drew semicircles on the carpet around his feet. In front of him bits of cord and tape were strewn across the bloodstains where Youngberg had first spotted the teen-age boy and woman lying on their backs, gurgling for air. Moore observed, but touched nothing.

Moore had arrived at the Hi-Fi Shop with the rest of the Tac Squad, just after the first ambulance had departed for St. Benedict's. Because of his previous experience working in homicide, he had been assigned by the squad leader to head up the initial investigation at the murder scene. After speaking briefly with Youngberg, he had secured the building, instructed a guard not to let anyone through the back door, then eased down the stairs himself to inspect the basement for evidence. A short while later the crime-scene technicians had reported to the scene with their processing equipment, and the new homicide investigator, D. K. White, who would be in charge of the actual case, had viewed the basement quickly from the bottom step. White had talked with Moore, then left immediately for the McKay-Dee emergency room to interview his eyewitness, the survivor, Mr. Walker.

While the technicians were combing the scene for evidence, the county coroner had arrived and pronounced the two remaining bodies officially dead, and funeral directors who were to transport the bodies to the State Medical Examiner in Salt Lake City had been admitted to the basement. Wearing gloves to avoid contact with the caustic that had blistered the victims' faces, they had slipped the bodies into plastic bags and sealed the bags to deliver to the pathologist's table exactly as they had been found at the scene of the crime. With the help of police officers, they had then carried the bodies slowly up the stairs, through the back door, and into the alley, where bright lights had opened up from reporters bunched a short distance from the building. In the flood of light and frequent flashes the bodies had been slid into the funeral home station wagon, and the driver had eased the car forward, cutting through the small crowd.

As Moore sat in the center of the room, it now seemed vaguely larger, though still dreary and smelling of death. Overhead, the dim light had been turned on, and the faint shadows cast by the crime-scene technicians glided among the stationary angles of gray thrown by the piles of stereo boxes. Through photography the technicians had already reconstructed the scene as they had found it, taking pictures of the bodies, the boxes, the bloodstains, before anything had been moved. Now with the bodies gone, they were systematically measuring and collecting the physical evidence. In clear bags and plastic bottles they sealed the lengths of cord used to tie the victims, the .25 caliber cartridges that had randomly ejected into some of the boxes, the .38 caliber slugs found imbedded in the carpet beneath where two of the victims had lain. They searched for a container of liquid that could have caused the burns on the victims' faces, but found none.

Hanging over the basement was a pall unlike any crime scene any of them could remember. Something in the room made it forbidden to speak. When their work demanded, they communicated, but it was official and terse, their movements methodical, as though they feared a casual move or an unnecessary word would allow empathy to seep into their thoughts and paralyze them with emotion. Some of them would later hear the voices of the victims pleading for their lives, and others would have nightmares about that single crime scene. The longer they were in the basement, the further each man receded into his own shell.

With his eyes Moore followed the beam of the flashlight around the room, silently noting the vacated positions of the bodies, a fresh gouge low on the north wall, the circle of pale blue residue on the stairs. He had crouched in the middle of dozens of murder scenes before, looking, thinking, filling his mind with a list of the Ogden criminal element and trying to match the murderer's style with someone on the list. Imagining suspects was that meager point of beginning where the momentum of an investigation got rolling. But as Moore looked around the room, he noticed nothing familiar, nothing that betrayed some subtle quirk of anyone he had pursued in the past.

During his two years as a homicide detective Moore had been assigned thirty murder cases, and when he left the Detectives to join the new Tac Squad, only a single case of his remained active. Even now, that one case was unresolved, and it gnawed at Moore. From the beginning the investigation of the case had been a strange ordeal, full of potential witnesses glancing worriedly over their shoulders at nothing, then suddenly becoming tongue-tied. Unlike the present murders, there had been but a single victim, and he had been murdered quickly and quietly in his sleep. But for sheer brutality, the weapon and the fashion in which it was employed rivaled what had happened at the Hi-Fi Shop. Having that one open file still gnawed at Moore, not because it marred his otherwise perfect record, but because he knew who the murderer was, and couldn't prove it.

He watched the beam flicker across the bloodstains in front of him. On the stairs footsteps were coming down into the basement, and then D. K. White, returning from his interview with Orren Walker, appeared in the room and called the technicians together for a briefing. When White had first seen Walker in the emergency room, a physician was extracting a dark blue, plastic shaft over six inches long from Walker's ear. The survivor had already been treated for a gunshot wound at the back of his head and chemical burns around his mouth, on his forehead and across his shoulder. With the pen safely removed, the doctor had dropped it into a plastic bag, sealed the bag, and laid it on the counter for White to take as evidence. A bloodstain ran upward from the tip of the pen almost five inches.

Though groggy from pain and fatigue, Walker had still been coherent after the operation. As White jotted quickly in his notebook, Walker had recounted the evening from the time he had entered the parking alley behind the Hi-Fi Shop until he had left there in an ambulance. His story was long, chronological, and specific; as he lay in the basement, Walker had promised himself that if he survived he would forget nothing.

He had described the two men as black, one short and one tall. The tall one had fine features and his skin was not too dark. The shorter one was very dark and husky, his face was rounder than the taller man's, and his features were coarse. Both of the men, Walker had estimated, were in their early twenties, and each wore his hair in a short, trim Afro. To enter the shop from the alley, Walker had remembered having to walk around a van pulled up nearly flush with the back door. The van had been light in color, maybe green or yellow, he wasn't sure.

As White now read from his notes, additional suspects began to surface in Moore's mind, though none of them seemed capable of committing a crime of this magnitude. He knew men who could shoot someone outright, men who, surprised or cornered or merely angry, could point a gun at another man and pull the trigger. But he could think of no one who would first torture and rape his victims, or tie them up and execute them one at a time.

When White had finished recounting Walker's story of what had happened that night in the Hi-Fi Shop basement, one of the technicians echoed Moore's thoughts.

"Who do we know around here who would be *savage* enough to do this?"

The murderer in the single case that Moore could not solve had seemed not so much savage as he had inhuman. The previous fall Moore had gathered enough evidence to interrogate the man, and had told him to his face that he knew he was the murderer. The man had sat stone-still, not a tremor in his face, not a tic of regret or a twitch of anguish that Moore could see, nothing but his narrow eyes seeming to glaze over. He had been the strangest suspect Moore had ever come up against. He had been fingerprinted, photographed, and interrogated twice again, but Moore had not been able to pierce that placid face and those glazed eyes. Nor had he been able to produce a witness or the murder weapon. For months after the initial investigation he had continued piecing together a strong case of circumstantial evidence, but not enough for a murder charge. The man had been set free, and Moore had known then that when he needed to, he would kill again.

What Moore didn't know was that the same man he had been circling all those months had knelt where he was now kneeling only a few hours before.

Dr. Richard Rees was an aggressive thoracic surgeon, brilliant and at times theatrical. If he detected anything salvageable in a patient, "Is there anything left of the squash?" he would say, tapping his head with a forefinger. He would stop at nothing to save the patient's life.

That night in Intensive Care, Rees was confronted by the heaving, rubbery-blue body of a young boy. A bloody tube gurgled out of the boy's neck, a nasogastric hose rolled from his nostrils and IV lines disappeared into each arm. In the back of his head was a bullet hole.

Dr. Rees scrubbed quickly in a nearby sink, called for a cutdown tray, hunched over Cortney's body, and began a meticulous but rapid procedure he called "shotgun therapy." He sliced Cortney's wrist and slipped an arterial blood sampling catheter into his radial artery for a computerized analysis of his blood gases. He cut into his subclavian vein and threaded a thin IV catheter toward the right ventricle of his heart. He shot Decadron and Lasix into the IV tubes to help control his edema. He administered digitalis to strengthen the action of his heart. He cut down on the saphenous vein of his groin and inserted a catheter to measure his venous pressure. He injected antibiotics to fight infection. He pumped atropine into his body to counteract his slow pulse and build up his blood pressure. He wired his heart to an electrocardiograph. He told the inhalation therapists, Chad and John, "Take him off that little ventilator, get the MA-One in here, he's got to have more oxygen!"

As Rees worked, he issued a constant flow of orders for instruments, drugs, and tubing for the lines he was installing in Cortney. So many things had to be done at once, the nurses didn't know whether to obey one order or remain next to Dr. Rees for the next.

Hands fluttered across the boy's body. Hands slicing, hands fasten-
ing, hands reaching, hands gripping, hands peeling. Hands attach-
ing, tying, pulling, suctioning, inserting, assisting. Shotgun therapy.
Pull all the stops. Do everything you know to keep the patient alive.

The flurry continued for two hours. While Dr. Rees and the nurses
plugged Cortney's body into the life-support machines, Chad and
John methodically squirted ethyl alcohol down his tracheostomy tube
and suctioned out the converted red liquid. It came slowly at first,
but after an hour the edema began to clear, and more of the oxygen
pumping from the new ventilator was now slipping into his lungs.
With tubes and wires curling into Cortney's body, the machines began blipping back his life signs, and the nurses monitored the sig-
nals, administering drugs as they dictated.

While Rees was operating, Byron Naisbitt returned with Dr. Wallace to the ICU. His demeanor had calmed, but the lines in his face
were deeper now and his eyes were red and misty. He gazed through
the glass at his son, barely visible beneath the flailing of skilled
hands, and saw that he was still alive. For a few minutes Byron
watched quietly as Dr. Rees performed his special magic; then he
stepped away from the glass. Around him people were running in
and out of his son's room, carrying things for his son's survival.
Standing there, he could do nothing but watch; watch and worry
and feel powerless to help his son.

He left the ICU and in the hallway talked briefly with a police
officer stationed there to guard Cortney. From the officer he learned
that the other survivor, Mr. Walker, was still alive at McKay-Dee
Hospital, and was able to talk. Byron began walking down the hall
toward the elevator.

"Where are you going," called Wallace.

"To the McKay," said Byron.

"Don't you think you ought to calm down a little bit first?"

Byron turned his head back halfway and continued walking. "I'll
calm down when I find out what the hell's happened!"

On the return trip from the morgue, when Byron had collapsed,
Fran Heward, the nursing supervisor, had left him and Dr. Wallace
in the nurses' lounge and hurried upstairs to phone Byron's brother,

Paul. Adhering to a tacit policy of the hospital, she would tell him only that there had been a serious accident involving his sister-in-law and that his brother needed his support. Shortly after Byron left for the McKay-Dee Hospital, Paul and his wife Maureen arrived at St. Benedict's. Mrs. Heward met them at the emergency room door and escorted them to the ICU. As they walked, she explained that Carol and Cortney both had been shot, that Carol was dead and Cortney was in Intensive Care, not expected to live.

When the door to the ICU swung open and they saw their nephew straight ahead of them, Maureen gasped, threw her hand over her mouth, and turned her back to the window. The boy in the window was long and thin and gray, and needles punctured his body. Dr. Hauser had returned to take another look at him and was conferring with Dr. Rees and Dr. Wallace in an alcove adjacent to the boy's cubicle. Paul, a quieter, more serious version of his older brother, left Maureen and walked over to the huddle of doctors.

"How is he?" he asked softly.

"Hello, Paul," nodded Rees. "He's got a lot of fluid in his lungs, and he's been shot in the head. We were just discussing whether he can tolerate Jim opening his head and taking a look inside."

"Do you expect he'll live?"

Rees hesitated, then shook his head. "No, we don't think so."

Paul walked back to where Fran Heward was still standing with Maureen near the entrance. "Where's By?" he asked.

"He's gone over to the McKay," said the supervisor. "He's trying to find out whatever he can from the other survivor."

"Have any of the kids been notified?"

"Just Brett, he should be here in a few minutes. I just hung up talking to him, but I haven't been able to get hold of the other two yet."

"Okay, where's a phone? I'll try to get in touch with Gary and Claire myself."

Brett Naisbitt exuded the same energy and jocularity as his father, although as a child it was manifested in unpromising ways. He was the little boy who was always in a fight, who laid the plastic vomit on the teacher's desk, who had a daily appointment with the principal to discuss all the bad things he had done in school that day. Nevertheless, Carol Naisbitt once told Brett's wife Diane, "Of the four children, I think I enjoyed Brett the most because he was so funny, and so unpredictable."

As a man, Brett had blond hair, green eyes, and a face lighted by a warm, pleasant smile. Though he was three inches shorter than his brother Gary, his shoulders were thick and wide. In college Brett had a quick mind and imagined himself studying to become a doctor, but instead of attending classes he preferred to ski five or six days a week in the nearby Wasatch mountains. He never graduated. He married Diane, a stunning girl with blond hair and blue eyes, when he was twenty and worked a succession of jobs as a house painter, roofer, coal shoveler, and motel manager. He also cleaned the kill floor of a meat-packing house, worked in a chemical lab, and journeyed into the Brazilian jungle to organize a diamond importing business. Now twenty-five, he had gravitated to medicine. He was an operating room technician working in general surgery and occasionally assisting neurosurgeons or the Ogden open-heart team. That morning he had scrubbed with Dr. Hauser on a craniotomy at the McKay-Dee Hospital.

For Brett and Diane it had been a pleasant evening of dinner with Diane's parents and some of her nine brothers and sisters. The family affair broke up about ten thirty, and Brett and Diane began a leisurely drive home to Riverdale, a suburb west of Ogden. They were traveling north on Harrison Boulevard, taking the long way home, when they heard sirens coming up one of the side streets from town. Then a motorcycle cop suddenly swung onto Harrison heading south. No sooner had the motorcycle made the turn than an ambulance swerved onto Harrison behind it. Both sirens were blaring as they came around the corner, and their lights were flashing. Brett commented that whoever was in the ambulance had probably had a heart attack. But Diane had other thoughts about the passenger in the ambulance.

When we saw the ambulance, I got this funny feeling. I even said to Brett: "That ambulance really has me worried. I think it's somebody in our family." Brett said, "Oh, don't be silly." I didn't know if it was my family or his family. I just had this feeling. So I said to Brett, "Please follow it." Which is silly, but I wanted him to. He kept saying, "No, that's stupid." And I said, "Brett . . . please . . . follow . . . that . . . ambulance." And he said, "Everything's all right, don't worry, it's none of our family." You know. He convinced me that it was all right. We later found out that it was his mother.

By now the ambulance had disappeared and Diane's plea began to seem rather silly even to her. They continued their drive out Harrison, then looped over to Washington Boulevard and back south again through downtown Ogden. They drove past the Hi-Fi Shop. Farther down Washington Boulevard they turned onto Riverdale Road and headed west. As they neared Riverdale, Brett began to notice the large number of police cars on the streets. With their lights flashing and sirens wailing, several had passed by earlier. Now they were pulling into deserted shopping centers, combing side streets and alleyways in search of something or someone.

"There's really a lot of action tonight," Brett remarked. "I've never seen it like this, something really big must've happened."

At home they put their newly adopted baby, Natalie, in her crib and went straight to bed. The ambulance was forgotten, the police cars were forgotten, and soon they were asleep. Then the phone rang. Brett was awake immediately.

"Brett, this is Frances Heward at St. Benedict's. I think you better get over here right away, there's been a bad accident and your dad needs your support."

"What happened?" said Brett. "Is he all right?"

"He's okay," said the supervisor, "it's your mother and Cortney, they've been in an accident and your dad needs your support. Hurry on up to Intensive Care."

"What's wrong with them?"

"Just hurry over here."

It hit me like a great big wave, a rotten, sickening feeling. It just turned me inside out. I didn't know what to think, or what to do, I just felt panicked. I started shaking immediately, could hardly control myself. I hurried and threw some clothes on, and Di grabbed Natalie and I drove them back to her mother's. On the way we tried to rationalize the situation. We figured, now they've probably been in a car accident, and they would have been in the station wagon, Cortney and Mom, and they had probably been to a show, and so they couldn't be hurt too badly because the theaters are close by and the station wagon is a big car. We had it all figured out that everything would be all right. So I dropped them off, and then I just raced to the hospital.

I came into the emergency room and they told me to go to ICU on the third floor. So I went flying up there, and I got out of the elevator and started running down the hall and Uncle Paul stepped out of the waiting room there and he grabbed me by the shoulders and he told me that there had been a shooting down at the Hi-Fi Shop and that Mother had been shot and killed, and Cortney had been shot and probably wouldn't make it. . . . You just can't believe something like that is real. You're sure it is, but you hope it's a dream, hope any minute you're going to wake up. It was like I was paralyzed. I just stood there saying, "No, no." And I started crying. Uncle Paul took me into the waiting room and had me sit down for a while. He had to convince me that Mother was dead, that there was nothing I could do for her. Then after that, I wanted to see Cort.

So I went in there, and he looked terrible. He really looked dead to me. They were doing the cutdowns on his wrists and ankles when I got there, putting in the monitors and the IVs and all that stuff. They had him wired from one end to the other, and he started looking more and more bizarre as it went on. It looked just like a Frankenstein movie, all the paraphernalia. . . . I was panicked, just barely keeping it all together. A million things are going through your mind, and adrenaline's surging through you, and then I had this wild rage when I thought about him being shot by those characters. I would have given anything to get my hands on them.

I had been there about twenty or thirty minutes when Dad came in. He had been over at the McKay talking to the other survivor. When I saw him standing there, I ran over to him and we embraced and didn't say much of anything for a while, I was just crying. Course, he was tough. He was what really got us through it all. We all kind of glided in on his coattails, his strength. . . . After a while I asked him what had happened, and he explained it, best he knew at the time. He just said that Cort had been down at the Hi-Fi Shop and got caught up in the middle of a robbery, and then Mother came down looking for him, and they got her too, and then the guy shot Mother and killed her; and he said that . . . I said are you . . . I *just kept asking him, "Are you sure she's dead?" you know. He said, "Yeah, she's really dead." And so I asked to see her, and he said, "Well, you can't, she's already . . . she's already gone." It just . . . it just . . . it's so hard to believe. It's like hearing a story about someone else.*

In another corner of Intensive Care, Drs. Hauser, Rees, and Wallace were at a disturbing, but familiar, crossroads: Did the boy have enough of a brain left to warrant saving? It was an old question, but one made fresh by the circumstances of each patient. On the one hand, Cortney was strong and young, able to endure anoxia better than an adult. The bullet had not entered his brain. His pupils had shown some vague reactions to light, and according to a blinking orange bulb on the respirator panel, he was assisting the machine on each breath. On the other hand, despite the physical damage done to his brain by the concussion of the bullet, and the damage to his internal organs precipitated by the acid, there was really only one question: Hadn't Cortney far exceeded the few minutes even a young brain can survive without oxygen? Once the brain has been deprived for its limit, it begins to die, the more specialized functions being the first to shut down. When those brain cells have died, they cannot be regenerated.

While the nurses administered to Cortney, the three doctors huddled at a table in a room next to the boy's, doing what they had done a thousand times before: second-guessing death. If they kept Cortney alive, could they make him whole again? If they couldn't make him whole, was dying now preferable to putting his family through an agonizing and futile coma? Was it more benign than bringing him back only to a state of profound mental and physical deformity? They couldn't answer these questions until after they had done everything they could to keep the boy alive. And then it would be too late to choose for him a quick, painless death.

A cup of hot coffee sat on the table in front of each of the doctors. Jess Wallace, as an emergency physician, had no further responsibility for Cortney, but was included in the consultation because of his original contact with the patient and his experience working with trauma.

"I've caught hell so many times," he told the other two, "it doesn't make any difference anymore. And I'll probably catch hell on this one, but downstairs, even in the first few minutes, I saw something in the kid that triggered me to move on him as fast as I could. Maybe it was his pupils, they seemed to react just a little when we shortened that dead air space."

As a neurosurgeon, Hauser's chief concern was the boy's pupils. They were the surest, outward indicator of brain damage. When he had examined the boy earlier, he had seen no deviation in their wide, fixed position.

"I'm still not comfortable with his eye signs," he commented. "But then again, it's encouraging to me to see his blood pressure's coming back."

"What the hell," said Wallace, "we talk about using our clinical judgment in cases like this and really it's more like ESP or witchcraft if we end up doing the right thing."

Rees had his arms folded and was leaning back in his chair, rubbing his eyes. "The fact is," he said, "I have never seen a patient this dead make a comeback. I really haven't."

Hauser agreed with Rees.

"I don't think that matters at this point," said Wallace. "I think you've got to keep going balls to the wall on the kid just to . . . how do I say this? . . . just to give some sort of psychological support to By."

Wallace had verbalized what was becoming apparent to the other two doctors.

"I don't see how the boy has a chance of making it," said Hauser, "but after this double whammy, I'm not at all sure how much more By can take, either."

Rees was yawning. "We've got to do something," he said. "I just don't know if he can make it through brain surgery."

"If I do anything about that pressure in his head," said Hauser, "it's going to have to be soon. Burr holes won't accomplish much if all we find is pulped brain, but if we can evacuate something besides brain, like maybe a blood clot, he might have a chance."

"Oh, hell," said Rees, "if he doesn't have the burr holes, he's not going to make it anyhow, I guess, so any way you look at it we've got nothing to lose. One thing," he continued. "By probably understands the situation better than most people, but I want to explain everything to him. I want him to be fully aware of what's going on, and what the possible consequences are."

Byron Naisbitt stood not far away, his arms around Brett, consoling him in a little alcove by the Intensive Care nurses' desk. Brett's tears had dried upon his face, leaving his eyes encircled by puffy flesh. Byron gripped him tightly, watching as Dr. Rees and Dr. Hauser came toward them.

"By," said Hauser, "we don't need to elaborate on how serious Cortney's situation is. I want to take him to surgery and open up his head so we can get a better idea of where we stand. Dick's got him stabilized as best he can, but we don't know if he's strong enough to tolerate surgery like that, he might not be. On the other hand, if we don't operate soon to try to relieve that pressure, it's going to kill him anyway."

Byron's face was expressionless. He stood with his arm around Brett and listened. When Hauser had finished, he said: "I understand what you're up against. Just do whatever you can for him."

"There's something else, By," added Rees, "and I think we should get it out in the open right now. I probably don't need to tell you this, but we want to make sure you're fully aware of it."

He paused for a moment and Byron nodded his head as though he already knew what the surgeon was going to say.

"If Cortney somehow pulls through all of this," Rees continued, "if we can keep him alive, we may be creating a monster. We may get him back to a certain point and then wish we hadn't."

Byron said nothing at first. He had realized much earlier that before the night was over, he would have to make a decision. He could allow his son to die peacefully as he lay. Or he could beseech the doctors to keep him alive, despite the consequences. It upset him to think that even if Cortney lived, he would be deprived of doing all the things he had wanted to do. But then he thought, being alive's better than being dead.

"Yeah, I've thought about that," he said. "But I want you to go ahead and do everything you can. We'll worry about the rest of it later."

For the surgery a single rule was established: The respirator assisting Cortney's breathing would be put on Demand, so that if the boy initiated a breath, it would assist him and flash the orange light each time. If he quit tripping the respirator, if the orange light went out, it would mean that even the central, more primitive part of his brain was gone. If this occurred during surgery, rather than keep alive the heart and lungs in a person whose brain had died, Dr. Rees would simply unplug the machine.

A three-member surgical crew, including an anesthesiologist, an RN, and an operating room technician, had been summoned to assist Dr. Hauser in the exploratory operation. But when Hauser phoned the operating room to give instructions for setting up the operation, he discovered that the OR technician wasn't qualified to assist in neurosurgery. Ironically, the only person in the hospital qualified to scrub for neurosurgery was Brett Naisbitt. Brett overheard Hauser's phone call and volunteered to scrub for the operation. His face still appeared stung, and Dr. Hauser questioned whether assisting in the operation would be too much for him to absorb emotionally. But Brett had already acquired a full set of pajama greens, the antistatic slippers, pants, top, and tie-back cap, and was walking down the hall to surgery to set up the scrub for the operation on his brother.

Though she stood a few inches taller, Claire Naisbitt seemed cast in her mother's image. She was petite and had blond hair and moist green eyes, and there were freckles dusted lightly across the bridge of her nose. She was a pretty girl, "a girl you'd see and not soon forget," recalled a high school classmate. Of the Naisbitt children Claire, now twenty-two, had always been the achiever: the cheerleader, the honor society member, the class officer, the award winner. At home she was the peacemaker among her brothers. But beneath her tact and achievements and appealing face lay concealed a certain soft sensitivity. She was quick to make someone feel better with a card or a kind word; she never forgot a birthday and was hurt if someone forgot hers.

Two weeks prior to her parents' trip to Hong Kong, Claire felt moved to write them a note. It was something she did occasionally, a thoughtful reminder to her parents of how much she loved and appreciated them. The note remained unwritten, however, until the day before their departure, when she finally sat down and wrote a card to her parents. At the airport to see them off, she handed the sealed card to her parents. It simply wished them a safe trip and added, "I just wanted you to know how much I love both of you."

Claire had envisioned her parents in the air, opening the note and merely smiling to each other as they began their trip to the Orient. But after the last passenger had boarded, and Claire stood at the window, waiting for the plane to take off, she was surprised to see her mother coming back off the plane. Carol ran inside the terminal and hurried up to her daughter.

"What in the world are you doing?" Claire laughed.

Her mother hugged her. "I just wanted to tell you how much *we* love *you*. Claire, honey, that was the sweetest note."

"Oh, that's just how I feel," said Claire.

"Well, it was thoughtful of you to do it. You're mighty special to us."

"You'd better hurry," Claire cried, "You're going to miss your plane!"

"Oh, they'll wait," said her mother. She kissed Claire and started toward the ramp. "We'll see you in a couple of weeks."

Claire waved and yelled, "Have fun!" She was glad she had written the note.

What Claire hadn't included in the note was that she and Scott Swift, a second-year medical student at the University of Utah, would soon be announcing their engagement. Claire knew that her excitable and highly organized mother had been planning her only daughter's wedding from the day Claire was born. In fact, Claire was still in high school when Brett and Diane were married, but her mother had decided then that it was time for Claire to begin planning for her own wedding by selecting patterns for her china, silver, and crystal. For the past six years, at birthdays and Christmas, Claire had received pieces and place settings in her chosen patterns. Now that she would be graduating from college in June, she had collected all of her fine tableware, but her mother had been unable to pry an admission from her that she and Scott were planning to be married. On more than one occasion Carol had complained to Scott's mother, "I just don't think I'll ever see my daughter get married." But Scott had already purchased the diamond, and they were saving the announcement as a surprise for Carol and Byron, sometime after they returned from their trip. It was hard for Claire not to share the secret with her mother, but for now the excitement would have to wait just a little while longer.

Even when Claire welcomed her parents home at the airport two weeks later, she had said nothing about her plans with Scott, although the first day they were back, Claire and her mother had attended the wedding of a friend of Claire's. After the wedding Claire had remained in Ogden over the weekend with Gary and Cortney to hear the stories and see the souvenirs their parents had brought back with them from the Orient. Through a friend the Naisbitts had been permitted a tour of a Hong Kong jewelry factory, where they had bought select pearls and jade. Then, after viewing the Red China border, they had flown to Saigon; but fighting erupted only twenty miles from the capital, and they had flown out the same day. On the return flight to Hong Kong they had landed in Bangkok and purchased yards of shimmering Thai silk. The stories of the trip included the side ventures, the quick impressions of the lands and peoples, the exotic dishes they had sampled. The pictures of the sights they had seen wouldn't be ready, if at all, until Monday.

Claire returned to school in Salt Lake City on Sunday afternoon. Monday was a typical day for her, attending classes in the final courses she would need for her medical technology degree from the University of Utah. That night she and her roommate, Jody Hetzel, went out for dinner and returned to their apartment to study until eleven thirty. Then they turned out the lights and went to sleep. In the silence just after midnight the phone rang.

"Claire, this is Uncle Paul." His voice was firm and dry. "There's been an accident," he explained slowly, "and we want you to come to St. Benedict's Hospital."

Claire sat up in bed. "Who is it?"

"It's okay," said her uncle, "just come on up."

"Right now?" she asked. It was thirty-five miles from Salt Lake City to Ogden.

"Yes, right now. But don't hurry," he added. "Be safe."

"Sure," said Claire. "I will."

I got up and started getting dressed, and I woke up Jody and I told her what my uncle had said, so she decided she'd better go with me. I felt really anxious. I remember hurrying, getting dressed, and just running out the door and jumping in the car. It was raining a little bit, and I was driving so I would have something to keep my mind occupied. We decided we were going to drive slow, but it didn't really turn out that way.

I felt sort of sick. I was trying to figure out who would be out that late at night. The only person that would be was my dad. And then I thought, Well, what could have happened to him? So I figured he had gotten in a car accident on the way to the hospital for a delivery. Right at first I didn't think it would be that bad. We didn't talk about it very much. I was wondering out loud why Uncle Paul had called instead of Mother, but then I decided that if something had happened to Dad she would probably be more concerned with him. But then I thought, If it was just a little accident why wouldn't she be able to call? Maybe Dad really was badly injured. I didn't think he was dead or anything. I tried not to think about that. I thought, Well, I don't know, I'll just have to wait and find out.

It must have taken us about thirty minutes to get to the hospital, and we walked right in the emergency room. I didn't have to ask any questions; it seemed like as soon as we walked in the door somebody was right there and said, "Come this way," or "Come with me," or something. So we walked down the hall, and somebody else met us, that must have been Dr. Wallace . . . he looked familiar, but I really didn't know who he was, and at that point I really didn't care. I just followed him and we . . . we went around the corner . . . and got in the elevator. And . . . um . . . while we were in the elevator . . . he . . . he put his arm around me . . . and he told me . . . he said that my mom had been shot . . . and that she was dead . . . and that . . . um . . . Cortney had been . . . shot, but he said that he was . . . not . . . he was . . . critically ill . . . or serious . . . or something . . . and he said that I was going to have to be tougher than anybody else, because my dad needed all the support he could get. It hit so hard . . . I felt like . . . somebody . . . dropped . . . a ton of bricks right on top of me. I just remember . . . just grabbing Jody . . . throwing my arms around her . . . and just crying. I guess she held me up. . . . It's the most horrible feeling . . . it's so shocking . . . you know, just so . . . so surprising . . . even if you sort of expect something bad like that. It's like your worst expectations have come true . . . that someone is dead, but I couldn't imagine how my mother had been shot. Maybe a car accident or a heart attack, or something. But how do people get shot? Things like that just didn't happen to people.

We got to the third floor and the door opened and we walked a little way down the hall and Uncle Paul was there and he came up and took me down to my dad. Brett was there in the waiting room, sitting on the couch. Dad was sitting in a big chair, and I just climbed up on his lap and hugged him. And I cried. . . . My dad . . . my dad said . . . he always says, "Don't fret, don't fret." And he told me, "Go ahead and cry and don't fret, and it'll be okay." Just what daddies will tell you. He said: "I've had my cry, you just go ahead. I've already been through it all, now it's your turn." He told me, too, that he had had to go down and see Mother. And I said, "Was it awful?" and he said, "Yes, it was awful." But he was glad that it was over. And I can remember asking him what she looked like. And he said: "Just fine. Don't worry." He would never tell me. I guess . . . I'm sure he thought . . . I don't know what she looked like, I really don't . . . even though he said, "Just fine." She may . . . maybe did and maybe didn't. He was always telling me, "Don't worry about that." He said: "You don't want to ever see her. You don't want to see her like that. You want to remember her the way she was. So don't think about it. Just think about Cortney and getting him well. . . ."

He held me for a while, and then I asked him about Cortney, and he took me in to see him. I couldn't believe it. . . . I'd been in ICUs before, but it's different when it's your own brother. I remember they had him on one of those cold-blankets, and he was shivering . . . and I remember how long and thin he looked . . . he wasn't completely cleaned up . . . and he didn't have any clothes on . . . he just had tubes everywhere . . . they were going in his arms and his legs, and it seemed like he was pretty yellow. And he had a trache in . . . I don't know why, but that really bothered me. And his eyes were closed and sort of black and blue, kind of sunken in and dark-looking. I remember he had burns around his mouth and kinda down his neck. He looked really tired . . . just totally exhausted. He just . . . he just looked . . . he didn't look like himself at all. He wasn't pink, and he wasn't . . . I don't know . . . he looked kinda . . . kinda dead. And then everything came crashing down on top of me again. I was nauseated. It's so weird to see somebody all tubed up. Somebody that you know. It's really awful. And he was coughing up junk all the time. I was thinking, Who is this? You're not my brother. I mean, you don't look like him. My brother's jumping up and down, running around.

I just stared at him right at first, then I talked to him and asked him how he was doing. I don't know if I dared to touch him. I think maybe I touched his toes, or something like that. Or else . . . maybe I went over and touched his hand . . . after Dad did. Yeah. I think I did touch his hand. But I remember I was just so . . . so shocked, I didn't . . . I just felt like I couldn't touch him. I didn't know what it would be like, I guess. I guess I was afraid of him.

They only let us stay in there for a minute, and then Dad walked me back into the waiting room and he went back in with Cortney. And then Gary came, and I saw him walk by the door and into the ICU.

In the basement of the Hi-Fi Shop, Don Moore and the crime-scene technicians had now heard the full eyewitness story of the murders, relayed by Detective White. It helped them in their search for evidence, but it did little to suggest suspects. For Moore there was nothing to link his single unsolved murder with the murders in the Hi-Fi Shop basement, other than the savagery it took to commit them. To connect the savagery of one with the savagery of the other, Moore would have had to perceive that a man with a soft tiptoe and an indifferent way of crouching to execute his victims could also drive a bayonet through a sleeping man's face.

If Moore had sensed that he had once tracked a murderer as cold and detached as the one described by Mr. Walker, it would have keyed vivid memories, taking him back in time a little over six months, to October 5, 1973. About noon that day, a Friday, he had been called in to investigate the death of a young black Air Force sergeant stationed at Hill Air Force Base, just south of Ogden. Sergeant Edward Jefferson was found in his Ogden apartment, reposed on a couch, murdered in his sleep. He was wearing only a set of white thermal underwear, and his hands were still folded peacefully across his chest. Tracking down leads, Moore had worked through the weekend and by Monday had focused his investigation on a rather mysterious figure whose full name no one seemed to know— just Dale from the West Indies. Agents from the Air Force Office of Special Investigations, OSI, working with Moore on the case, had finally identified him as another young black airman, a twenty-year-old Trinidadian named Dale Pierre.

From records and witnesses Moore had pieced together the following story on Pierre: Pierre had been at Jefferson's apartment the previous Sunday afternoon, taping some music, when Jefferson's key ring, including the keys to his apartment and his 1971 Grand Prix, had suddenly disappeared. Though the apartment was searched thoroughly, the keys were not found until Pierre returned the following day and brazenly suggested they search again. During this second search the key ring had miraculously reappeared. Jefferson became suspicious, investigated the matter, and discovered that Pierre had stolen his key ring, gone to the base locksmith, forged the name Curtis Alexander, and duplicated the keys to his apartment and his car. Jefferson changed the ignition on his car and had his landlord install new locks in his apartment. He then confronted Pierre about the incident, and a third airman, a friend of Jefferson's, overheard the two arguing, but was not close enough to hear what was said. Two days later Jefferson's body was discovered on the couch in his living room, a pillow over his face and a light coverlet pulled up over the pillow. His face was puffed and bruised, with bits of brain mired in a thick pus oozing from his nose and eye sockets. A bayonet had been driven repeatedly through his face, the first blow killing him instantly. The murderer had used such power and the weapon had been driven so deeply, that the blade had gone all the way through Jefferson's brain, the hilt itself fracturing the man's skull.

Moore had viewed the Jefferson murder as particularly cold and unfeeling, a matter of expediency rather than passion. He saw the present murders similarly, but here there was a new dimension he had not been aware of in the Jefferson case: after hearing the eyewitness's story, Moore surmised that the killer had actually enjoyed seeing the people suffer, that he had calculated the damage that would be done each time he fed them the caustic or pulled the trigger. It was this aspect of the new murders that prevented Moore from imagining Pierre as a suspect. Though Pierre may have enjoyed murdering Jefferson, Moore had had no witness to attest to it.

Three days after Jefferson's body was discovered, the OSI agents working with Moore located Pierre and had him brought to their office, where Moore saw the elusive airman for the first time. He was short, about five five, and thick-limbed, well-muscled from lifting weights, but rather oddly put together. As thick as his body was, his head was still too large, and his forehead sloped too steeply and ran too high to meet the back of it. His back was slightly arced, ending in a large, protruding ass that would have suggested a waddle if it hadn't been for the strut he affected. There was nothing menacing in Pierre's physical presence; to the contrary, his nonchalance made him appear unusually docile. But there was something haughty in his demeanor, an air that suggested he was far too busy to have his time wasted. He strolled into the office and nodded casually at Moore, then settled easily into a chair and with his finger massaged the bridge of his nose, a gesture slow and calm and innocent. Moore felt that Pierre, being interrogated for first-degree murder, was little more than annoyed at the inconvenience.

Prior to joining the Ogden Police in 1969, when he was twenty-four, Moore had taught hand-to-hand combat for the Army Special Forces. He stood six six and weighed 225. Everything about him, including his silence, was large and intimidating. He had large hands and large fingers, a massive head, and huge eyes covered by thick, dark eyebrows that seemed to weigh heavily on his eyes, slanting them out toward his temples. His eyes were a medium blue, and when he glared at a suspect, they actually bulged out and seemed to flash a lighter, hotter blue.

Moore knew little about Pierre, and seeing him now gave him no reason to think that Pierre would be any different than other subjects he had interrogated. They frequently acted cocky at the beginning. Sitting sideways on top of a desk, Moore opened by advising Pierre of his rights, then explained to him that he was a suspect in the Jefferson murder. Pierre sat still and said nothing. As always, Moore was firm and direct, never taking his eyes off Pierre's face. A few feet from Moore, in a chair against the wall, Pierre struck a similar pose, never taking his narrow, flinty eyes off Moore's. Though Pierre spoke an English of confusing rhythms and inflection, Moore could understand him, and the two men conversed stiffly but affably about Trinidad and Pierre's job in the Air Force. When Pierre had answered a question, he would close his mouth and sit quietly, waiting for the next one. He volunteered nothing, never became animated or smiled, and never looked away from Moore's face.

Pierre admitted knowing Jefferson and being at his apartment a few days before the murder, but he denied stealing the keys or having them duplicated. Toward the end of their first meeting Moore asked Pierre where he had been the night Jefferson was killed. Pierre pensively tapped his index finger at the groove between his nose and his thick upper lip, a habit he had when he was thinking. After a moment he said that he had borrowed a car belonging to his roommate, who was away on leave, and gone to Salt Lake City by himself to shop around for a used car on the used car lots. Then he had returned to his barracks and remained there till the next day when he had gone to work on the flight line. Finished with his explanation, Pierre dropped his hand away from his face and continued staring at Moore. Although his alibi couldn't be substantiated, Pierre's expression betrayed not even a hint of concern. In Moore's experience, this was unique.

"When you interrogate somebody that's involved in a crime," Moore explained later, "they try and bluff their way out, they try to tell stories, they tell lies, they look off into space, they fidget with something, they concentrate on the telephone. Whatever. But Pierre wouldn't. He could look you right in the eye for fifteen minutes and never take his eyes off you."

During their second meeting a few days later Moore covered the same ground they had been over during their first session, and Pierre gave the same answers, still denying any involvement. When they had finished and Pierre was leaving the office, Moore asked him to sign the name Curtis Alexander four times, which Pierre did willingly and in a clear, exquisite hand. It was like Pierre to be cunning and careless at the same time, to show off his penmanship at the risk of facing a murder charge. After handwriting samples were taken

from a number of the victim's friends, each was compared to the
signature left at the locksmith's, and Pierre was positively identified
as the author of "Curtis Alexander."

But Moore needed something stronger than the signatures to arrest the man for murder. He needed witnesses, someone who had
seen Pierre near the apartment on the night Jefferson was killed, or
who had heard an altercation between the two men. Searching for
those witnesses, Moore discovered that Pierre was a loner, that he
had no friends, that little was known about him because he rarely
associated with anyone. When he wasn't on the flight line, he was
either at the movies or shooting pool. Perhaps stirred by his reti-
cence and his origins in the West Indies, rumors even circulated
that Pierre, a baptized Protestant, practiced voodoo. Most of the airmen avoided him. Those who knew anything about him were afraid
to talk. One man, who knew Pierre and Jefferson and had been
cleared of suspicion with a polygraph, would visibly shake every time
Moore talked with him. He told Moore he was afraid that the same
person who got Jefferson would get him, too. Another airman, when
told about the bayonet driven through Jefferson's face, told Moore:
"Pierre is a crazy dude, man. It sounds like some of the crazy things
he would do without even flinching." The impression Moore got of
Pierre, that he was a tough guy, a loner, somebody capable of Jefferson's murder, derived not so much from *what* the few people said
about Pierre, as it did from *how* they said it; always tight-lipped, in
a whisper, as though no matter where they were Pierre could easily
hear them. But impressions would not hold up in court. Lacking
witnesses and a murder weapon, Moore would somehow have to
draw a confession from the man.

The evidence Moore now had against Pierre was the sort that
festers into cynicism in a detective's mind: enough to convince his
street-sharpened instinct that Pierre was the murderer, but too little
to sway that sense of due process in the judicial mind. In the hands
of an experienced interrogator, one able to seize inflection and nu-
ance, one able to read the intricate music of the nervous system in
a man's face, such evidence could be used as nimble fingers to play
the suspect, stroke him, massage his conscience, sometimes terrify
him, sometimes befriend him, and ultimately to pull from him an
admission. Moore considered interrogation an art form of finesse

and timing. Upon questioning a suspect, he first filled his head with every fact of the case, then faced the subject and observed closely each response, waiting for his cue to come in with a soft sympathetic word, or to switch on his blue eyes and fly into a rage.

Their third meeting opened as the other two had, slowly, Moore asking the same questions he had asked twice before, and Pierre offering the same answers. Pierre was as controlled and indifferent as he had been the first two times they had met. Moore watched him, pretending not to notice his obvious annoyance at having to answer the same questions again. Twenty minutes into their encounter Moore asked Pierre about the locksmith, and Pierre admitted for the third time that he had been at Jefferson's when the keys were lost and again when the keys were found, that he had helped look for the keys both times. But, he calmly stated, again for the third time, he did not steal the keys, he did not have the keys duplicated, he did not steal Jefferson's car, he did not kill. . . .

Suddenly, Moore hurled his six-foot-six-inch, 225-pound body across the desk, his blue eyes on fire.

"You're lying to me, Pierre!" Moore shouted, his face inches from Pierre's. "I *know* you stole Jefferson's keys, I *know* you went to the repair shop, I *know* you had these duplicates made, I *know* you forged the name Curtis Alexander!"

Moore paused for a second to let his enraged, bulged eyes flick from one of Pierre's eyes to the other.

"Jefferson knew it too, and he caught you, didn't he! And he had all of his locks changed, didn't he! And he threatened to bust up the car ring you had going, so you killed him, didn't you! You drove a bayonet right through his Goddamn head! Didn't you!"

Moore later recalled what happened next. "I got up close to him, started violating his body space, reached out and touched him on the shoulder and said, 'I know you're involved in this!' But Pierre didn't mind that. He didn't fidget or move around or act nervous or anything. He just got that much closer to me, and then he rose up and looked me right in the eye with those eyes of his and said, 'I didn't commit any murder.' That's when I could see a noticeable change coming over him. It was visible, you could see his eyes becoming more fixed, and staring at you, and he just quit talking, and this cold, cold atmosphere came over him.

"I've run across acts of defiance where somebody'll just look you right in the eye and dare you. I see that all the time. But this was different. I can't put my finger on it, but you could just watch a change come over him. As soon as we started going into his criminal activity, you could actually see it coming. Of all the subjects I've ever interrogated, he was by far the toughest because of the way he looked back at you. I think Pierre could probably intimidate people just with that look. That look, that whole attitude, it was an eerie, eerie feeling that would emit from him. He could probably scare the daylights out of somebody. I've never run across it before or since."

Now kneeling in the basement of the Hi-Fi Shop six months later, if Moore had only known that the man who had knelt there just hours before him was in the Air Force, or if he had somehow gotten a clear description of the man's eyes, he might have connected the two murders and shortened the twenty-four hours it took to capture Dale Pierre.

A speaker clamped to his partially raised window, Gary Naisbitt was slumped in the front seat of his car, hypnotically absorbed in a mindless and forgettable drive-in movie. The conversation with his father had left him with a dull sense of relief, and the movie helped to numb his thoughts. It was novocaine for his mind that wore off when the movie ended just after midnight.

Stopped at the traffic light on his way back to Centerville, Gary noticed a police car situated curiously in the middle of the street. Its blue lights were flashing and the officer was glaring seemingly at him. The light turned green and Gary hesitantly entered the intersection. Suddenly the police car swung around, shot in front of Gary, and forced off the road the vehicle that had been next to him at the light: It was a light-colored van. Gary slowly pulled away from the van and the flashing blue lights, watching as the ordeal faded in his rearview mirror, and proceeded to Centerville. He had been home fifteen minutes when the phone rang.

"Gary?" said the voice on the other end.

"Yeah?"

"This is your Uncle Paul."

"Hello!"

"There's been an accident," continued his uncle. "I want you to come to St. Benedict's Hospital as fast as you can. Don't do it recklessly, I want you to get here."

"Sure," Gary said. "How bad is it?"

"One of them," said his uncle, "is very bad."

That automatically told me that at least two people were involved, and that accounted for Mother and Cortney not coming home. It implied that she had found him, and I just figured they had been in a car wreck on the way home. At the time I had this distinct feeling that Cort would somehow be okay and that the one that was really bad would be Mother.

So I got dressed again and drove to the hospital about seventy-five or eighty miles an hour. I was fairly calm, but my legs were shaking. I walked into the emergency room and hardly even broke stride. I was trying to affect a jovial mood, but I was in turmoil inside, I had the nervous shakes, because I had no idea what to expect. I asked them, "Where's the Naisbitt group?" and they said, "Up in ICU, third floor." Then no one said a word and there was no expression on anyone's face as I walked down the hall and got in the elevator.

When the elevator door opened on the third floor, the first person I saw was John Lindquist, a close friend of the family and a mortician. He said, "Hi, Gary," and I said, "Oh, you're a bad omen." He said, "You haven't heard?" I said, "No, just getting here." And he never said another word, just got in the elevator and closed the door.

I walked down the hall trying to be calm, trying to get hold of myself. I passed a room filled with all kinds of relatives, aunts and uncles and cousins, but I didn't take the time to stop, everybody was crying and everything. I just kept right on going, on into the ICU.

Cort was the first thing I saw, I didn't see Mother anywhere, but Cort was right there in front of me, all covered with tubes and people. He was all bandaged up and wired in and stuff, and he looked like Cort, but he looked like he had just run a three-minute mile. And I thought, Well, a car accident of some sort . . . Mother found Cort and they had been in a car accident. I didn't go in and take a look at Cort. It was just a quick glance.

Dad was back in a little alcove where they had a light box and he was looking at some X rays with Dr. Wallace. They were X rays of Mother, and they were postulating whether the two white blurs were the bullet and a bone fragment or an unjacketed bullet that had split in two. So I walked over to Dad, and I was pretty much matter-of-fact, I think that was my way of keeping from going all to pieces. I said, "Well, here I am, what's wrong?" He said, "Let me tell you what's happened, Gary . . . your mother's dead and Cortney's been shot, he's still alive, but we don't know for how long." I didn't know how in the world they could possibly be shot. The first thing that flashed through my mind was that Mother must have really gone berserk, shot Cort and then committed suicide, but that seemed a little farfetched. The thought couldn't have lasted more than a split second, because it was just the next sentence that he said, "There was a robbery at the Hi-Fi Shop and they were both involved." He didn't have to tell me that Mother had backtracked to find Cort at the Hi-Fi Shop.

I was too tied up with myself to see how Dad was taking all of this. I can't say for sure that I put my arms around him and said, "I'm sorry," though I possibly could have, and I hope that I did, though I can't say for sure. I just can't remember. I asked him, "Well, how about Cort?" and he said: "He's still alive, but he's not in very good shape. They made him drink some stuff and his throat's all burned up, and he can't breathe, but he's been stabilized for now and they're going to do an operation to see if they can relieve some of the pressure that's going to develop in his brain, get rid of some of the blood." He was very professional, very controlled. Maybe slightly forced, but he wasn't enraged.

I know I controlled my emotions for a few more minutes, but then I broke down and cried and I couldn't help it. Dad had already done his crying and now he was taken up with the medical problems of trying to save Cort. I know that I used Cort's situation as an escape. I assume that's what he was doing too, but only because there was hope in Cort's case. Mother's story had already been told.

IV bottles dribbling life into Cortney were unhooked and placed on the bed beside him. His arterial line was disconnected. The respirator was replaced with a hand-squeeze bag and portable oxygen supply. Cortney was now mobile. A nurse sprung the chocks on the gurney, and with an entourage of tubes and technicians keeping pace, he was rushed around the corner and down the hall to surgery.

In the operating room green tile covered the floor and climbed the walls halfway to the ceiling. At the center of the room hung a glaring surgical lamp, three feet in diameter. It was ringed by eight smaller lights concentrated on a point directly below the center of the large dome. At the convergence of light was Cortney's shaved head, smooth and rounded but for a mottled lump now swollen to the size of a child's fist. His gray body was propped in a stiff sitting position, his legs wrapped tightly in elastic bandages, his arms extended and supported as though he were presiding from a throne. With tubes and wires sprouting from his neck, his wrists, his groin, his bladder, his forearms, his nose, and his heart, he looked like an electrically operated boy-king. His head was crowned with a stainless steel brace, three-pronged, like a Christmas tree stand, the rubber-padded screws cranked down tightly against his skull to hold it fast. Only half closed and covered by a thick, protective jelly were his eyes.

Before Brett Naisbitt could set up the scrub for Cortney's operation, another OR technician, qualified in neurosurgery, had been located and had come in to assist Dr. Hauser. Brett, however, had remained in his pajama greens, hoping he would be allowed to watch the operation with his father and uncle; it seemed easier than waiting outside for scraps of Cortney's progress.

The operation was to consist of drilling two holes through the underside of Cortney's skull in back, and another at the point of the bullet's impact. Once into the region of the brain, Dr. Hauser would evacuate the collection of blood he hoped to find and try to explore the extent of physical damage. The more blood he could evacaute, the less of Cortney's brain would have to be removed to accommodate the swelling.

Dr. Hauser was a finicky surgeon. He enjoyed surgery, and he insisted on organizing each operation down to the smoothest possible coordination of time and instruments. Those assistants who caused the slightest interruption in his impeccable planning found him to be impatient and tactless. Unfortunately, trauma surgery was always a hurried affair, never performed under optimum conditions. It was a circumstance Dr. Hauser had learned to tolerate. But the atmosphere of the operating room that night was exacerbated by the background of emotion and tension now focused on the operation. To this was added the unique and unsettling presence in the operating room of the patient's father, uncle, and brother. Dr. Hauser finally decided the whole affair was so singular and impossible that it would be better to allow the boy's family to observe the operation than to submit them to an agonizing wait outside.

Cortney's head was soaped and scrubbed with disinfectant for a full ten minutes. Then with Dr. Rees monitoring Cortney's life signs, and Byron, Paul, and Brett Naisbitt scrubbed, green-suited, and silently watching, the deft neurosurgeon began a ritual of placing sterile green towels all around Cortney's head, beginning just above his eyebrows and hooking each to the skin with a scissor clamp. When he was finished, the lower rear of Cortney's head was isolated for surgery and the lump at the back rose singularly above the green covering.

Beginning the procedure for drilling the first two holes, Dr. Hauser made a vertical incision at the back of Cortney's head and neck and began filleting the tissues, stretching them back with hemostats. Slicing further, stretching back, he reached a thin layer of tissue, the pericranium, just outside the skull, and scraped this away. Then he took a Hudson brace-and-bit, a hand drill resembling a carpenter's tool, and cranked slowly into the bone, augering out bits of skull and periodically flushing the hole with a saline solution, until he reached the leathery covering of the brain, the dura mater. He swabbed the dime-size hole he had just drilled, and with a pair of bone rongeurs began snipping off chips of skull to enlarge the hole to the size of a silver dollar.

As Dr. Hauser repeated the drilling and snipping process on the opposite side of the midline, Byron, Paul, and Brett stood immediately behind him, gazing over his shoulder. Except for the metallic click of the instruments and the breathing behind each mask, the shiny, sterile room was silent. A few feet from the operating table Dr. Rees scanned the lighted board on the machine that could see inside Cortney's body. The orange light at the top continued to blink slowly. Byron's eyes moved from the orange light to the back of his son's head to the side of Dr. Hauser's face. As yet, Hauser had said nothing.

With two holes now opened in the back of Cortney's head, Dr. Hauser reached into each defect with a double-pronged hook, gaffed the dura mater twice and held it taut while making the dural incisions. Next he hooked a black silk suture into each flap of the sliced dura mater and spread the flaps to expose the surface of Cortney's cerebellum. A clear cerebrospinal fluid was released through the two dural defects, but there was no evidence of blood clot.

"There isn't the accumulation of blood I had hoped to find," Dr. Hauser spoke to Byron through his mask. "But we've still got the wound itself to look into."

Hauser extended the scalp incision upward in the shape of a hockey stick to include the wound made by the bullet. The outer layer of skull in that area was fractured, but a burr hole drilled adjacent to the wound revealed that the inner layer of bone, although cracked, was still in normal alignment. As he drilled the hole, Hauser explained to Byron what he was finding.

"Frankly, the wound itself is not as bad as I expected it to be," he said. "Somehow the bullet didn't enter the brain. It smashed through the outer table of the skull and shattered the inner, but the inner wasn't even depressed. It turned the bullet to the right, over here."

"What does that mean?" asked Byron.

"Right now it doesn't mean anything," Hauser explained. "It's just remarkable that the bullet or at least part of his skull wasn't forced into his brain. That could've done significantly more damage."

Dr. Hauser was quiet again as he cleared the overlying bone from the area of impact and sliced open the freshly exposed dura. There on the surface of Cortney's brain was a scarlet spot the size of a quarter. Byron and the rest crowded closer, leaning down to view the damage done to Cortney's brain by the bullet. As they watched, Dr. Hauser called for a probe and carefully positioned the needlelike instrument in the middle of the bright contusion. He slid the probe cautiously beneath the surface of Cortney's brain. It met with little resistance. Continuing to examine the wound, Dr. Hauser spoke to Byron over his shoulder.

"By, it looks like the concussion of the bullet has turned a chunk of Cortney's brain, I would say about half the size of my thumb, to jelly. It's all pulped brain and dark blood."

"What does that mean?" Byron asked again.

"I hate to keep being evasive," said Hauser, "but I really don't know. It's good that the bullet didn't enter his brain, but I'm afraid that more damage can be done by the shock waves, which traveled from the lower right here where the bullet hit across to a point roughly in this area." Hauser drew a circle in the air above the upper left portion of Cortney's head. "That's the contrecoup injury," he continued. "The impact of the bullet causes the brain to smash into the skull on the opposite side. Now at the point of impact this pulverized mass of brain tissue will have to be scooped out to avoid infection and to give the rest of the brain a little more space in which to swell."

The back of Cortney's brain glistened beneath the bright lamps. Dr. Hauser turned away from the incision and looked at Byron above his surgical mask.

"I'm afraid these devitalized brain cells are in an area that controls vision. If the boy lives, he could well be only partially sighted."

Byron listened to the neurosurgeon. Then he asked, "What about the contrecoup injury?"

"As for the contrecoup injury, it's impossible for me to say what the damage will be, but the shock waves traversed areas that involve speech and the control of the right side of his body. He could be paralyzed on that side."

Cortney had been a graceful skier, a competent sailor, and a good wing-shot in the pheasant fields. In AAU swim competition he had won ribbons and medals for the breaststroke and freestyle. A year ago he had placed first in the Mt. Ogden Junior High Science Fair with a telescope patterned after that on Mount Palomar. He had ground the six-inch mirror and silvered it himself, then engineered an electronic tracking system so the telescope could automatically follow a particular heavenly body. The *Ogden Standard-Examiner* had run an article, complete with a picture of Cortney and his award-winning telescope. The newspaper piece was entitled "REACHES FOR STARS—Hard Work, Patience Pays Off For Energetic Science Student." Cortney had aspired to be an aeronautical engineer since he was five years old, and Byron knew that he had soloed for the first time that same afternoon. Now Cortney was sitting hunched forward on an operating table, the back of his head sliced open and the exposed surface of his brain revealing a bright purple concentration of dead brain cells caused by a bullet from a murderer's gun. And the most that Byron could hope for was that his son would be blind, paralyzed, and unable to speak.

"One thing's certain," Dr. Hauser was saying. "He's suffered severe brain damage. If he lives, it may be weeks, or months, before we know the extent of it. The bullet itself is lodged over here a little to the right, as you saw on the X rays."

Dr. Hauser extended the incision further to the right, where the missile had burrowed in and now rested in its own groove. He extracted the bullet from under the scalp, then removed the devitalized brain tissue at the point of impact, along with a fair quantity of thick, dark blood.

"This clotted blood makes me feel a little better about his situation," Dr. Hauser admitted, "having it to remove instead of brain to help relieve the pressure in his head."

Dr. Hauser then tied one sublayer of black silk sutures and stitched together the long, angled incision in Cortney's scalp and neck. The operation was over. A nurse rolled the bullet up in gauze to give to the police for evidence, and Cortney's head was carefully wrapped before he was wheeled back to Intensive Care. The procedure had lasted just over two and a half hours, Dr. Rees quietly monitoring Cortney's life signs, and the orange light on the respirator blinking slowly and methodically.

Outside the doors to Surgery, Gary and Claire sat in wheelchairs, fidgeting the chairs back and forth, sometimes spinning a short distance down the hall and coming back again. Each drifted about, absorbed in private thoughts as time passed slowly during these early, dark hours of the morning. The original shock had left them numb, and now they were focusing what hope and energy they had left on the survival of their younger brother.

It was an agonizing wait. Police roamed the halls, and a guard had been posted a few feet away in front of an elevator.

Claire asked the guard, "Why are so many police around here?"

"It's just a precaution," he said, "in case they try to come back."
Claire was unsure what he meant.

"You mean if they find out they didn't kill everybody?"

"Yes," said the guard, "witnesses. Somebody went and told the press there were survivors."

Rebuffed by police and hospital personnel for more facts about the murders, reporters had located the ambulance driver, a crusty veteran of ten years, who had told them it was the worst scene he had ever walked in on.

"Couple of 'em was dead we seen right away," he had related. "The woman and the boy was groaning, making growling noises, trying to breathe like. Reminded me of the Korean executions over there, those Chinamen, when we was over there in Korea. You know, hands tied behind your back, shot 'em right in the head. That's what it reminded me of. I didn't think I'd ever see it here, frankly."

When asked about the victims, the driver had disclosed there were two survivors, a man at McKay-Dee and a kid at St. Benedict's.

"I guess it's okay to talk," he had added, "nobody told me not to say nothing."

Since midnight, radio stations along the Wasatch front had been broadcasting vague accounts of what was alleged to be the most heinous crime ever committed in Utah, the Ogden Hi-Fi Murders. And each broadcast reiterated the survival of two of the victims. Though medical personnel huddled inside ICU and Surgery were oblivious to any threats of violence, the police and personnel in other parts of the hospital anticipated a second attempt on Cortney's life. The killers were still at large, and the elevator behind the officer was a service elevator that descended directly into the unguarded basement. It opened fifteen feet from the doors to Surgery, where Cortney lay.

"Do you think they'll try anything?" Claire asked the guard.

"If they were crazy enough to do what they did in the first place," he answered, "they may be crazy enough to come back and try to finish them off."

Periodically, their father or Brett had slipped into the doctors' change room, which adjoined the waiting area with the surgical suites, and delivered reports of Cortney's operation to Gary and Claire. One moment their hopes soared over the knowledge that the bullet had not entered Cortney's brain, only to be apprised a short while later that the impact alone had turned a portion of his brain to pulp. It had gone back and forth that way throughout the operation. Gary queried Brett and his father for the minutest details. Where are they drilling the holes? What caliber is the bullet? How far was it deflected? he wanted to know. Involving himself with facts was Gary's way of dealing with the tragedy; it crowded everything else out of his mind. But Claire was finally overwhelmed by the discussions of facts. She understood them, but she did not want to hear them.

"This is too detailed for me," she had blurted out. "I don't want to know these things. I just want to know if he's okay."

Her father had put his arm around her and said, "Yes, yes, so far he's okay."

The operation was now over, and it was almost 5:00 A.M. The large surgical lamp was finally turned off. Byron walked out of Surgery, pulled off his surgical mask, and eased the green cap from his head. Gary and Claire were waiting by the entrance. Byron put his arms around them and walked them down the hall away from the operating room, as Brett followed closely behind.

"Well, now, Cortney's pulled through the surgery," Byron told Gary and Claire, "and I'm grateful for that. I got the impression that Dr. Hauser felt it wasn't as bad as what he thought it was going to be." He stopped and moved to the side of the hall. "They still don't have any idea what's going to happen to him. If he lives, Hauser thinks he'll probably have a little trouble with his eyes. The bullet struck in his visual center and that was some of the dead tissue they had to remove. Then the shock waves from the bullet Hauser feels may have bungled up his speech center and he could be a little stiff on his right side. They just don't know. I'm explaining all of this to you because I want you to know what we've got left to work with."

What Byron hadn't explained was his fear that the damage done to Cortney by the bullet was minor compared to the edema choking off his lungs. Oxygen to the brain was the critical factor, and Cortney's ashen-bluish color and fixed, dilated pupils when his father had first seen him in ICU indicated Cortney had gone far too long without it.

The Surgery doors suddenly flew open and Cortney's body was rushed out. Except for the white sterile gauze now wrapped around his head he looked the same: prone once again, still wired with tubes and bottles, an attendant squeezing oxygen into his lungs. Byron watched the cart go by, then turned back to his three children.

"Why don't you kids follow Cortney back to ICU and make sure everything's okay. I have to run downstairs for a minute. I'll meet you back in the waiting room."

He gave them a gentle push in the direction of the nurses' desk, and the three of them obediently started down the hall, turning the corner some distance behind Cortney and the technicians tending to him. Then Byron called the nursing supervisor again, stepped into the elevator, and pushed the button for the basement. Before the mortician could transport his wife's body to the State Medical Examiner in Salt Lake City, Byron wanted a final moment with her alone.

I just wanted to . . . just wanted to see her again. I didn't particularly want to see her in that state, but . . . just to see her again . . . just to . . . I guess just to make sure. I don't know. You don't know why the hell you do the things you do in those circumstances. But there seemed to be a purpose at the time. And whatever purpose it was, it fulfilled the purpose. I looked at her and just had some tender, warm feelings. And some heartache feelings. That everything was over with. And that's the way it was. That the partner I had had for life was no longer with me.

It had been nearly thirty-six years since Byron had met Carol one summer day over a scoop of ice cream. Carol's parents owned an ice-cream company and root beer stand in Ogden where Carol and her three sisters car-hopped root beer and ice-cream cones during the warm summer months. Which is why Carol's friends had to coax her that day to go with them for ice cream at a rival dairy across town.

"There's this cute guy working down there," they had giggled, "you gotta go see him."

"I was thinking," Carol told Claire many years later, "How obvious would that be if I drop in for an ice-cream cone over there?"

But after a good deal of coaxing from her friends, Carol had finally relented.

The cute guy loading and serving ice cream at his uncle's dairy was Byron Naisbitt, a tan, broad-shouldered youth of fifteen.

"She came out there to get an ice-cream cone one day," recalled Byron. "Then she kept coming back to get more ice-cream cones, so I just kept serving her ice-cream cones, and we just struck up a relationship."

Byron and Carol dated for the next two years and were engaged when Byron was seventeen. (In the frame of his closet mirror, Byron still kept a picture of Carol that year when she was a senior in high school.) Carol, who was born on Christmas Day, was exactly fifty-one weeks older than Byron. She had finished her second year of college and Byron his first, when they were married in the Mormon temple in Salt Lake City. Carol then quit school and went to work as a secretary to put Byron through an accelerated premed program and later medical school at the University of Utah. After graduation, internship, and residency they had returned to Ogden to live and raise their family, which had already grown by two.

From the time they were married, Byron and Carol had made a striking couple, he ruggedly handsome, she petite, pretty, and bubbly. Though she had suppressed it all those years they were in school, Carol had a taste for clothes, and now that those years were behind them and they could afford it, Byron found pleasure in indulging her that joy.

"He would go and sit while she modeled different outfits for him," a neighbor remembered. "Byron was proud of Carol, he liked to see her well-dressed. She always looked like she had just stepped out of *Vogue* magazine."

Despite her taste for high fashion Carol was the handy one around the Naisbitt household. As another friend said, "She'd be more apt to fix the toilet if it leaked than By would." Carol kept her own toolbox, neatly organized with an assortment of tools and other hardware she needed for her projects. When the Naisbitts were ready to build their first home, Carol shopped for a contractor, decided they all cost too much, that she couldn't trust them, and that she could probably build a better house herself. She designed the house and took bids from subcontractors. Each morning she sent Gary and Brett off to school, put on jeans and a work shirt, dressed three-year-old Claire and took her with her up to the construction site, where she read the plans, learned the vernacular, and supervised each phase of the construction. The Naisbitts still lived in the second home Carol had built eleven years before.

Once a house was built, Carol relished creating a warm and elegant atmosphere with Persian rugs and fine period antiques. The house where they now lived was a showcase of her imagination and personality. She had remodeled every room at least once, doing most or all of the work herself. Had she turned an avocation into a vocation, which admiring friends had encouraged her to do, she would have become an interior designer. In addition to being tastefully decorated Carol's home was organized down to the last nut and bolt in her hardware collection. Every one of the children's closets and drawers were neatly labeled Socks, Underwear, Sweaters, Pajamas, and so on. The medicine cabinets, linen closets, kitchen pantry, and her own toolroom were similarly organized. In the kitchen she kept notes of things to tell people, and when she saw them next, before another word was said, she would get out her list for that person and gripe at, remind, apologize to, or thank them.

Byron found amusing the amount of energy Carol could generate and the projects she was unafraid to tackle: her decorating; her Junior League, bridge club, and church activities; her constant comings and goings with the children for swimming practice and Scouts, her collecting for the March of Dimes; her baking cakes all night with Claire for the Ogden High football team. Once, on a camera safari in Africa, Byron had had to jerk her inside the tent as she stood flat-footed, determined to photograph a bull elephant with his ears lowered to charge. At night, when the two of them were in bed asleep, her energy level often was still so high she would awake with "the fidgets" and attack the closets at three in the morning, cleaning and straightening until she was sure she could get back to sleep. As years had gone by, her late night workouts had become more strenuous. She would scrub the bathrooms, vacuum the downstairs, sprint in a circle through the dining room, living room, den, and kitchen, then race her Exercycle until she had just enough energy to walk back upstairs and fall into bed. On nights when the fidgets were only mild, Byron would roll over and find her jogging in place beside the bed.

As he stood in the morgue, Byron moved a little closer to look at Carol before she was taken away.

I looked at her, but so far as I was concerned, that wasn't my wife the way I knew her and I just blocked it out. I saw her the way she was in life . . . a real dedicated mother, probably too good of a mother. And a good, devoted wife. She could do anything. If she didn't like what the carpenter had done to the house, she'd just change it herself the way she wanted it. And if she couldn't find something she was looking for, she'd make it herself, curtains, bedspreads, it didn't matter. When we were in school, she made all of her clothes and some of mine. She was pretty handy, and sharp . . . sharp, sharp. If she thought she was right, why hell, that was the end of the program. She wouldn't back off to anybody. And I suspect that's the way it was down yonder. She may have been frightened, but she wouldn't back off, I don't think . . . not where one of the kids was involved.

I'd draw it through my mind how I felt about her having to tolerate and go through this stuff, but that's just . . . that's just the way I felt towards her. I silently let her know how I felt about her situation, how bad I felt that she had to go through it. No one should have to die like that, at the hands of someone else, someone who terrorizes you and tortures you, that's no way to die. There's lots of terrible ways to die, but that's no way. No one should have to tolerate that. No one should have that right over another person. . . .

And I made promises to her. I promised her that I was going to make sure that the family did as well as we could without her, knowing full well it was never going to be the same, knowing full well that everything around was going to be different. I made a pledge to her that I would make sure that everything that could possibly be done for Cortney was going to be done, and that we were going to keep the family together. And we'd do the best we could with just a partial household. I promised her that we wouldn't fold, that even though we were handicapped and we didn't have her spirit

*in our household, her input, her happiness and all of the things she
meant to all of us, we'd try to do the best we could.*

Byron closed the tray and walked the long white tunnel for the
last time. This time his legs carried him past the nurses' lounge and
into the elevator, the same elevator where hours before Andy Tolsma
had told him that Carol was dead. The elevator took him to the third
floor, and when the doors opened, he could see that the knot of
relatives that had gathered in the waiting room was beginning to
unravel. They had received word that Cortney had survived the surgery, and now they were drifting back to their own homes and families. He passed by, touching some of them and nodding as they
mumbled condolences.

A police officer standing in the hallway came up and said for him
not to worry about Cortney, nothing else would happen to the boy.
Guards would be posted by his room twenty-four hours a day, and
patrol cars would keep surveillance over the Naisbitt home.

Gary, Brett, and Claire sat on a couch talking softly and waiting
for their father. It was easier for them to talk now, though their
faces were pale, their eyes red-rimmed and still teary. When their
father appeared in the doorway of the waiting room, their conversation stopped and they went to embrace him.

For a while Byron said nothing, just gripped his remaining children tighter around him. He wanted to explain to them something
he didn't fully understand, and to reassure them that things really
hadn't changed when he knew they had.

"There's something I want you kids to realize," he said. "Death is
a part of living. If you're going to be here, you just as well figure on
dying. That's just part of life on this earth. There's no sense making
a big thing out of it. It happens to everybody." He paused. "What's
happened to your mother and Cortney was horrible and there aren't
any rational explanations. There's no way to understand why these
people did what they did. But what's important for us now is to stay
close and love each other. That's what families are for. Just because
you have a disaster in your life, that doesn't mean you go your own
way and try to deal with it. If you have a lot of love and affection in
your family and everybody comes around and gives love and affection to the other people, then everybody bolsters everyone else. And
you know things aren't going to fall apart that way. Because they

can't fall apart as long as one person has feelings for another person."

Claire was crying softly again, and her father squeezed her tightly against him.

"We still have each other," he told her. "We'll always be together. We can always do things together. One thing we can't do is worry about your mother anymore. We were married in the temple for time and eternity, and I plan to see her in another place and another time. We'll all be together. That's our belief, and it makes life easier. Right now we just have to concentrate on getting Cortney well again, we've got to get him squared away and salvage what can be salvaged."

Byron thought back to memories of the six of them as a family: summer sailing on Bear Lake, winter weekends at nearby ski resorts, the annual family vacation to someplace special, like the Caribbean or Hawaii. He didn't want to mention those times; he just wanted to remind them that they had led a good life together, that there were things to remember from their past that would somehow make their future seem less dark.

"We have lots of fun memories," he said, "and we'll always have those, nobody can take those away from us. Just think how lucky we are to have them, all the fun memories we've had as a family. We've had lots of fun times, and we'll have lots more." He stopped here and took a deep breath. "Our family will just be smaller, that's all. It'll be different, but it'll be okay. Just don't fret about things. Everything will be okay. . . ."

The words stopped, and the four of them stood in silence. The room was nearly empty.

"Now then," Byron said, "I want you all to go home and get some rest. There's nothing more to be done here except wait and you can do that at home."

"I'd rather stay here," Gary said.

"There's no reason you have to stay," said Byron.

"I know," said Gary, "I just want to."

"All right. Brett, why don't you and Claire drive Jody home and then take Claire back to the house."

Claire still had tears in her eyes. "Dad," she said softly, "I don't want to go home alone."

"You'll be okay," said her father. "The police are watching the house, so there's nothing to worry about." He could see his daughter was on the verge of collapsing. From the outside, it appeared she had taken it the hardest of anyone. "Go on back, lock the doors and get some sleep. Brett, you make sure she gets in okay."

"What about you?" Gary asked. "You look like you could use a little rest yourself. Why don't you go back to the house with Claire?"

"No," said Byron, "I . . . I'm going to stick around for a while just to see what develops." He shook Claire lightly, playfully, and said, "Brett'll get you all squared away, and Gary or I will be along in a little bit."

Claire nodded quietly, hugged her father, and turned toward the door. Brett followed her. As they moved near the door, their father said to Brett: "When you get Diane and Natalie back to your house, lock the doors and keep a gun loaded. This is not going to happen to my family again."

When Claire entered her father's house, she was awed by the silence. She tried to avoid thinking about her mother, but she couldn't help wondering what life was going to be like now without her. She wanted to be strong like her father, so she concentrated on Cortney as he had told her to do. If thoughts of her mother began creeping again into her head, she would say to herself: "Mom's at the store, she'll come home. She's just at the store."

Brett returned to his wife, Diane. He was sweaty and his hair was matted down from the surgical cap. His eyes were bloodshot but dry. He entered his in-laws' house and Diane was standing in the kitchen. Brett's Uncle Paul had called her from the hospital and told her what had happened. She didn't know what to say, and Brett said nothing. They stood across the room and looked at each other for a moment; then Diane went to him and put her arms around him, and everything that Brett had been keeping inside released at once and his eyes filled with tears.

The doctors who had been with Cortney all night finally left the hospital. Although Gary remained in the waiting room for a while, he soon realized his father had been right: there was nothing he could do but sit and wait, and though he felt he should remain near Cortney he had no idea why. Waiting could be done at home with

Claire, and that at least seemed to have a purpose. He left the hospital and drove back to his father's house.

Of the crowd of medical technicians and nurses who had rushed about the ICU, working for the past seven hours to save Cortney's life, many were gone now, and for the first time since late the previous evening, the place was quiet and still. For a minute Cortney's cubicle went black, except for the thin beam of a small flashlight. A special nurse checked his pupils carefully, then turned the lights on again. From his eyes she went down his body all the way to his feet, routinely suctioning the secretions in his airway, listening to his lungs, glancing at the heart monitor, changing IVs, giving medication, checking reflexes, charting everything she had just done, then beginning again with a dark room and the flashlight shining in Cortney's eyes.

In these moments just before dawn Byron stood alone outside the glass front and watched. Not even twelve hours had passed since he had come home from his office and found Carol worrying that Cortney had not yet shown for dinner. When the lights came back on, he could see Cortney's body in the window, long and thin and yellow, his half-open eyes buried in circles of gray, the bloody tracheostomy tube poking up out of his neck. In a corner next to Cortney's bed the orange light on the respirator blinked back at Byron. Though he hadn't mentioned it to his other children, Byron had remained at the hospital for a single reason: If Cortney was going to die, he wanted to be there. He didn't want his son to die alone.

Through the blinds in the window of the ICU he could see a thin corona of blue light silhouetting Malan's Peak rising behind the hospital. Daybreak was not far away, and Ogden was beginning to stir beneath the white cross of St. Benedict's. The streak and twinkle of the city lights were melting before the first rays of the sun, as the city came alive and prepared for the business of the day.

Up on that east hill overlooking Ogden, in a little room on the third floor, Byron Naisbitt sat alone waiting for his son to die.

ARREST

Morning was approaching, but the streets still were quiet and nearly dark. Only faint light had begun filtering over the mountains, and the image in A. K. Greenwood's binoculars had evolved from shadow to a featureless block of gray. Greenwood was hunkered down in the front seat of his squad car aiming the glasses across an open field at a small house in west Ogden. He had been watching the house in the dark for a long while now and nothing had happened. With daylight beginning to creep into the darkness, Greenwood was thinking of the panic the city would be waking up to in another hour. As leader of the Ogden Police Tactical Squad, it was his responsibility to capture the killers.

About ten thirty the previous evening the Tac Squad had stopped for their nightly "lunch," and had just been served a hot meal at Fred's Burger Chalet, when Greenwood had received a felony-in-progress call from the dispatcher. Three minutes later the seven-man squad had responded to the front and back of the Hi-Fi Shop, as well as positioned two cars along the adjacent side streets.

In the alley Greenwood had found the rookie Youngberg, who had given him two facts to go on: the killers were black and they drove a light-colored van. Immediately, Greenwood had notified his men and all patrolmen, all detectives, the Weber County Sheriff's Office, and the Utah Highway Patrol to stop and search every van that moved in the city of Ogden and along the streets and highways outside the city limits. As soon as the victims still alive had been rushed to the hospital and the crime scene preserved, Greenwood had huddled in the alley with other officers, scrutinizing every member of the black criminal element in Ogden who was then active in robbery, burglary, or drugs. Informants around the city had been dragged out of bed in the early hours of the morning. At four o'clock had come the first break in the case: a beige van had been found parked to the side of a house not far from the Hi-Fi Shop. In the basement of the house was an apartment, and in the apartment lived a black man known to every officer in the Ogden Police Department. He had just been paroled from a federal penitentiary, where he had been serving time for armed robbery. With the Tac Squad surrounding the house, Greenwood had gone down the narrow flight of stairs and arrested the man at gunpoint. But when questioned, the man had seemed as stunned by the brutality of the murders as the police themselves had been. Greenwood had started over.

Next he had set up surveillance on certain houses around the city. In the houses lived known black criminals who roughly met the descriptions given by the eyewitness. That any of them would return home in a van or be caught moving stereo equipment was a long shot, but at the time there had been little else to do except play the long shots and hope for something to break. The rest of the night had passed quietly, the Tac Squad watching and waiting.

Greenwood was still sitting in his squad car, alone, his binoculars trained on a suspect's house, when the rays of the sun began spilling over the mountains.

At seven o'clock, with Ogden beginning to stir, he called off the surveillance around the city and ordered the Tac Squad back to the station for new assignments. Don Moore and his partner Mike Empey were to report to the State Medical Examiner's office in Salt Lake City at nine o'clock to identify the victims for the autopsies, then collect and preserve all clothes, bullets, hair samples, and other evidence as it came from the bodies. Greenwood assigned his other tactical teams to check on recent van sales and rentals with every new and used car dealership and every truck-leasing agency from Ogden to Salt Lake City. Advised by the chief that he was to have unlimited funds and manpower in his search for the killers, Greenwood borrowed three men from the detective division to begin the tedious interviewing of owners and employees of the stores adjacent to the Hi-Fi Shop.

Greenwood himself set up a command post at an old desk in the records room at the station. Early that morning an appeal had gone out over public radio asking citizens to call the police if they had any information that might lead to the arrest of the killers. Calls had started coming in, slowly at first, then in greater numbers as the day wore on. Greenwood and another officer answered the phones, took down names, addresses, phone numbers, and descriptions, then transferred their notes to a master list of leads to be assigned and investigated by other officers in the field. The list grew quickly to five pages, seventy-five items to be run down, checked out, then checked off. The pressure to capture the killers already was mounting, and by noon Greenwood was still sitting at the old desk in the records room answering the phones and calling his men on the radio, no closer to the killers now than he had been when he first arrived at the Hi-Fi Shop over twelve hours before.

By midmorning Cortney's condition since his neurosurgery had changed neither for the better nor for the worse. For the moment, he was stabilized, his head bandaged, his eyes half-open, and the respirator still pumping air into him each time he initiated a breath. Connie Garner, the nurse in charge of Intensive Care, had been called in during the night to "special" Cortney, and was still at his bedside, catching up on the charting of his medications and continuing the routine of one-to-one care that Cortney required. To keep his temperature down, a cooling mattress had been slid into place beneath him and turned on. A monitor next to his bed continuously recorded his blood pressure, while another monitor recorded his heart rate. Connie checked his blood gases and electrolytes, his venous pressure, his temperature, and the hourly output of sputum being suctioned from his tracheostomy tube. Ampicillin was being administered via his groin catheter and Decadron through the vaporizer attached to the respirator. Every two hours Cortney was repositioned from his back to his side, or his side to his back.

As part of her routine Connie regularly checked Cortney's reflexes, including scraping the sole of his foot to test what is known as the Babinski reflex. If the sole on the foot of a baby up to two years old is stroked, the toes will flare, the big toe separating from the others. A normal adult, given the same stimulus, will either jerk his foot away or curl his toes inward. If the same flaring reaction, the Babinski reflex normal to a baby, is seen in an adult, it is a sign of extensive brain damage. That morning, as Connie ran a sharp instrument from Cortney's heel to the ball of his foot, his toes flared like a newborn's.

Before dawn Carol Naisbitt's body had been removed from the morgue in the basement of the hospital and taken to the State Medical Examiner in Salt Lake City for the autopsy. On the third floor things had begun to quiet down. Dr. Wallace had completed his shift in the emergency room and after looking in on Cortney had gone home. Dr. Rees and Dr. Hauser, who had been with Cortney until just before daybreak, were soon due back at the hospital to check again on his progress. Byron was now sitting alone in the waiting room adjacent to Intensive Care. Since dawn he had been in and out of Cortney's cubicle, talking to the nurses, watching Cortney's vital signs as they came off the machines, and reading the doctors' and nurses' entries on the chart. For a long while now nothing had changed. Cortney's supported breathing had become regular, and the machines looking into his body were sending back the same results they had recorded the hour before, and the hour before that. Around ten o'clock Byron went back into Cortney's room and looked again at the most recent vital signs on Cortney's chart and the readouts on the machines.

"Do you expect any change for the next hour or two?" he asked one of the nurses.

She shook her head and said no.

"I might head home for a short while then," said Byron. "Will you call me if there's any change?"

Byron then left the hospital alone. The drive home was but a few blocks, but along the way he had time to think about the sudden change that had occurred in his life.

I knew that I was alone. I knew that Cortney was bad and probably wouldn't live. What I tried to do right in the beginning is not feel sorry for myself. I just tried to remember all the good, fun times that our family had always had together. And just let anything that was adverse leave my mind. My wife had lost her life, and a sixteen-year-old son who was just starting to flower into a young man, who had just started taking an interest in what's going on. . . . I was devastated not knowing what his situation was. But I knew there was no sense to keep bringing it all back. If you let that happen, that's bad news. That is bad news. Then you never recover. If I found myself thinking about those things, I just put them away. Because it wasn't going to change. I tried to promise myself that I'd just take things and try to look at things as objectively as they actually were, and not read anything into them that wasn't there, and try just to make a life of what was left.

I had some feelings of being hurt. And I had some feelings of, oh, I don't know, just . . . I had some feelings of tenderness and awareness for the persons that I had lost. I was wondering . . . I felt that Shorty was fine, my religion let me know that she was fine, that I wouldn't have to be really worried about her welfare, and that sometime later I would be with her again. But I just felt bad that she had to go through what she did. I was upset about that. And I just had some very tender thoughts toward her. And just wished that things could have been different, but they weren't.

On the way home I realized that my house was going to be empty, and when I got there, it was. It was really empty. I mean you open the door to an absolutely different existence. There was something missing in my house, and in my life. No one was going to greet me and no one was going to be there. I had a vacant feeling, it was a hollow feeling, and it was a sad depression. Just a . . . just a feeling that I've never had before.

I went into the house and everything there from one standpoint or another reminded me of Shorty. She decorated the house, it's got to reflect who she was and what she thought. Her house, her closet full of her clothes, everything in the house was just her. And now there's no one there taking care of the house or fixing a meal or taking care of anything. It's just empty. And your life is empty with it.

I went upstairs, and I don't even know if I got into bed or just flopped on it. But I didn't feel that tired. I never felt the fatigue that I felt sometimes when I was in residency, working. I shed a tear or two by myself. No one ever knew, that I know of. I tried to keep that to a minimum. I cried and that was the end. Then I didn't cry anymore. But I don't think there's any harm in crying. I think that's a good thing. Sort of lets your soul come clean, and then you feel better. I suspect the events of the night before ran through my mind, and I'm sure that I had some feelings about that. I've wondered several times what would've happened had I not been on call and gone to get Cort myself. Probably would not be around. Who knows what the hell would've happened then, if I had gone rather than Shorty. There's no reason to think about that, but it's gone through my mind. Chances are, had I not been on call and sticking by the phone. . . . Maybe even the two of us would've gone. I hope that maybe one of us would've stayed in the car outside and then terminated things differently. I don't know, who the hell can say. You can't say what would've happened. Only thing we know is what did happen.

After that, I had a little prayer. I just wanted to make sure that the Lord knew that I understood, as best that I could understand, what had happened. And I wanted Him to know that if He was now looking after my wife, that I knew she was in good hands. And that I believed that I would see her later, that it's just a matter of time here and then we'd be together again. And that's comforting insofar as I'm concerned. And I wanted to be appreciative because Cort was alive and I hoped that he would be able to live, to be a functioning person. That's when I felt that Cort would be all right. I was sick at heart, no question about it. And yet, I had a feeling within me right from day one that he was going to make it. So I didn't dwell on the fact that he wasn't going to make it. I expected a phone call from the hospital any minute. I expected it, but I had a feeling that I wasn't going to get it. I had a feeling inside of me that he was going to make it. And that he'd be all right. And that feeling never left me.

I lay on the bed and probably did sleep for a minute or two, or for a while anyway, just completely relaxed. I don't know if I was completely relaxed, but I felt relieved. Then I was anxious to get back and see how he was going to stabilize. So I got up, got showered and dressed, and went back to the hospital.

The trash Dumpster for Barracks 351 at Hill Air Force Base squatted on an island in the parking lot, approximately thirty feet

from the north entrance to the barracks. It was a large metal recep-
tacle, where airmen assigned to bay orderly duty in the barracks
dumped the trash after they had finished their duty each day. It was
also a favorite target of twelve-year-old Charlie Marshall and eleven-
year-old Walter Grissom, partners in a "bottle picking" enterprise
that netted each of them almost five dollars a day, three or four days
a week. The two boys lived next door to each other on the base,
where their fathers were sergeants in the Air Force. In an afternoon
after school they hit an average of nine Dumpsters in two or three
hours, wading waste deep among the trash and rifling the large
brown bags for the pop bottles discarded by the airmen. The bottles
netted five cents, sometimes ten cents, apiece at the Pantry Pride
across the street from the base exchange. Bottle picking was hard
work, but the way Charlie and Walter looked at it, once they cashed
in for the day, the hamburgers and movies and pinball machines at
the BX were free.

That Tuesday afternoon Charlie and Walter started work about
three thirty, and after a half hour in two of the Dumpsters, the cardboard box and the canvas bag they were lugging were already half-
full. With two of the four Dumpsters in the area emptied of their
bottles, the boys proceeded to the third, the white, eight-foot metal
cube sitting in front of Barracks 351. It was filled to a man's waist,
but the two boys climbed in, one on each side, and began to pick
through the trash. Before they could snatch up their first bottle,
Walter spied something sitting on top of the pile.

"Hey, Charlie, look here," he said, "somebody's lost a purse."

The two boys turned the purse inside out, but it was empty. Walter flipped it back into the pile, and as he did so, he spotted another
purse on top of the trash. This one held eleven cents plus a credit
card. Walter slipped the card into his pocket to give to his mother,
"in case somebody lost it." The bottle picking temporarily abandoned, the boys began sifting through the trash looking for more
wallets. A fistful of credit cards was scattered like leaves across the
top of the pile, and the boys flicked them aside in the search. Charlie's hand suddenly darted into the pile and plucked another purse
from just beneath the surface of trash. It was a lady's clutch purse
made of rough-cut cowhide with a rectangle of purple in the center.
As Charlie lifted the purse, a checkbook fluttered into the trash and

Walter retrieved it. With the purse in his hand Charlie climbed out of the Dumpster and Walter followed. In the brighter light they could read the name Michelle Ansley written across the top of each check. Walter replaced the checkbook in the purse and found the purse filled with credit cards, pictures, and a driver's license.

"Let's keep everything in this lady's purse," Walter told Charlie, "and give it to my mother so she can turn it in." Then Walter climbed back into the mouth of the Dumpster. "I'm gonna see if there's any more stuff in here."

He eased himself down into the trash, but before he had got halfway in, his eyes focused on a small triangle of leather poking up out of the trash pile. Spreading the trash aside, he picked up the wallet and looked at it. It was a man's wallet made of hand-tooled bound leather, and there were dark wet stains on it. Walter flipped through the wallet's thin, clear plastic pockets and found a driver's license in the name of Cortney Naisbitt. In the next pocket, made out to the same Cortney Naisbitt was a card labeled "Student Pilot License." Charlie was still holding the clutch purse when Walter hopped out of the Dumpster and showed him the fourth wallet.

"Maybe there's been a robbery," said Charlie. "There's so much stuff here."

"Yeah," said Walter, "we'll give all this stuff to my mom and she can tell us what to do with it. Let's see if there's anything else."

Once more the two boys hoisted themselves into the Dumpster to rummage through the trash, but there were no more wallets to be found, only small bottles of cosmetics and a set of keys, all of which they left in the pile. But there were pop bottles still to be collected, and the boys searched the Dumpster until they were satisfied they had found them all and put them in the cardboard box and the canvas bag. Then they climbed out of the Dumpster for the last time, and Walter stuffed Cortney Naisbitt's wallet into his pocket and threw the clutch purse in with the bottles in the cardboard box. Charlie grabbed hold of the canvas bag and began dragging it toward the next Dumpster in front of the bowling alley across the street. Walter tried to follow, but was struggling with the heavy box. After carrying it a little way, he set it down to rest. As he was preparing to lift the box again, a young airman returning from work on the flight line saw him tugging with the heavy box. Airman Robert

Paul Weldon, blond, eighteen years old, lived in Barracks 351. About to enter the barracks, he had seen the boys trying to lug their bottles across the street and wondered how anyone so small could hope to lift something so heavy. Weldon walked over to Walter and picked up the box filled with bottles.

"Where do you want it?" he asked.

Walter pointed to the Dumpster by the bowling alley.

"Over there, that's where we're going."

With Weldon now toting the box, Walter ran ahead to Charlie.

"Hey, some guy's carrying my box for me," he told his friend.

Charlie set his bag down just as Weldon caught up with the two of them.

"Geez, we found all sorts of things in that last Dumpster," Walter told the airman.

"Yeah?" smiled Weldon. "Like what?"

"Bunch of purses and a wallet and some credit cards, some little things of lady's eye-paint. . . ."

"Where'd you put the purse?" Charlie interrupted.

"I got it in my box," said Walter.

Weldon set the box down next to Walter. "Well, lemme see."

Walter reached in and yanked the purse out of the box.

"This is it," he said, "and here's the other one." He pulled the wallet from his pocket.

Weldon examined the wallet and the purse while the boys watched. Both of the billfolds still held identification with addresses and phone numbers.

"I tell you what," said Weldon, "if you guys want to give them to me, I'll make sure they get back to their owners."

"No way," said Walter, "we can do that ourselves."

"How do I know you'll do it?" asked Weldon.

"How do we know you will?"

"I promise I'll call them," said Weldon, "and I can take the wallets by when I'm in town."

"My dad can drop 'em by the base police on his way to work," said Walter.

Weldon said again that he thought it would be better if he tried to locate the rightful owners of the two wallets, and finally Walter agreed to give him the clutch purse, but the man's billfold Walter was keeping for himself to show to his parents.

"You sure you don't want me to call on that one, too?" asked Weldon.

"Yeah," said Walter, "I'm sure."

The two boys got ready to scour their fourth Dumpster for the day, and Weldon started back across the street toward the barracks, looking through the purse for the owner's phone number as he walked. He found the girl's number imprinted on the checks, and without thinking he would be drawing attention to himself as a suspect if the purse had been stolen, he borrowed a dime and from the phone booth on the first floor of the barracks called the number printed on the checkbook. A girl answered the phone.

"Hello," Weldon said politely, "this is Airman Weldon out to Hill Air Force Base. I've found a billfold and a checkbook belonging to a Miss or Mrs. Michelle Ansley. Could I speak to her, please?"

"Michelle was murdered last night," said the girl.

Weldon was so stunned, for a moment he couldn't talk.

"I . . . I didn't know about that. All I was trying to do was find the correct owner."

But the girl was gone now and a woman had grabbed the phone and was interrogating him.

"Who are you?" asked the woman, "and how did you get this number? Where are you calling from?"

"Ma'am, my name is Robert P. Weldon. I am stationed at Hill Air Force Base. I found the billfold here by the barracks just a few minutes ago."

"Hold on," said the woman, "Michelle's brother wants to talk to you."

A young man about Weldon's age took the woman's place and continued the interrogation. By now, Weldon was so frightened he began repeating his name, rank, and serial number.

"My name is Robert P. Weldon," he said. "I am assigned to the Fifteen-fiftieth Organizational Maintenance Squadron at Hill Air Force Base. I am a helicopter mechanic. My duty phone is three-four-seven-oh. I live in Barracks Three fifty-one. My room number is three seventeen."

The other man kept asking questions, but Weldon was too frightened to say anything else. Finally, he asked the man a question.

"Are you going to call the cops?"

"Yes," said the man.

"Okay," Weldon swallowed, "I'll call the air police."

Corporal Cecil Fisher, a member of the Ogden Tac Squad, had just completed an assignment and had reported back to Greenwood's command post at the station about three thirty. He was standing next to the dispatcher when another citizen called in response to the appeal aired by the police on the radio.

"Fisher," said the dispatcher, "you're wanted on the phone."

From the telephones on Greenwood's command desk, Fisher picked up a receiver.

"This is Corporal Fisher."

"I think I know who did this Hi-Fi job," said the voice on the other end.

Fisher waited for the man to continue.

"I'm not a rat or anything," he said, "and if somebody'd just robbed a place or done something else that wasn't so bad, I probably wouldn't even call, but on this I want to help if I can."

"It's good that you called," Fisher reassured him. "What can you tell me?"

"I heard on the radio you're looking for two black guys driving a van."

"That's right," said Fisher.

"I know who these guys are, they drive a light-blue van, a Chevy with mag wheels. One's name is Dale Pierre, he's the short one. The other one is William Andrews. Andrews has the van."

"How do you know it's them we're looking for?" asked Fisher.

"I know for a fact," said the man. "I heard them talking about it. They said they weren't going to leave any witnesses."

The caller stopped talking, waiting for Fisher to say something. Though at that time he went into no further detail about what he had heard the men say, some time later he explained how he had known that Pierre and Andrews were the killers.

"A couple months before this thing happened, Andrews and I were

on barracks cleanup duty. We were both being punished for something. While we were working in the barracks there, he'd come down
to my room sometimes and I'd go up to his. Kinda got to be friendly.
So, I don't know, I guess one night he needed a ride into town, and
he was tripping on some speed and other drugs. He was a pretty
heavy doper. Anyway, I had my girl friend with me. You know, you're
not allowed to take girls into the barracks, but we both went up and
stopped in and had some joints, right? And he showed me his stereo
he had, and he said, 'Pierre got that for me.' So apparently Pierre
stole it. And he showed me a lot of clothes and stuff Pierre had
gotten for him. He thought Pierre was a real neat guy. Then he
showed me a couple toy cars he kept his drugs in. I didn't even
know he kept his stuff right there. He was just bragging up everything. And I guess we were talking about how it'd be nice to have
money, and he told me about a bank that him and Pierre and somebody else had planned to rob. They had it all planned out, then they
went and reneged on it. Then after that, we somehow got to talking
about stereos and for some reason he said, 'One of these days I'm
going to rob a hi-fi shop and if anybody gets in my way I'm going
to kill 'em.' I really don't think Andrews would shoot anybody or
make 'em do anything. I don't think he was smart enough. He was
just kind of a screw-up. I didn't really know Pierre and I'm glad I
didn't. I think everybody did what they could to stay away from
him."

"Hold on a minute," Fisher was saying, "let me get these names
down." After a moment he said, "Okay, do you know where we can
find these guys?"

"They live in the same barracks," said the caller. "Three fifty-one,
out at Hill Field. Andrews's room is two eighteen, and Pierre lives
on the same floor, but I don't know his number."

"Okay," said Fisher again. "I have to give the information to my
sergeant and see how he wants me to handle it. Is there a number
where I can reach you?"

"I'm calling from a pay phone at the K mart, but you can reach
me at my girl friend's number in a few minutes." He gave Fisher
the number. "If you need me, call me there and we'll talk."

Fisher notified Greenwood immediately. Greenwood then contacted the prosecutor, Robert Newey, and told him they had the

names of two suspects. Could they arrest the two men on the information provided by the informant? Newey advised Greenwood that the information would not support an arrest warrant unless the informant would agree to testify in court. Ten minutes after he had hung up, Fisher called the informant back at the number he had given.

The same man answered.

"The DA says we can't arrest this Pierre and Andrews," said Fisher, "unless you'll agree to testify in court."

It seemed that the man had already considered this possibility, for right away he said, "Okay, you got it."

"Kelly, I want to prepare you for what you're going to see when we go up to the hospital."

Claire, sitting with Gary in the living room of the Naisbitt home, was speaking to sixteen-year-old Kelly McKenna. School had just let out and Kelly had gone straight to the Naisbitt's.

"Cortney doesn't look the way you remember him," said Claire. "I don't know what you've heard at school, but Cortney's been shot in the head, and they made him drink some stuff that's burned his mouth. And he's got tubes running everywhere. It'll be a shock for you to see him. So I want you to be ready for it when we get up there."

Claire went no further with her description of her younger brother, but Kelly had heard little she had said after the first sentence, anyway. He was already preparing himself for the sight. Gary and Claire both were talking to him calmly, but their faces looked raw. Once or twice their eyes filled with tears and spilled down their cheeks. Kelly, too, was crying. For the next few minutes there was some small talk, and Kelly remembered the word "sorry" being used a lot. Then Claire stood up and wiped at her eyes.

"Why don't we go on up there to see him," she said.

Gary shook Kelly's hand and thanked him again for coming by. "I think I'll stay here," he added. "I'll talk to you later."

On the way to the hospital Kelly felt light-headed. He wanted to say something to Claire, something appropriate and something from his heart, but he didn't know how to express his feelings. He was afraid he would say something wrong, so he said nothing at all. Claire drove in silence, as Kelly tried to imagine what his childhood friend now looked like. He saw pieces of Cortney's body scattered over a white room. He thought part of Cortney's head would be gone, blown away by the gunshot, and that his mouth would be nothing but a large, wide cavity. Kelly was preparing himself to see something not human.

Though Kelly was more gregarious and socially inclined than Cortney, the two boys had been closest friends since before they had started elementary school together ten years earlier. Kelly, six feet tall since the eighth grade, had thick, dark red hair, hazel eyes, and perfectly straight, white teeth lined by a thin silver retainer. When he smiled, a dimple sank deeply into each cheek.

"I've known Cort all through elementary school, ever since I can remember, since I've been a young, young kid," Kelly once said of his relationship with Cortney. "For a while we kinda split up because we had different interests. Cort's always been into math and stuff, and I could never really delve into it like he could. You know, he always liked to read books on electronics and planes and aeronautics and stuff like that. That's how he was. I was more the goof-around type, I guess. And that's why I think we split up for that while. Then I started getting back together with him kinda. I like the outdoors, which he does too, he likes to go sailing and stuff like that. We were taking hikes and went up to their cabin a couple times and messed around. Then I started going with him out to the airport for his flying lessons. I didn't mind listening to him talk about flying because that was interesting stuff. He'd tell me about all the controls and explain everything to me. Then I'd watch him and Wolf take off and fly around. He was always in a really good mood when he landed, and he'd talk about everything they'd been doing up there. He'd talk about it all the way home."

Cortney had called Kelly the previous afternoon just before leaving for the airport. He thought he might be soloing for the first time, and he wanted Kelly to come along. But Kelly was at the library studying for a history test. When Kelly returned home, having passed up dinner to continue studying, his mother gave him the message that Cortney had called a little after three. She added that a few hours later, about six thirty or seven, Mrs. Naisbitt had also called

wanting to know if Cortney was with Kelly. Kelly told his mother
he hadn't even seen Cortney in school that day. When his parents
left for a late dinner out, Kelly went into the kitchen and fixed himself a sandwich. The kitchen radio was on and while he was eating,
a news bulletin announced that there had been a murder downtown
in the vicinity of the Hi-Fi Shop, and that the station would have
more details on the eleven o'clock news. Kelly was only half listening. It occurred to him that someone had probably been knifed on
Twenty-fifth Street. Before the next newscast was aired, he was in
bed and almost asleep.

The next morning Kelly skipped his first two classes for an appointment with the orthodontist. While he was sitting in the chair,
the dental assistant asked him if he knew the Naisbitt family. Kelly
said sure he knew the Naisbitts, Cortney was his good friend. What
the assistant said next made Kelly sit up so quickly, he came right
out of the chair. Mrs. Naisbitt had been murdered, she said, and
Cortney was in critical condition, not expected to live.

"It really shocked me," Kelly remembered later. "I just kinda went
blank."

By the time he arrived at Ogden High that morning, disbelief over
the Hi-Fi Murders had escalated into one rumor affirming another.
The "official word" on the murders and on Cortney circulated
through the halls with an authority that perpetuated itself. There
was talk of nothing else. But even after the horror had become familiar and the students understood what had happened, few of them
wanted to believe it. Kelly wouldn't accept the "official word" until
he had heard it from Cortney's father. The official word was that
Cortney had died.

"It was like looking through the back end of binoculars," Kelly
later said, describing the walk down the hall toward Intensive Care.
"You know, you're looking through and you see it smaller? I remember, I was walking down that hall and I was feeling awful that
day and you got an armed cop sitting out in front of the door and
the door's closed and 'No Smoking—Oxygen' and stuff like that,
and you walk in and see just nurses running back and forth, and
then you walk into Cort's room, the curtains are pulled, and you
walk in there and there he is, he's got tubes running through him

and the nurses are whispering in his ear, 'Keep going!' He was all burned up inside. I remember looking at his lips, you could see inside the skin, all this white . . . it was just all white inside of his mouth, all burned in there. The nurses were just waiting around for him to . . . they were kind of keeping him alive, but they didn't have any hope at all for him. I could see that on everybody. They were just kinda waiting for the time to come."

In the tiny ICU cubicle four or five nurses hovered over Cortney. One was changing the bottles of IV fluid, one was checking and rechecking the machines for Cortney's vital signs, one was charting, one was suctioning. In the midst of all of this Cortney lay perfectly still. To Kelly he looked dead, "like they were pumping juice into a slab of meat on the table." But what stood out in Kelly's mind was not Cortney or the nurses; it was the noise. Every piece of hospital equipment he had ever seen in the movies was blipping and hissing in the tiny room. Cortney's chest was rising and falling with the Aqua-lung sounds of the respirator, and the long seconds between each breath caused Kelly to hold his own.

Kelly stood at the foot of Cortney's bed on the left side, afraid to advance any farther. He could see the reddish scrapes from the rope burns around Cortney's wrists. And from his wrists and seemingly every other part of his body, Cortney had tubes and wires curling away into the noisy machines. The head that Kelly had imagined would be blown apart was intact and wrapped tightly in a white bandage. The lips too were there, but they were surrounded by raw, open sores.

Neither Claire nor Kelly should have been in the room with a patient as critical as Cortney. Claire knew it; the nurses knew it. But from the beginning the rules regarding Cortney seemed to have been abandoned. As Kelly stood behind Claire and stared at his friend, the nurses worked around them as though they weren't there.

Claire took hold of Cortney's hand and bent down close to his ear. "Hi, Cort," she said. "How are you?" She held onto his hand and looked into his face. "I brought someone to see you. Kelly came up with me to visit."

She turned back to Kelly. "Why don't you say something to him, Kelly," she said softly. "I know he can hear you."

The two exchanged places, and Kelly put his left hand on the pillow next to Cortney's head and slipped his right hand in among the wires and tubes in an awkward grasp of Cortney's forearm.

"Cort, how you doing?" he said.

Cortney's eyes remained closed, and the tracheostomy tube protruding from his neck gurgled.

"Listen, buddy, I'm really sorry about what happened, you know. I mean, if there's anything I can do for you, you just let me know. Anything at all."

He could think of nothing else to say, but just then Claire took hold of Cortney's hand again and whispered to Kelly, "Maybe we better go."

Kelly nodded.

Looking back at Cortney, Claire said in a louder voice: "Kelly and I are going now, Cortney. I'll be back tonight to see you." She squeezed his hand and moved away from the bed.

"Talk to you later, Cort," said Kelly. "Take it easy."

As they turned to leave the room, nurses filled their places at Cortney's bedside as though they had never been there. Kelly looked at Cortney a last time and Cortney's body still lay motionless. Then the respirator hissed again, and Cortney's chest swelled quickly and collapsed.

It was now four o'clock in the afternoon. A few detectives were sitting around a table at the police station discussing the Hi-Fi case, when Chief Leroy Jacobsen walked into the detective office with the latest news: a call had just been received from the Office of Special Investigations at Hill Field, where several items belonging to the victims had been found in a Dumpster adjacent to Barracks 351. When he heard the barracks number, Glen Judkins snapped his fingers. Three months earlier, in January, he had arrested an airman living in Barracks 351 for car theft. Then he had returned to the same barracks for a second car theft, and a third, and another arrest. All in the same week. All the same airman. The case was still vivid in his mind because the airman who had stolen the cars always returned to the car lot the next day pretending he was ready to buy the car he had stolen the night before.

"I really think he felt it was a cover-up," Judkins explained later. "Like I've been in and tried that car out and I come back real indignant because my car's gone. And if I'm indignant enough, someone's not going to come up to me and say, 'Hey, did you rip off the car down there?' I think that was part of his master plan."

For Judkins, the case unfolded as follows:

On January 23 the airman took a yellow 1973 Corvette for a test drive at Lyle's House of Hardtops, a used car lot in west Ogden. The next morning, when the owner arrived and discovered the same Corvette missing, he called the police. But before the police could answer the call, the airman himself appeared back at Lyle's. He was driving the same car he had driven the day before, a green 1970 Buick Riviera, the car he wanted to trade in on the Corvette. When the owner told him the Corvette had been stolen, the airman insisted he have that car. The owner called the police.

When Judkins pulled onto the Lyle's lot, the first thing he noticed was that the green Riviera parked next to the office had New York license plates front and rear, and a Utah inspection sticker in the corner of the windshield. He went inside the office and talked to the airman, but now he wasn't interested in the Corvette so much as he was curious about the Riviera parked out front.

"Go ahead," the airman waved, "take a look at it."

Judkins recorded the car's serial number and a description of the car, and called it in to the dispatcher, who ran the information through the national crime computer. In a few minutes Judkins learned that the green Riviera the airman had driven onto the Lyle's lot to trade in on the stolen Corvette was also stolen.

The airman denied stealing either of the cars, but offered no resistance. After searching beneath the driver's seat of the Riviera and finding a loaded South American-made Colt .45, Judkins read the airman his rights, shook him down, placed him in handcuffs, and drove him to the station. In his pocket the airman had three sets of keys, one of which fitted the green Riviera. The next day his bail was set at the standard $5,000, then halved, and he posted bond after a week in jail and was set free.

Shortly after the airman was released on bail, the yellow Corvette and a red Riviera missing from another car lot were located on the base not far from Barracks 351. The two remaining sets of keys that

Judkins had found on the airman a week earlier fitted the two stolen cars. Judkins swore out the necessary warrants and complaints, went to the base, and placed the airman under arrest for the second time in a week, this time on two counts of grand theft auto. He tried to interrogate the airman, but when he asked about the stolen cars, the airman stopped talking and glared at him as though he were in some sort of trance.

"You've seen a dead man with his eyes open?" Judkins said later. "That's what he looked like."

On both of the new counts the airman was unable to post bond, and spent nearly six weeks in jail before he was released. He was still incarcerated at the time of his preliminary hearing, when the weight of the evidence against him was sufficient to have all three cases bound over for trial. But the judge agreed to consolidate the cases and apply his previously posted bond of $2,500 to all three counts of auto theft. On March 20 he was again set free on bail, free to return to his room in the barracks and his life in the Air Force. Today, April 23, the man was still out on bail, awaiting trial. His name, recalled Judkins, was Dale Pierre.

Judkins later wrote in his Hi-Fi report: "As soon as the Chief mentioned the barracks number, I was aware that this was the barracks that is occupied by Dale S. Pierre. Having arrested Pierre on prior occasions, I was familiar with his description, which seemed to closely match that of one of the suspects involved in the homicide." Chief Jacobsen assigned Judkins, Detective Lee Varley, and the homicide investigator, Deloy White, to respond to Hill Field and investigate the finding of the items belonging to the victims.

In the records room down the hall Greenwood's command post had not received word of the discovery in the Dumpster. A half hour before the call from Hill Field had come in to the detective division, Greenwood and Fisher had been tipped by the informant that the men they were looking for were named Dale Pierre and William Andrews. They were still being advised by the prosecutor how to proceed with this first break in the case. While the prosecutor's office was preparing the complaint and arrest warrants, Greenwood had sent one of his men to the McKay-Dee Hospital with the mug files to show to Mr. Walker. The police had no pictures of Andrews, but out of the pages of other faces Walker tentatively identified Dale Pierre as the short man of the two, the one who had pulled the trigger on all five of the victims in the basement. He added that the man who had shot them had spoken with a distinct and peculiar accent.

With Pierre tentatively identified, and an informant willing to testify to Pierre's and Andrew's involvement in the murders, Greenwood notified the base commander at Hill Field that the Ogden Police were preparing warrants for the arrest of two airmen, and that in the meantime, with the commander's permission, they would be sending out police officers to observe the suspects. The commander's reply surprised Greenwood, who later recalled his reaction.

"Unbeknownst to me, the call on those wallets had come to the detective division rather than the command post. And Deloy White had been assigned to go out and get that evidence. But he didn't know what we had on the names. He had no idea. You see. That we already had the names. And we didn't know that he had been assigned to go out and get the wallets. I guess he was already there before I ever heard that those wallets had been found. So we had the names that were given to us by the confidential informant, you know, and I'm ecstatic. But you've got to have corroboration, a mere suspect is no good. You've got to have something to tie that suspect into the crime. Anyhow, I'm preparing to send people out, and before I can get them out there, I find out that White's already there and searching through the Dumpster. Well then, that's when I jumped straight in the air and clicked my heels, because right there I knew we had 'em."

The Dumpster had been cordoned off by the air police, and Varley stood outside while Judkins and White waded around inside, sifting through the trash one piece at a time. Items taken from the murder scene were scattered all through the trash, and as each was discovered, Judkins or White handed it out to Varley who placed it in a separate evidence bag and sealed and labeled the bag for safekeeping by the evidence officer. Before the afternoon was over, Judkins and White had discovered, and Varley had bagged, a dark blue ball-point pen imprinted with "Hi-Fi Shop," one white pullover shirt, two leather purses, a pair of white lady's-gloves, a temporary driver's license of Carol Naisbitt, a single .38 caliber casing, eleven .25-caliber casings, two key rings with fifteen keys, and sixteen charge cards in the name of Dr. Byron H. Naisbitt.

The three detectives still were unaware that an informant had called the command post and identified two airmen, Dale Pierre and William Andrews, as the murderers. Nor did they know that the suspects' quarters had been given as Barracks 351, just thirty feet away. While they worked their way through the Dumpster, they watched the wall of windows along the north side of the barracks. Before long they noticed consistent activity in a particular window on the second floor at the east side of the building. The shade was pulled back and they were being watched.

Barracks 351 housed part of the 1550th Organizational Mainte-nance Squadron, 475 men assigned to maintain the helicopters used in training airborne paramedics. When evidence recovered from the Dumpster out front was linked with two airmen from the 1550th residing in the barracks, the squadron's first sergeant, James Ste-vens, was summoned to advise Air Force security and the Ogden Police on the suspects. Was Pierre short? they wanted to know. How tall was Andrews? Could he confirm that the two men had been spending a lot of time together recently? That Pierre spoke with an accent? That Andrews owned a light-blue van? Could he fill them in on the suspects' habits, their room numbers, the nearest exits? Stevens could tell them all of this and more. He wasn't surprised that Pierre had murdered three, maybe four, maybe five people. For months now he had been trying to get Pierre out of his squadron and out of the Air Force.

A career noncommissioned officer with eighteen years in the Air Force, Stevens had been brought in from a racially troubled squad-ron in Korea to restore discipline in the 1550th. He had arrived at Hill a month after the Jefferson murder the previous October, and the commanding officer of the 1550th, Colonel John Neubauer, had briefed him on Pierre and the facts of the Jefferson case. They had discussed Pierre frequently. Based on information from the Air Force investigators and the Ogden Police, both had concluded that Pierre was a killer, that he lacked the same conscience, the fear of retribution, possessed by the other airmen. On more than one occasion Neubauer had confessed to Stevens: "I lie awake at night worrying about that guy. I just wonder who he's going to kill next."

Stevens had a voice of megaphone intensity and eyes greatly magnified by thick glasses. He smoked cigars. When dressing down a cocky airman, he would first crowd the airman with his potbelly and glare at him with his magnified eyes, and then out of his mouth would blast a cloud of cigar smoke and a salvo of orders and threats peppered with "Do you hear me, boy!" and "Is that clear, son!" It worked on everyone but Pierre.

"I got the impression that whatever happened to him was just *che sarà*," said Stevens, "like a fatalistic approach. But it was something you sensed more than you really knew. I could stick that cigar in my mouth and try to look mean, hit him up one side and down the other, but I just wasn't getting through to him. The other guys I'd do that to I could see a little tremor, or *some* kind of reaction, hatred or fear or something. But with Pierre it just rolled off him like water off a duck's back."

Their problem was that Pierre had officially done nothing to violate the provisions for separation from the Air Force. Not until late January, when Pierre was arrested for auto theft by the Ogden Police, did Stevens and Neubauer feel they had grounds to begin processing him for an early "undesirable" discharge. Though they had to await a conviction before Pierre could be discharged, Stevens and Neubauer had begun the paper work for his separation while Pierre was still in jail. However, when Pierre was released on bail on March 20, still awaiting trial, he surprised them by requesting an early out under a new regulation, which provided for the resignation of an airman who was unable to adjust to military life. Under this regulation he would receive an honorable discharge. Though Stevens and Neubauer wanted Pierre separated from the Air Force with an "undesirable," even more than that they wanted him out of the Air Force *as soon as possible*. Under the new regulation no conviction was required. Pierre immediately had been taken off the flight line and assigned to permanent bay orderly duties in the barracks. Stevens called it "hang-fire status" which was to apply until he could have Pierre separated from the Air Force.

Two days after Pierre had gone to Stevens with his resignation request, Andrews had also asked to be separated from the Air Force. Andrews was a different case, Stevens felt. He would have been "a darn good trooper." Andrews, though, seemed never to act on his own, drifting with whatever was happening around him. In a crowd he could be tough. As Stevens remembered, "You could get him to be really scared to death until he got out and talked to some of his buddies."

Stevens began processing Andrews's separation papers and assigned him to bay orderly duties with Pierre. The two of them reported to the TV room five days a week at seven thirty in the morning to learn whether they would be mopping and vacuuming one end of a hall or another, or policing the grounds around the three-story building and the Dumpster out front. And at the end of the day Pierre and Andrews had still more janitorial duties to perform. Each of them had received an Article 15 for failing twice to report for duty on the flight line. As punishment the two men had been reduced to the grade of airman basic and ordered to serve two penalty hours each afternoon from four o'clock to six o'clock for the thirty days of April. During these two hours Stevens had them GI the floors, clean the latrine, and perform other janitorial details around the barracks orderly room.

Now, as he sat in the OSI headquarters briefing his supervisors on Airmen Pierre and Andrews, Stevens mentioned the Article 15 each of the men had received and the penalty hours they were now serving every afternoon in his orderly room.

"But last night," said Stevens, "neither one of the gentlemen showed up."

Though the Ogden Police now had enough evidence to arrest Pierre and Andrews for murder, because they were on a military base, there were legal complications that slowed the process. If the affidavits supporting the arrest and search warrants were sworn to under oath by the officers involved and they were signed by a civilian judge with proper authority, the intermediate step of review and authorization by the base commander was necessary before service of process could follow, and then only according to procedures and guidelines set down by the commander and his advisers.

The base commander, Colonel James M. Hall, Jr., met with his military legal advisers at the OSI offices around six o'clock in the evening. Charges of murder, especially this murder, against airmen under his command made Colonel Hall even more cautious than usual. Weber County Prosecutor Robert Newey notified Commander Hall that the necessary warrants and complaints were being processed and would be delivered to him personally by Sergeant Greenwood of the Ogden Tactical Squad. In the meantime, requested Newey, would the commander issue an order to his base security police to detain the two men should they make any attempt to leave the base? Commander Hall refused to issue such an order. His position was that, legally, he could do nothing to stop the men from leaving the base until the proper papers from civilian authorities were in his hands and he had had adequate time to determine their legality. Any attempt to detain them prior to a review of those civilian documents, therefore, was not possible. The commander agreed to provide the Ogden Police with additional manpower for surveillance of the barracks, but if the suspects attempted to leave the barracks or the base before the warrants arrived, by military law they would have to be permitted to go.

About six thirty that evening a member of the air police assigned to guard the barracks watched as Dale Pierre and William Andrews, together with a third airman, walked out of the barracks' west exit, crossed the lawn to a parking lot adjacent to the next barracks, got into a light-yellow Ford Pinto, and drove off. By the time Detective White was notified of their departure, the three men had cleared the base gate to the east and driven off into the glow of early evening.

The Ogden evening was warm, and Jean Hamre, who lived in the foothills behind Weber State College, had taken the opportunity to wash windows long smeared by the winter snow and rain. From the deck where she stood spread a panorama of the city and the colors from a setting sun still reflecting from the sky and the Great Salt

Lake. This area of Ogden along the east bench was high and people often drove slowly up and down the streets and gazed out at the setting sun, or at night down upon the twinkling lights of the city. Some parked to take in the view. So it was not unusual when a car Mrs. Hamre had never seen before cruised by on the road above her home and at the end of the street pulled off onto a lookout point and stopped. But the three men who got out of the car *were* unusual; none of them seemed interested in the view. Immediately, the three began arguing. They were far enough away that Mrs. Hamre could hear nothing of what they were saying, but she became intrigued with the drama being enacted at the end of her street; so much so that after five minutes of "glancing up that way occasionally" and seeing that the men "seemed to be arguing and pleading with each other," she went inside the house, got a pair of binoculars, and watched the pantomime through the window.

One of the three, a tall, muscular man wearing a denim jacket, sat on a rock, while the other two stood on either side "arguing violently" with him. Of the two men standing, one was tall, very thin, and light-complected. With a stoop in his shoulders and a pair of gold-rimmed glasses resting on his thin nose, he looked studious and frail. Every few minutes he would walk off, stand alone briefly, then walk back and plead again with the man sitting on the rock.

"The one on the right as they were facing me I would say was about five nine or five ten," Mrs. Hamre said in her statement to the police the next day. "Kind of a stocky frame, with a high forehead, almost a receding hairline. He had on olive green pants, and a Hill Air Force Base T-shirt. He's the one I watched and noticed most. He just stood there with his hands in his pockets."

After twenty-five minutes the scene ended. The three men climbed into the yellow Pinto again and drove back the way they had come. Not once did any of them gaze out at the sunset colors now almost melted into the horizon where the lake met the darkening sky.

"First thing that come to my mind was there was gonna be a shootout," recalled Polo Afuvai, one of the seven Tac Squad officers. Afuvai was sitting in an unmarked squad car outside OSI headquarters, while Greenwood and Moore were inside being briefed by

Commander Hall on the assault that was about to take place. "We went down there with the attitude that's what was gonna happen. But the ol' hands was sweaty, you know, and perspired as hell. I was wet that night, all right. I had sweat glands I'd never known about."

Bill Thorsted, another member of the Tac Squad, was in the squad car next to Afuvai's, waiting. "Your armpits were wet clear down to your belt," he remembered. "Knowing they're in there, but not knowing what they're going to do. I was thinking, if they don't know what's happening outside and then they find out, probably the first thing that's going to go down is a hostage situation."

Over a mile away White and a dozen other detectives waited with shotguns in the perimeter of Air Force security surrounding the barracks. The base was dark now. Hours earlier, when the suspects had slipped away, it looked as though the net that so quickly had been thrown around them had just as quickly been cast aside. But the police had stayed hidden, and as darkness was settling about the base, White's contact inside had notified him that Pierre and the other two men had just returned to their rooms in the barracks.

Nearly two more hours of waiting had then passed. The detectives standing in the perimeter had kept close watch over the lighted balconies and the fire escapes. If Pierre and Andrews tried to leave the base again, this time they would not go alone. Just after ten o'clock White had received the message he had been waiting for: Greenwood and the Tac Squad had finally arrived at OSI headquarters with the arrest and search warrants for the two suspects.

Inside OSI, Greenwood was now conferring with Colonel Hall. After reviewing the warrants the colonel had issued an order that the police surrounding the barracks had authority to arrest Pierre and Andrews if necessary to prevent them from escaping. The next step was to devise a plan to get them out of the barracks.

Colonel Hall, pointing to an area map and a blueprint of the barracks, briefed Greenwood, Moore, and a dozen colonels, majors, and OSI agents on his plan of attack. Sharpshooters were to be positioned so that the balconies outside the rooms would be cut off as escape routes. Air police and base security would establish a defense perimeter around the barracks to isolate and contain a possible gun battle. Greenwood and his men, if they wanted them, were to be provided with automatic weapons and body armor for their assignment inside: draw out Pierre and Andrews. Knock on their doors, kick the doors in if necessary, but locate them in the barracks, keep them away from the other airmen, and disarm them if possible. The colonel assigned one of his majors to lead the assault.

An hour earlier White and some of the other detectives had observed Andrews through the window in his second-floor room getting dressed. Then the lights had gone out and the shades had been pulled. Since that time neither Pierre nor Andrews had been seen by any of the police or Air Force personnel. Pierre's room had been dark since nightfall. Though no one knew where in the barracks Pierre and Andrews were hiding, with armed guards surrounding the building they were certain the two men were still inside. But as Greenwood stood listening to the colonel's briefing, and as White waited in the perimeter for the assault on the barracks, the voice of a base security guard suddenly broke on all radios: a light-blue Chevy van had been spotted rolling fast across the base headed for the west gate.

Thorsted was still idling the engine of his Tac Squad car in front of OSI headquarters when an OSI agent jumped into the car.

"They got to the van and they're trying to escape!" yelled the agent.

The young Tac officer threw the car into gear and jammed the accelerator, the OSI agent shouting directions to the gate. Afuvai and the rest of the Tac Squad waiting outside the OSI building took off after Thorsted. They could hear over the radio that Air Force security agents were already closing in on the van. Thorsted kept driving for the gate but was still a mile away when he heard that the security agents had stopped the van and ordered the occupants out at gunpoint.

The occupants were a staff sergeant and a friend on their way home. The van, identical to Andrews's van, belonged to the sergeant. When Thorsted and the OSI agent heard the arrest over the radio, they stopped immediately, turned around, and rushed back to the OSI office. On the way Thorsted was trying to make radio contact with Greenwood to report the false alarm on the light-blue van. But just as quickly as the van had been sighted and then stopped, another report came in over the agent's walkie-talkie: Pierre and Andrews were in custody.

When the news hit the OSI office that Pierre and Andrews had been captured, Colonel Hall was just entering the final phase of his briefing. He paused to listen to the report, and then to the amazement of everyone else in the room, continued with a pointer stick, coordinating his plan of attack. The major who had been assigned to lead the assault with the Tac Squad interrupted the colonel twice.

"Colonel, sir," he said, "the suspects are in custody."

"Yes," acknowledged the colonel, and went right back to his briefing.

He was still talking and pointing with his pointer stick when Greenwood and Moore ran out of the office.

No one knew who had given the signal to move on the barracks or why it was given. But seconds after the light-blue van was reported leaving the base, the detectives surrounding the barracks had rushed the east entrance and proceeded up the stairs to Andrews's room on the second floor.

Deloy White led this first group of eight or ten detectives, some with revolvers drawn, others carrying shotguns. As they approached the closed door to Andrews's room, half of the men swung silently around to the opposite side of the door, while the other half backed up White. With everyone in position, White tapped on the door with the barrel of his shotgun. There was no answer from inside, but after a moment the doorknob turned, and the door opened slightly. White followed the motion with his gun until, through the crack in the door, he saw a man's face. The man was standing only a few feet back from the door, looking straight up the barrel of White's shotgun. His hands were in the air with the palms open and facing White. As soon as he saw the hands were empty and no one else was in the room, White lowered his gun. The man identified himself as William Andrews. One of the detectives behind White advised Andrews that he was under arrest for murder, and then read him his rights and asked him if he understood those rights.

"Yeah," said Andrews.

The same detective then explained his rights in greater detail, and again Andrews said that yes, he understood. But he made no attempt to speak again or protest or resist arrest. After the tension that had been building all those hours waiting outside in the dark, some of the detectives felt that Andrews was almost disappointingly meek.

Glen Judkins, the detective who had arrested Pierre for car theft, was standing in the back of the line outside Andrews's door. Although he could hear White and one of the other officers reading Andrews his rights, because of the line of detectives in front of him he couldn't see the suspect. Just then the line had turned about and Judkins suddenly was first in line and running down the hall with Detective Lee Varley, going after Pierre.

Pierre's window on the south side of the barracks had been under surveillance since five o'clock that afternoon. All officers involved knew that Pierre's room was 223, on the other side of the hall from Andrews's and at about the middle of the building. But as Judkins and Varley passed the poolroom on their left, an airman stepped into the hallway in front of them.

"Pierre's not in his room," the airman whispered, "he's on the ground floor, southwest corner."

Assuming the rest of the officers had got the same message and were immediately behind them, the two detectives ran past 223, down the hall, and took the west side fire escape to the first floor.

The room in the southwest corner of the first floor was 106, the first door on their right as Judkins and Varley came off the fire escape. The door was closed, and since Judkins had to assume that Pierre was armed, he waited outside for the rest of the detectives to catch up. With more men to back him up, the odds were greater he could arrest Pierre without a shot being fired. Too, he didn't *know* if Pierre was even in the room. Everything had happened so fast, and the airman who had whispered the information had seemed so sure, that Judkins had just followed his instincts. He and Varley could have been waiting with their guns drawn outside an empty room. Then they heard voices coming from within. They waited a few minutes longer, and no one else had arrived to back them up, when suddenly the door to 106 opened. A black airman stepped into the hall.

Judkins knew it wasn't Pierre. He motioned with his gun. "Take off down the hall," he said in a terse whisper.

The airman flinched at the sight of Judkins's gun and moved

quickly away. But no sooner was he away from the door than a second airman peered out into the hall. This second airman was tall and thin, had a stoop to his shoulders, and wore gold-rimmed glasses.

"Hey, man," he said to the first black, "who you talking to?"

Then he looked up and saw Judkins holding a .38 on him. Judkins jerked his head.

"Down the hall," he whispered again.

As the airman eased into the hall and walked slowly away, he left the door ajar. The door was hinged on the right, in front of Judkins, and swung outward, toward him. Judkins and Varley had worked cases together before; each knew how the other would react. As they stood in the hall, Judkins motioned to Varley to look through the crack in the door. Varley leaned to his right and peered in with one eye. He could see a single individual still in the room, but the man was sitting on a couch hunched forward with his back to the door, like he was tying his shoe. Varley couldn't see the man's hands. He signaled to Judkins that there appeared to be only one man left in the room, but indicated there might be more that he couldn't see. He motioned for Judkins to look in, but as Judkins did so, the man on the couch suddenly turned toward him. Judkins recognized Pierre. He kicked back the door and crouched low in the doorway, gripping his .38 in both hands.

"Put your hands on the wall!" he yelled.

Pierre moved quickly to his left. Judkins watched his hands until they were placed flat against the wall above a dresser. Knowing that Varley was covering him, Judkins slid his revolver back into its holster and popped out his handcuffs.

"Now put your hands behind your back, Pierre."

Pierre brought his hands down from the wall in unison and held them behind his back.

"What's this all about this time?" he asked Judkins.

"Hang on," said Judkins, "the warrants will be here in a minute."

With Pierre handcuffed, Varley holstered his gun, and the three men stood in the middle of the room, waiting for the other detectives to arrive. For the minute that ticked by, none of them spoke. Then the room suddenly filled with men wearing coats and ties, and carrying shotguns. One of the men told Pierre he was under arrest for first-degree murder, then held out the arrest warrant for Pierre to see. Pierre looked down at it for a moment, then raised his head and seemed to lock his eyes on a point somewhere just above the officer's shoulder. The officer then handed Pierre a card with the Miranda warning printed on it, and asked Pierre to read it. But Pierre only nodded like he understood and continued to stare.

As the officers brought the two men out of the barracks that night and placed them in separate squad cars, something none of them had ever heard in connection with their work now was beginning to break all around them. Applause. From the barracks to the east, hanging over the balconies clapping and whistling, were hundreds of airmen.

The airmen were still cheering when Greenwood pulled up in front of the barracks. Pierre was just being led into the parking lot, and Greenwood directed his men to put Pierre in the backseat of his car. Through it all Pierre's expression had never changed. He had not spoken a word since he was arrested. When he was placed in the squad car, he continued to stare straight ahead. Airmen, some of them curious, some cutting up, strolled past the car and peered into the backseat at the man sitting there. Pierre ignored them.

Greenwood, mad that the detectives had moved on the barracks before the order had come down, but pleased that the arrests had been made so quickly and smoothly, climbed into the backseat of the squad car with Pierre. By now Pierre had been read his rights twice, but Greenwood read them to him again. Pierre gave no sign that he had heard Greenwood. When Greenwood next asked him if he wanted to say anything, Pierre remained silent, but this time he shook his head no.

In the other car Andrews was telling a uniformed officer that he and Pierre the night before had only driven into town with another airman named Keith Roberts, dropped Roberts off in town, driven around a bit, returned to the base to see the movie *Blackbelt Jones,* then gone out to a nearby 7-Eleven for a couple six-packs of beer and been back to the barracks and in bed by about midnight. Andrews didn't elaborate, and the officer, although by now he had given Andrews his Miranda warning three times, didn't press him for details.

Commander Hall had determined that the search warrants drawn by Prosecutor Newey and signed by a county judge were valid and could legally be executed on the base. With Pierre and Andrews in custody Greenwood assigned three officers to ride in the squad car transporting Andrews back to the station, and two others to accompany him and Pierre. The remaining detectives and Tac Squad personnel broke into teams of four or five and began searching the three rooms, Pierre's, Andrews's, and the one in which Pierre was arrested. The crime-scene technicians, who had been at the base processing evidence since the first items were recovered from the Dumpster, joined in the searches. Shortly after the searches began, the two squad cars bearing Pierre and Andrews departed from the barracks parking lot.

On the way back to the station, a fifteen-minute drive, Pierre spoke once. Greenwood had been making small talk since the car had pulled away from the crowds gathering in front of the barracks. He was asking Pierre where he was from, how he liked the Air Force, what he did all day on the flight line. Pierre sat facing forward, not speaking, seemingly not hearing. The base was dark and the driver of the car, Jerry Burnett, was smoking a cigarette in the front seat, while Greenwood sat in the back asking question after question of Pierre and hearing nothing from Pierre's corner of the car but silence. Burnett was not familiar with the roads at Hill Field. As he approached a darkened intersection, he slowed to consider the three possibilities, wondering aloud, "Now how the hell do you get off this base?"

Greenwood was looking out the window to see if he recognized any landmarks, when from the other corner of the backseat he heard, "Turn left here, sir."

Pierre was giving directions. Burnett turned left and proceeded along another dark road. As he approached the next intersection, Pierre spoke again.

"Turn right here."

Burnett and Greenwood later described the tone of Pierre's voice as "polite." At every turn, until they arrived at the base gate, Pierre "politely" directed his captors across the sprawling air base. But once they had cleared the gate and were on the open highway headed for Ogden, Pierre resumed his placid expression, staring straight ahead, mute.

* * *

Word of the capture of Pierre and Andrews already had got out, and though it was nearly midnight, the squad cars transporting them to the station were greeted by a crowd of some two hundred Ogden citizens. The two cars edged through the crowd and into the police garage at the center of the building. While Pierre remained seated and still in the backseat, Greenwood got out of the car, walked around, and opened the door for him to get out. As the two men passed the elevator at the end of the garage, news photographers and cameramen gathered in the hallway opened up with bright lights and flashes. Pierre would appear in the paper the next day, his eyes closed and his face bunched up in a wince of annoyance. Behind him in a coat and striped tie would appear Greenwood, one eye and the flat corner of his mouth visible to the right of Pierre's cocked head.

A minute later Fisher guided Andrews through the crowd by a grip on his triceps. Andrews was snapped with a glint in his eye and a smirk across his face.

No one even attempted to interrogate Pierre. No one asked him where he had been the night before or what he had been doing from six to ten. Once inside the station, no one spoke a word to him. As Greenwood came into the hallway with Pierre, Chief Jacobsen pulled the Tac Squad leader aside and asked him to address the crowd waiting outside. "Just make a statement about the arrests and the charges against these guys," he told Greenwood. Another officer took hold of Pierre and ushered him onto the elevator and up to the ninth floor to be booked. Neither of them said a word on the elevator. When Pierre was booked, the officer locked him in a holding cell alone until morning and left.

It was now one o'clock. Downstairs, on the first floor, Andrews was taken to a small room used by the city meter-maids and seated in a chair, his manacled hands dropped down behind the chair back. The officer who stood next to him was a powerfully built man of thirty-nine, with blond hair, wire-rimmed glasses, and a ruddy face. R. E. "Pete" Peterson taught classes in interrogation techniques to other officers, and he was ready to begin the tentative questioning of Andrews. Peterson had two gray eyes, one real and one glass. On hard cases he had been known to pop that glass orb out of his head and aim what remained of the skin-flapped hole at the suspect.

Peterson gave Andrews his rights and asked him if he understood them. Andrews said yes. Then Peterson explained them again, this time in greater detail. Andrews again indicated that he understood. Peterson began his questioning, Andrews answering slowly, thinking long about each question before saying a word. When asked where he had been Monday night, the night of the murders, he told Peterson that he and Pierre had been at the movies watching a picture called *Blackbelt Jones*. Peterson himself had talked with one of the airmen at the barracks when Pierre and Andrews were arrested. The airman had told him that he had seen Pierre and Andrews at the base movie house together on *Sunday* night watching the same *Blackbelt Jones*. Peterson stopped Andrews and told him that he and Pierre had been seen at the movies not Monday night, but Sunday night. That's right, they had, said Andrews, they had gone to the same movie together two nights in a row.

Andrews then surprised Peterson by volunteering that he had been in the Hi-Fi Shop the previous Saturday afternoon. Andrews said that if they found his fingerprints on any of the stolen property, it was because he had handled *all* of the merchandise in the store that day.

Peterson was easy on Andrews, treated him "delicately" so there was no chance of "dirtying up" the case. "But you could see he was boiling inside," he said of Andrews later. "Until we had him arrested and down here, I don't think he fully realized what he had done. He reminded me of a guy who was trying to play it as cool as possible, but he wasn't a cool character. When I confronted him with a piece of evidence, he would just stare at the wall and I'd have to bring him back again. Then he seemed to remember and he would talk and then suddenly he would seem to go 'Oh, my God' as realization came back. I think he wanted to talk about it, to get it off his chest, but he just wouldn't let himself. I was looking for him to blame it all on Pierre. But he was scared to death of him. Whenever I asked him about Pierre, he would tighten up. I think he would have talked if he hadn't had so damn much fear of Pierre."

After thirty or forty minutes Andrews finally said that he could not help them anymore. Peterson said, "Cannot or will not?"

"Both," said Andrews.

* * *

Pierre and Andrews were in custody, and the victims' personal belongings had been found in the Dumpster just outside their barracks. But still unaccounted for was twenty-four thousand dollars in stereo equipment. Back at the base, officers from Detectives, the Tac Squad, and Tech Services continued to search.

Moore, Empey, White, Varley, and a crime-scene analyst named George Throckmorton had been assigned to Pierre's room. The previous night until almost daybreak Throckmorton had been in the Hi-Fi Shop basement, sketching the scene, measuring, photographing, gathering evidence. In seven years of police work it was the first time he had found himself silent, concentrating on technical questions just to bend back his emotions. It was the first time, too, that he would refer to the atmosphere of a crime scene as "sacred." The mood was different now. Where he and the others had been careful not to disturb anything in the basement, and had even spoken in hushed tones, everything in Pierre's room was to be torn apart.

The room was austere: two writing desks, two dressers, two lamps, two bunks. It was designed as living quarters for two men, but Pierre was the sole occupant. The walls were beige, and unlike the rooms of other airmen they were clean of all posters and pinups. On one wall hung a single framed picture of Pierre sitting in his uniform next to an American flag, affecting a valedictorian pose. Stacked on the floor were karate magazines, a few pornographic directories with black-and-white snapshots of naked women, and a whorehouse guide to the neighboring state of Nevada. Under it all stretched a plain, gray-brown carpet.

The bunks were taken down and the mattresses pulled apart. The footlockers and wall lockers were emptied. The lamps were studied, a small refrigerator was examined, all drawers in the desks and dressers were opened and turned upside down. Pierre's closet was ransacked and the contents spread across the floor. The ceiling was checked for removable tiles. When an area of the room had been scoured by one officer, another came along behind him and did the same again. And then a third officer, and a fourth, until the room had been searched five times over. But other than a blue parka spattered with a white chemical residue and a substance that looked like dark blood, the only evidence they found were brochures of stereo equipment. On the back of one brochure was a list of three Ogden stereo stores. Beneath the name of each store was a checklist of stereo components and their makers. The Hi-Fi Shop was first on the list.

Down the hall in Andrews's room another team uncovered a pair of rubber surgical gloves hidden on a closet shelf between two pillowcases and a T-shirt. A brown paper bag was wadded up inside the wastebacket and contained several clear plastic album covers with the Hi-Fi Shop label. But as with Pierre's room there were no weapons and no sign of the dozens of large speakers, amplifiers, and turntables taken from the Hi-Fi Shop.

When Pierre's room had been thoroughly searched, Throckmorton said that only one thing remained to be done, and that was look under the carpet. It was after one in the morning, and most of the men had been without sleep for almost two days. The carpet covered the entire floor, and the only way to look under it was to shift the bunk beds, dressers, and other furniture around the room, each time peeling back the free corner of the carpet. That meant moving all of the furniture at least twice, some of it four times. After the furniture was wrestled across the room the first time and piled in the southeast corner, Throckmorton ripped up the flap of carpeting in the opposite corner and found nothing. Everyone but Throckmorton and Empey left the room. On his way out Varley turned to Throckmorton and said, "You can't hide a stereo under a rug."

Twice more Throckmorton and Empey dragged furniture from one corner to another, but each time they lifted the carpet and pulled it back, they found nothing. After the third corner had been looked under with no results, Empey left to join up with his partner, Moore, and return to the station. Throckmorton continued to work alone, finally going out into the hall to ask an OSI agent there to help him move the last piece of furniture, a dresser, off the southeast corner of the carpet. As the agent tilted the dresser back, Throckmorton reached down and pulled the carpet out from under it and then began stretching it back toward the center of the room. But before he had raised it far, there appeared between the carpet and the padding a white envelope.

"Well look what I found," said Throckmorton.

He picked up the envelope and opened it. Inside was a rental agreement between Dale Pierre and Wasatch Storage. Wasatch Storage was a maze of garagelike units at the corner of Twenty-sixth and Wall, only a few blocks from the Hi-Fi Shop. Pierre had rented Unit 2 the previous day, April 22, the day of the murders.

"That has got to be where all the equipment is," Throckmorton said to the agent. Then he stepped out of the room and yelled down the hall to White. "Bingo! Deloy, we got 'em!"

Sometime after two in the morning Deloy White went back to the station and got a search warrant for Unit 2, Wasatch Storage. By now all of the officers who had remained at the barracks to search the rooms of Pierre and Andrews had returned to Ogden. Most of them knew that the rental agreement had been found, and they were waiting, filling out their reports, until the search warrant had been obtained and it was time to serve it. They all wanted to be there when the door to the storage shed was lifted.

As late as it was, the search warrant was quickly granted. Then, led by Deloy White, a procession of police from all departments headed out the back of the station and drove the three blocks to Wasatch Storage. Unit 2 had a military padlock on it. With thirty to forty police waiting in front of the unit, White produced a key chain he had taken from Pierre at the time Pierre was arrested. One of the keys fit the lock. White sprang it open and slid the door up.

Half a dozen flashlights flickered into the small garage. It was piled like a treasure trove with expensive stereo components. When they saw the glistening metal stacked in front of them, the officers cheered, and the mass of them took about three steps forward, but then they stopped.

"Let's everybody get back," one of the captains was saying. "We know it's here, we can't process it all tonight. Let's come back in the morning when we can all think straight."

When the shed was closed again, White put on his own padlock and the crowd of officers dispersed, slapping each other on the back and offering congratulations. But even before they had got back to the station, the good feelings had begun to disappear. Mike Empey later recalled the mood when he returned from the storage shed. "There were comments from several officers that even though the case was pretty much wrapped up, that the evidence had been found and the property recovered, there were still all these people whose lives were ruined, and no matter what we did there really wasn't much to change that."

Kevin Youngberg, now with thirty-three days' experience in police work, was assigned to guard the storage shed. Across the street from Wasatch Storage was an alley next to the old, abandoned Ranch Cafe. Youngberg backed a patrol car into the alley where he had a clear view of Unit 2. It was early Wednesday morning; everyone else left, went home to sleep, some for the first time since Sunday night. Later, they would learn what was in the shed, and the doctors and nurses at St. Benedict's would finally know what had caused the burns around Cortney's mouth and the bloody foam spilling from his lungs. None of the police had seen anything specific, just a maze of stereo equipment illuminated by flashlight. No one had noticed the stereo dust cover resting upside down in the middle of the pile. Nestled in the dust cover was a black and yellow car mat, and wrapped in the car mat was a small green drinking cup. Next to the cup was a large bottle, only half-full, with a label that read, "Tough on Clogs, Won't Hurt Pipes." It was liquid Drano.

Youngberg sat in his patrol car alone watching the shed for the rest of the night.

FUNERAL

That was a mistake to go down to the police station. Lynn wanted to go down and see them, and he didn't think he could get in unless I went. So I thought, Well, I'll go down and just look at 'em. That was the one thing I regret doing.

Shortly after Pierre and Andrews were captured late Tuesday night, radio and television stations broadcast news of the arrests, and local newspapers featured the story with front page headlines Wednesday morning. The panic that had been mounting in Ogden during the twenty-four hours following the murders now was turning to anger, and one angry citizen was Byron Naisbitt's brother-in-law, Lynn Richardson, father of Hi-Fi Shop owner Brent Richardson.

When Lynn learned that Pierre and Andrews had been captured at Hill Field, he telephoned Byron. The two suspects were locked up on the ninth floor of the Municipal Building in downtown Ogden, and Lynn wanted to look at them. He wanted to go down to the courthouse, up to the ninth floor, "and look the bastards in the eye," he said later. "It was such a hideous, senseless crime, I wanted to see if they walked on four legs or not." He called Pierre a "yellow mad dog," and added: "They both were cowards, you know, they could be nothing but cowards to act like that. Talk about them being black, they can't be black, they're yellow. We wanted to see who could be that completely yellow."

Byron doubted that the police would allow them in to see Pierre and Andrews, but he agreed to meet his brother-in-law at the station. The police were holding Carol's jewelry, which Byron had to claim at the station anyway, and though he wasn't sure why, he too wanted to look at the alleged killers, especially Pierre. He wanted "to see what kind of a person could do this type of thing to another human being."

When the two men arrived at the police station, Lynn was directed to Police Chief Jacobsen's office and Byron to the sergeant's desk, where he identified and collected Carol's jewelry. After signing a release, he then joined his brother-in-law, who was already talking with the chief. As the office door closed behind him, Byron held out his hand so the other two men could see what the killers had overlooked. In his palm lay three rings and a watch.

"I'm glad they didn't get these, too," he said. "They'd be hard to trace probably."

The watch was a 14-karat gold Rolex. One of the rings was set with jade and a diamond, and the other two were plain gold bands, one bearing a large diamond solitaire that Byron had given to Carol for a recent anniversary.

"There was probably more on her fingers here," Byron sighed, "than all of the stuff they hauled out into that truck."

Lynn kept looking at the jewelry in Bryon's hand and shaking his head. He had been enraged when he first entered the chief's office, but now he had begun to cool down.

"They didn't care what they got," he said. "They had such a lust to kill that that was the main thing in their minds, was to kill."

Jacobsen agreed with Byron that the jewelry would have been difficult to recover, and for a few more minutes the three men wondered aloud how it could have been overlooked. But the police chief doubted that Byron Naisbitt and Lynn Richardson had come to his office to discuss why the killers had not taken more than they had. He saw in Byron's face a familiar look, "like he'd had his guts ripped out," the same look he'd seen three or four times in the past, when the family of a rape or a murder victim had come to the station wanting to confront the perpetrator. Jacobsen was waiting for the question, and he didn't have to wait long. When the discussion of the jewelry ended, Byron said, "What's the possibility of seeing them?"

"Why do you want to do that?" asked Jacobsen.

"I just want," said Byron, "just to look those guys in the eye, just to look them right in the eye and see what kind of guys they are."

"We want to see who could pull such a cowardly trick as that," said Lynn.

Jacobsen could see that neither of the men was carrying a gun, but looking at the depression and anger in Byron's face, the tears in his eyes, he wondered whether the man, if given the chance, might try to kill Pierre or Andrews with his hands. The chief had no love for the suspects either, but he knew that allowing Byron and Lynn upstairs would solve nothing and might lead to a scene embarrassing for them later. Yet, because he sympathized with them, he was reluctant to tell them simply to go home; he wanted them to decide for themselves that they didn't want to look at Pierre and Andrews, after all.

"I can understand why you want to see them," he said, "but let's not have that kind of trouble."

Byron wasn't sure what the police chief meant: he didn't even know himself why he wanted to see the killers.

Lynn said, "I'd just like to give the bastards what they've got coming."

"I'd want to do the same thing if this happened to me," said Jacobsen. "I know how you feel inside, I know what you want to do. I would, too. But I'd be sorry for it later."

Jacobsen assured them that the evidence against Pierre and Andrews was substantial and growing. He reviewed for them the items the police already had found in the Hill Field Dumpster, and the stolen equipment they had recovered from the storage unit rented by Pierre. With that kind of evidence against them, Jacobsen explained, Pierre and Andrews would not go free.

"If you want," he added, "I'll give a call to the sheriff upstairs and tell him you're coming. But I'd like to put a stop to this whole thing right now."

"All we want to do," said Byron, "is look at them."

"And why do you want to do that?"

"I don't know," said Byron.

Jacobsen paused for a moment, looking at Byron. Then he said, "Dr. Naisbitt, if I let you in to see Pierre, would you kill him?"

The question startled Byron. "No," he said. "Hell, why would I want to kill him? I just want to look at him."

"Do you want to get in the cell with him?" asked Jacobsen.

"Nope," said Byron, "I don't. I just want to look at him eye to eye."

That's an odd sensation to ask to see somebody that's murdered your wife and damaged your son. You know. I think that's odd. And I don't think I'd do that again. When they asked me if I saw him if I'd kill him, I thought: What the hell would I want to do that for? If I had that in mind, I'd be just like he was. That wasn't the purpose. And when I come to think about it, I'm not even sure what the purpose was. There was no real purpose. Nothing could have been gained by seeing him. When they said, "Would you kill him?" that made me realize right then, I was down there foolishly. Foolishly, foolishly. No reason to be there.

"I didn't come to kill anybody," said Byron. "That's the farthest thing from my mind. I think maybe I'd just like to see what kind of a guy would do this kind of thing."

"If it's that important to you, then, I can have someone take you up," said Jacobsen. He asked Byron, "Is it that important to you?"

Byron didn't answer at first, just continued looking at the chief. After a moment he said: "No, I guess it isn't. Not to me." He dropped the envelope containing Carol's jewelry into his pocket and turned to his brother-in-law.

"Let's get out of here."

Before they left, Byron told Chief Jacobsen that he appreciated the police work that had tied up the killers so quickly.

"I figured you would find them," he said, "but I didn't know it would happen this fast. Now these guys will get a trial and I guess that will determine what happens to them."

We followed their counsel and went home. They had good judgment, and it was poor judgment on my part. I started to feel, This is ridiculous, what the hell am I doing here? So we went home, and I was glad we did. And I never discussed it again with anybody, about going down there, or wanting to, or the reasons, or anything else. I don't know what I was expecting to happen if I'd been allowed in. I'm not even sure. Not even sure. I don't know how they would have reacted. I don't know how I would have reacted, how I would've felt. I felt that I would have had plenty of control, there's no question about that. Regardless of what they did or said, I probably would've never even spoken or made a sound. Just looked at 'em.

But that was a mistake. And I've been glad a lot of times that I never did see those guys. Because after I got home and thought about it, I really didn't care about seeing them. It wasn't that important to me. I had plenty to do with my wife being dead and Cortney on the verge, without worrying about those guys, and I figured that the sooner and the farther they were out of my mind, the better my life was going to be. Because there was nothing I could see to be gained by confronting them. If they could have done Cortney any good I'd have confronted them in a second. If they could have done him any good at all, I'd have confronted them ten times a day. Or whatever it would take. But it wasn't going to change his situation, and it wasn't going to change mine. I was swayed a little bit by someone else, and I didn't let that ever happen again. I tried to have complete control over how I felt and thought and acted from that point on.

Shortly after Byron Naisbitt and Lynn Richardson left the police station, Pierre and Andrews were taken from their ninth-floor cells to the city courtrooms four floors below, where they were to be arraigned on charges of first-degree murder. The Information citing the charges against them was read and then each of the defendants was asked if he would like to consult with an attorney. Andrews requested an interview with the public defender's office, and Pierre stated that he had an attorney from another case but hadn't been able to contact her. To allow Pierre and Andrews time to contact their attorneys, the judge continued their arraignments until the following day, Thursday, and they were returned to their cells on the ninth floor.

Pierre's attorney was Rita James, a bright young woman who talked fast, smoked continuously, and punctuated her speech with short bursts of laughter. She had recently been divorced from an Air Force lawyer at Hill Field and was practicing law in a remodeled house in Ogden. That week she was away on vacation.

"See I was in Georgia visiting my parents when the Hi-Fi Shop happened," she said later. "And you know how you get these weird feelings? Well, when I read about it in the paper, I had this weird feeling I was going to be involved in it somehow, and that's not hindsight, because I told my mother that at the time. And then the next day it came out that Dale had been arrested, and he was waiting for his attorney to get back from vacation. [Laugh] You know, I'm reading this in the Warner-Robbins paper in the middle of Georgia.

"Prior to this there were a couple matters that he needed some counseling on, and of course he was in the military so he went to the base lawyers, the JAG office, and they felt that he ought to talk to civilian counsel about it. So he came to me. The first time, he was one of several suspects in this other homicide out at the base. They wanted him to take a polygraph on the deal, and none of the JAGs out there were that familiar with polygraphs. I don't even think I opened up a file on him at the time. The only thing I recall is the police saying something about Dale having a set of keys to Jefferson's apartment and cars and everything, you know, a complete set of the man's keys. And then several months later he was arrested for auto theft and had me represent him on what later turned out to be three auto theft counts.

"Now the auto thefts were in January of 'seventy-four, two Rivs and a Corvette. The MO was really brilliant. Bear in mind Dale always denied having stolen the cars. But the MO was go out in your uniform to a car lot, give them your correct name, test-drive a car that you couldn't conceivably afford with the number of stripes you got on your sleeve, tell 'em you want it and you're going to go to the credit union to get the money; then the car disappears that night. Then it's found on the base with a temporary sticker on it that you get. That's an incredibly dumb way to go about stealing a car. He didn't strike me as being that stupid. Nor did he strike me as being violent or nasty or evil or anything like that. You know, some people do give you the willies when you meet them. But he didn't. He never struck me as being anything but quiet. Maybe a little strange. Even though he maintained he hadn't stolen these cars, he couldn't come up with any sort of credible explanation for what they were doing [laugh] with his license plates on them, and his temporary stickers on them. He seemed to have more intelligence than that, so I was trying to see if there might be any possibility of, you know, not so much an insanity defense, that obviously wasn't there, he didn't strike me as being insane, but some mitigating mental problems so he could cry on the judge's shoulder. [Laugh] You know, and perhaps try to get some sort of help for him as opposed to a prison sentence. But I never could really get enough information out of him to be very helpful."

After Cortney's surgery the night of the murders Dr. Hauser had warned the Naisbitts that if Cortney survived till morning, the next major crisis would occur Wednesday night or early Thursday, when the swelling in Cortney's brain would reach its peak and the brain would begin distorting into the cavity at the base of his skull. If the pressure did not subside quickly, the respiratory center would shut down and Cortney would die.

When Dr. Hauser returned to the ICU late Tuesday morning to examine Cortney after his surgery, he found that Cortney was beginning to respond to verbal commands. But later that night he again visited and entered the following note on Cortney's chart:

> While rt. sided weakness persists, he is now moving all extremities on command. For several reasons, suggest that in spite of continued improvement, his official status be continued as critically ill.

Dr. Hauser was always pessimistic with the families of head-injury patients. Insults to the brain were not only serious but unpredictable. In Cortney's case, underlying all of Hauser's usual reservations was his original diagnosis upon examining Cortney in the emergency room: he had never seen a patient exhibit those same signs and live.

The nurses continued to check Cortney for signs of the swelling in his brain, looking into his pupils to see if they were equal and reactive to light. What made it difficult to compare Cortney's pupils was that his right eye had filled with blood and drifted off to the side.

Early Tuesday evening one of the nurses noted that Cortney's eyes were open and he was moving his lips, as if trying to form words. But the eyes did not track and there was no sign he could comprehend what was happening around him. After a few moments he closed his eyes again and sank back into his bed.

Through the quiet hours of Tuesday night and Wednesday morning, Gary stayed at the hospital after his family had departed. At two thirty in the morning he was in the room with Cortney, watching the nurses work around his brother, watching his brother's mouth pucker and open, then close again. At six o'clock he was back in Cortney's room, and Cortney opened his eyes and appeared to recognize him. But the moment was brief. The seeming recognition quickly faded and Cortney's eyes closed. When Gary had seen Cortney earlier in the night, Cortney had been breathing on his own, free of the respirator. Now he was back on the machine and assisting it only sporadically.

Shortly after Cortney had been put back on the respirator early Wednesday morning, his father returned to the hospital and was in ICU accompanied by Dr. Wallace. They watched as Cortney breathed off the respirator, only occasionally initiating the breath himself. A nurse turned Cortney and positioned him. At seven fifteen Dr. Hauser was back at his bedside. He examined Cortney again and found the boy's condition to be as he had predicted. He wrote on the chart:

> Apparently, at some point since I last saw him he has required MA-1 to take over. This is doubtless a reflection of increased intracranial pressure. This cerebral edema is expected to reach its maximum—assuming it is reversible—sometime tonight.

The doctors feared that even if the pressure in Cortney's head peaked and later subsided, his respiratory center still might be destroyed. Cortney then would be dead, except for his lungs filling every few seconds with air from the respirator. Byron told Gary he had given instructions to the ICU staff to allow Cortney to die if that's what he was going to do. He didn't want his son artificially supported by a respirator if the boy's brain had ceased to function to the point that it no longer had the primitive capacity to ask for oxygen. Wednesday afternoon Dr. Rees wrote an order on the chart that Cortney was to be taken off the respirator every hour for fifteen minutes to see if he was continuing to breathe on his own. The order was to run until the critical period had passed.

After predicting that Cortney's cerebral edema would reach its maximum sometime Wednesday night, Dr. Hauser returned to the hospital at six thirty that same evening. He noted that while Cortney still opened his eyes occasionally, he would not follow verbal commands as he had twenty-four hours earlier. The pressure inside Cortney's head seemed to be mounting despite the large doses of steroids he was receiving.

During the night Cortney alternated between what appeared to be intervals of sleep and fits of restlessness, the difference between the two being little more than a contortion of the face or a twitch of the arm. The monitor next to his bed indicated that his heart was in sinus tachycardia, beating faster than one hundred times a minute. Following Dr. Rees's order the nurses continued to take Cortney off the respirator for fifteen minutes each hour.

Just before midnight a resident on his surgical rotation stopped in the ICU to look at Cortney. He had been in the operating room the night of the murders, assisting Dr. Hauser in placing the burr holes in Cortney's head. Since then he had frequently checked on Cortney's progress. That night Cortney was responding to pain in his right Achilles for the first time, an improvement since the resident had seen him earlier that morning. As the resident was examining him, Cortney suddenly opened his eyes and the resident thought he mouthed the word "hi." The movement of Cortney's lips was so indistinct, the resident actually wasn't sure what he had mouthed, or even if the movement had been purposeful. But on Cortney's chart he wrote, "Definite code," meaning that if Cortney stopped breathing or his heart went into fibrillation, every effort should be made to save him. Later, Dr. Hauser would request that the resident cease from writing on Cortney's chart.

When Dr. Hauser saw Cortney again during rounds the following Thursday morning, the swelling in Cortney's brain appeared to be subsiding and he seemed vaguely more responsive than the evening before. The monitor to his heart was still indicating sinus tachycardia, but he was tripping the MA-1 on every breath. After examining Cortney, Hauser and the other doctors surmised that Cortney's period of continuous reliance on the respirator had possibly been caused not so much by the pressure on the respiratory center of his brain as by his total exhaustion. His body had been so tired it simply lacked the energy to draw a breath. Hauser remained chary of Cortney's condition and gave no hope to the Naisbitts for Cortney's survival. But he recorded on Cortney's chart:

> Holding his own. Feel the point of maximum cerebral edema has passed.

Claire arrived at the hospital later that morning, and when she found that the swelling in her brother's brain already had peaked and he was still alive, she was overjoyed, thinking that now Cortney would live and recover. *I remember one thing I was told. I think it was one of the doctors said, "Well, we think that if he lives till Thursday, he's going to make it." I guess they were worried about his brain, you know, whether it would start going down by then, or something, the edema. I guess that's why they told me that, and I thought, "Really?" You know? I mean, I really took it to heart. And when he lived till Thursday, I thought, "Wow, that is really neat!" But Dad'd say, "That's only one milestone, you don't know what he's got to go through." And I really didn't.*

Thursday morning the Ogden City courtroom was packed with spectators, many of them standing. But before the armed guards would bring Pierre and Andrews down from their ninth-floor cells for arraignment, the room had to be cleared and everyone searched before they were permitted to reenter. Once inside, no one was allowed to leave. Pierre's attorney, Rita James, had not yet returned from Georgia, and Andrews still had not qualified for representation by the public defender's office. The judge again granted a continuance until Monday to allow the two defendants an opportunity to confer with their lawyers. Afterward, outside the courtroom, Prosecutor Robert Newey told reporters that if Pierre and Andrews were convicted, he would demand the death penalty.

Like most death penalty statutes in existence at the time, Utah's was new and untested. Two years earlier, in June 1972, the Supreme Court of the United States had handed down its famous decision in *Furman* v. *Georgia,* a decision that appeared to the general public to hold the death penalty unconstitutional. But the *Furman* decision had not been nearly so decisive. The court had split five to four against the Georgia death penalty statute, each of the nine justices writing a separate opinion, a rare occurrence on the high court. Two of the five justices striking down the statute would have declared unconstitutional any statute authorizing capital punishment on the sole ground that capital punishment was "cruel and unusual." But the remaining three members of the majority indicated in their opinions that the aspect of the statute which they objected to was not the penalty itself but the amount of discretion left with the judge or jury in deciding who would die and who would not. The arbitrariness inherent in this discretion, not that the death penalty was cruel and unusual, was at the core of their rejection of the Georgia statute. The implication derived from their three opinions was that should the death penalty be administered according to stricter guidelines for judge and jury, guidelines that allowed less discretion and more uniform application, these three justices would not be opposed to the implementation of the death penalty.

After the *Furman* decision was handed down, the legislatures of most states, including Utah, revamped their old death penalty statutes, using as a guideline the sum of the reasoning in *Furman.* In Utah the new death penalty statute provided that if the defendant during the phase of the trial establishing guilt or innocence was convicted of murder in the first degree, then a separate, or bifurcated, hearing was to be held in which the judge or jury would listen to evidence, mitigating and aggravating, to determine whether the defendant would serve a life term or be sentenced to death for the crime. Circumstances that the jury were to consider as mitigating were listed in the statute and included the absence of a prior criminal record, extreme mental or emotional disturbance, mental disease, intoxication, influence of drugs, and the youth of the defendant. At the time of the murder, if the defendant committed another murder, or was engaged in the commission of rape or aggravated robbery, or killed for pecuniary profit or other personal gain, or for the purpose of preventing a witness from testifying, such factors were to be weighed by the judge or jury in favor of imposing the death sentence. Utah's statute had been newly drafted to reflect the recent changes dictated by the *Furman* decision, and Newey told reporters gathered in the hallway outside the courtroom that, assuming the evidence was sufficient for conviction, the new Utah death penalty would be given its first test by Hi-Fi murder suspects Dale Pierre and William Andrews.

In the same building a few floors below, Greenwood's command post had been dismantled and D. K. White had taken over the investigation. On Friday a third airman who voluntarily had been talking to police since the night Pierre and Andrews were arrested was himself charged with carrying a concealed weapon and tampering with evidence. The airman was Keith Roberts, a tall, thin black who wore gold-rimmed glasses. Roberts fit the description of the third airman given by Jean Hamre, the woman who had seen three blacks arguing near her home as she was washing windows Tuesday evening. Another woman who worked in a lingerie store just down from the Hi-Fi Shop had seen Roberts in a maroon coat walking back and forth in front of the shop from seven to nine the night of the murders. Roberts also had been seen just prior to six o'clock that same night, dropping Pierre and Andrews a half block from the Hi-Fi Shop, then driving off in a light-blue van. As more evidence involving Roberts was gathered, the charges against him were changed from carrying a concealed weapon and tampering with evidence to aggravated robbery and first-degree murder.

In these first few days after the murders citizens continued to call the station offering information they thought might be of help to the police. The young girl who had talked with Pierre in the alley behind the Hi-Fi Shop while her mother was picking up the day's receipts from the Kandy Korn next door was being hidden by her parents at a friend's house west of town. She was only thirteen, and when her parents discovered that she had talked to one of the killers while the victims were tied up in the basement, they feared the man would try to find her. When the police located her first, she told them the man had a funny way of talking, and she pointed to his picture in the mug file. It was Pierre.

A teen-age boy who had been in the Hi-Fi Shop the Saturday before the murders told the police that that afternoon he had seen two black men in the store discussing stereo equipment with Stan Walker. While the tall one had stayed in the sound room talking to Stan, the short one had walked toward the front of the store, looking around and writing something on a piece of paper he held on top of an eight-track tape. The short man had asked the boy if he worked in the store and the boy had said no. Then the man had walked back through the sound room to the back door, turned to his right, and peered down the stairs into the basement. Hours before Pierre and Andrews were captured, the boy had identified the short man who had peered down the back stairs as Dale Pierre.

Perhaps the most interesting piece of information received by the police came from a sergeant employed in the evenings at the Hill Air Force Base theater as a ticket taker. In a statement to the OSI the sergeant said that on the second of April he had been doorman at the movie house when he sold a ticket to a black airman wearing fatigues with the name "Pierre" sewn above the shirt pocket. (The name had caught the sergeant's eye because two days earlier, working his daytime job as military locator, he had received a phone call for an Airman Pierre and found that there were only two Pierres living on the whole base.) The movie showing that night had been Clint Eastwood's *Magnum Force,* and a particular scene in the movie was now of great interest to the Ogden Police.

In the scene a hooker is sitting in the backseat of a taxicab counting a roll of money and laughing. The cabdriver stops in front of a building and a tall man, the woman's pimp, jumps into the backseat with her. He is wearing a thick, floor-length fur coat and wants to know where she's been. She appears terrified and immediately begins to plead with him, saying that she's been working a convention, and she was just now looking for him to give him his cut. The pimp starts hitting her, and the driver suddenly stops the cab and runs away. The pimp then pulls a can of liquid Drano out of a pocket in the fur coat and forces some of the caustic down the hooker's throat. She tries to claw and kick at the pimp, but in a matter of seconds she begins to weaken and the pimp pushes her to the floor. She is coughing and choking as the pimp alights from the car. In the movie the hooker dies within less than a minute of ingesting the Drano, her hand falling limply out of the open car door.

*   *   *

At Byron Naisbitt's request Dr. Richard Iverson, a psychiatrist and friend of the Naisbitt family, examined Cortney one evening near the end of Cortney's first week in the hospital. The night before, Byron had been alone in the room with Cortney, talking to him as he always did, when suddenly Cortney had opened his eyes and looked at his father. What had happened next Byron did not understand and none of the other doctors had been able to explain it to him. He wanted a psychiatrist to examine Cortney and give his opinion.

Iverson stood at Cortney's bedside, testing certain reflexes, watching Cortney closely, talking to him. Cortney lay still. "I was looking at a boy with obvious paralysis, his eyes semiclosed, a bandage on his head," remembered Iverson. "My initial impression was a boy in a coma, but after I looked at him I decided to ask him some questions. At one time, our home was next to the Naisbitt home and we had a swimming pool, and Cortney used to come over and swim in our pool, as well as play with my two sons. So I started talking about our swimming pool and some other things we did, and suddenly I noticed a slight twitch of Cortney's mouth, a little blink of the eye, and maybe a little movement of the forehead. This indicated to me that what I said had some type of emotional impact on him. But that was all I got, and then things were turned off."

Byron's experience the night before had been different, and this is what he could not understand.

He spoke, see. When he was up in Benedict's Hospital, Cortney spoke to me. Then I don't know what the hell happened, and no one was able to explain it. I was questioning him, and I was trying to find out if he knew anything or could testify or whatever. Hell, everybody was interested. The police wanted to know if he could talk. The family wanted to know what had happened. Everybody thought he was going to be blind, because of where he was shot, and I was anxious to know if he could see, or hear. But he talked to me, and I can't remember what night it was. I remember he nodded yes, that he recognized me and could hear me. Then I asked him if he remembered what happened to him, and he shook his head that he knew, and then he started to say what had happened to him. I don't know how that worked with the trache in. I can't get the sequence on that. You can talk if the trache's covered, but maybe I was just asking him the questions and he signed back. . . . No, he talked to me. Cortney talked early. I wouldn't forget that. The sequence is all shot, but just right within the first few days he regained consciousness and he could hear and he could talk. And I asked him if he remembered what happened, and he shook his head yeah he knew. So I said, "How many were there?" And he said, "There were three and two had guns." And then he said that they grabbed him and kicked him in the gonads and punched him in the stomach and took him downstairs and tied him up and forced him to drink this stuff and then said that they were going to kill him, going to shoot him. And I said, "Who were they going to shoot, all of you?" And he said, "Yes." And I said, "Who do you mean by all of you?" And you could just see him think who the hell was down there. He was thinking and thinking, and then it looked like here is this picture of his mother getting shot in the head. And then all of a sudden, he let out this little squeaky moan, his eyes kinda glazed over and he just fell back and never said another word. I thought he had just put it out of his mind right then and there. That's the way it looked to me, because he was talking until he came to the point that he remembered that his mother was killed. There's no reason why he wouldn't be able to talk again, except that he just couldn't face the scene of his mother's death. He made that little screamy noise and sank back in the bed and then he laid there just kind of catatonic. He didn't respond after that, so I just figured that he couldn't handle it, it was so painful for him. At least that's what I thought. Because they couldn't explain it, see. They did scans on his brain, an arteriogram and all that kind of stuff, to see if he'd had a hemorrhage or what the hell had happened to him. But they still didn't know. I figured he just shut it all out and went into his own little world.

Cortney hadn't spoken since. He hadn't opened his eyes or moved his arms or moaned or stuck out his tongue or done anything to respond to his surroundings. Having made contact once, Byron couldn't understand how Cortney could shut off so suddenly and completely. The night Dr. Iverson came to observe Cortney, Byron told him what had happened during that single episode. He wanted to know how Cortney could speak for those few minutes then, and now would not even open his eyes.

"This sudden withdrawal is a very complicated issue," said Iverson later, "and I don't know if anyone has the answer. It could have been due to some acute intracranial pathology caused by the bullet, or by the effects of cerebral edema. Some people might call it acute psychotic withdrawal. I've seen a lot of brain-damaged people— trauma, drugs, tumors—but Cortney's unique in terms of having had brain trauma coupled with severe emotional trauma. I'm not sure that we even have a word for it. I think we have to diagnose him: posttraumatic stress disorder manifest by avoidance of activities or talking or contact that arouse recollections of the traumatic event.

"I remember after I saw Cortney I went out and read his chart, and the other doctors were just wondering when he was going to die. That I can remember very vividly, because when I walked in there, I even had to ask myself: 'Hey, are you being objective? You know this boy, you're good friends with his father. Do these things you're seeing in him really exist?' My impression still was that, yeah, this young man has an injury that's going to leave some brain damage, but I felt that his withdrawal and not talking was not due to that. When he talked to his dad, he thought about what happened, and remembered what happened to his mother, and the feelings that were generated built to a head, and then suddenly the emotions were so strong that he just shut off thinking and talking and withdrew from reality. Whereas physical damage to his brain would be more or less permanent, there was always a chance he would eventually learn to deal with these emotions. So I told the other doctors, 'Sure, he's had some brain trauma, he's had some surgery, but I think the *reason* he isn't talking, and the *reason* for this withdrawal that makes him look like's he's going to die, is due to an overwhelming reaction to having been there, to having seen what happened to his mother and the other people, and then the trauma to himself.' Cortney's the only case like that I've ever seen."

A month earlier Byron Naisbitt had buried his mother. Carol had helped plan the funeral and had told Byron and the children then that when she died she did not want to be displayed in an open casket. She liked the African mahogany, she had said, with the beige, satiny interior, but she wanted no one to see her lying inside of it.

Byron himself had said that when he died, at his funeral he did not want the casket to be open. Now, one month later, he was burying Carol and these decisions had to be made.

Carol would be buried in her temple clothes: a white veil, a small green apron, and a white robe that would be draped over one shoulder. But the dress she would wear Byron was to choose. Though the mortuary offered a selection of burial dresses, Byron wanted something different. He didn't know exactly what he was looking for, but he had been shopping with Carol often enough that he knew what he liked on her and what he didn't, and nothing at the mortuary looked right. He wanted something brighter, something happier for her. On Wednesday morning, after he left the police station, he found Claire and said to her, "Come on, we're going to go buy a dress."

In downtown Ogden, Byron and Claire went from store to store, shopping for the final dress that Carol would wear. While Byron waited outside the dressing rooms, Claire modeled dress after dress for him, as Carol had always done before. Claire was so much like her mother that just by watching her twirl slowly in the various styles, Byron could feel what would be right for Carol.

"My dad likes to pick out clothes," remembered Claire. "For my mom, we'd go through and I'd try them all on, and he'd say, 'No I don't like that,' or 'Yes. I like that.' "

The one that finally seemed right to Byron was long and white with a high collar and a sprinkling of daisies. It was a wedding dress.

Once the dress was selected, Byron and Claire ordered Carol's casket in the African mahogany with the beige interior. Next they had to decide whether to leave the casket open, fulfilling an obligation they felt toward those who came to pay their final respects, or close it in keeping with Carol's wishes. Because of the autopsy there were noticeable lines across Carol's forehead, and the morticians could not conceal the swelling in her face and neck or the chemical burns around her mouth. Byron felt that given the circumstances of his wife's death, she looked good, but an autopsy unavoidably changes the countenance, and considering that, he doubted that Carol would want to be viewed. Still, he wasn't sure the right decision was to close the casket.

"If it's closed," he said to Claire, "people might think it's because she doesn't look very good."

"But she does," said Claire. "And besides, I don't care what people think."

"Neither do I," said her father.

Byron talked with Gary and Brett about it too, and finally decided that the casket would remain open, but only for family. Friends who came to offer their condolences would not see Carol as she lay in the casket.

Carol's viewing was at Lindquist and Sons Colonial Chapel, from six to eight o'clock Friday evening. Byron had asked his children to be at the chapel earlier that afternoon, so he could speak to each of them alone, and they could spend the last few moments with their mother quietly.

Brett and Diane were the first to arrive. When they walked in, Byron was sitting next to the casket at the front of the chapel, where he had been sitting since midmorning. In the ICU a few nights before, Byron had also talked with Brett and Diane privately and had said something Diane never forgot, because thereafter her father-in-law never again mentioned his own feelings.

Brett's dad had asked us to come into the side room, in case Cortney could hear us. And he said: "I know I seem strong but it's only because I have to. You're married, and you know what it's like, the relationship of the marriage, so you'll understand more than anyone in the family how I feel, what I've lost."

For the viewing on Friday, Diane hadn't known whether the casket would be open or closed. Only when her father-in-law asked them to be at the chapel early did she learn that the casket would be open for the family and that she would have to view her mother-in-law.

I'm afraid to look at dead people, but Brett's dad was very comforting. It was the day of the viewing, and he called us on the phone and told us to come and say our good-byes. He said, "I've been talking to her for several hours, and . . ." He called her Shorty, it was always Shorty, and the kids called her Mums. And he said, "Come say good-bye to Mums." And I said, "I can't." He said, "There's nothing mysterious about death, it's a natural thing." He said:

"Shorty's here and she understands and she's happy. We've been talking for several hours." It was comforting to me because I felt that he really had been talking to her and that everything was all right. He said, *"She doesn't want us to be unhappy, she wants us to be strong."* That made me feel better. I mean, I looked at her differently. When I looked at her later, I felt that maybe she was really there and she could see us.

As Brett and Diane walked down the center aisle of the chapel, Byron stood and came over to them and the three of them embraced.

"Everything's all right," he said. "Just go on up and spend a few minutes with her and say your good-byes."

The chapel was large with many gold-cushioned pews on either side of the aisle. Chandeliers hung from the cathedral ceiling, and the afternoon sun was filtering through amber windows. At the front of the chapel, floral arrangements lined the shelves and then surrounded Carol's casket as it sat upon a hardwood bier at the entrance to a side room joining the chapel from the left. During the funeral the family alone would be seated in the side room with the casket.

Diane walked at Brett's side, clinging to his arm. When they reached the casket, Brett looked down at his mother in her white dress with the high collar and the daisies. The white veil had been pulled back from her face, and she was wearing small diamond earrings. On her left hand Byron had replaced the large diamond ring he had retrieved from the police station a few mornings before. Although it had been four days since his mother had been murdered, none of it yet seemed real to Brett. He still felt that he could leave the mortuary and find her at home. Or that if he called the phone number at his father's house, she would answer.

The funeral was just unbearable almost. . . . It was just hard saying your final good-byes. I remember getting real angry all over again and having a hard time coping with all that. I was almost beside myself with hate. You just felt such an emptiness, even though you could hardly bring yourself to believe it had actually happened. It was such a waste. Anyhow, they opened the casket for the family and she looked pretty good.

They all went through a coroner autopsy, and that upset me a

*little that she had to go through such a thorough one. They hacked
'em all up, and that was kind of bad. You could see the seams across
the front of her head where they'd, you know, taken her skull out,
and taken her brain. I guess they put them back, but it's just hard
to make it look like she really was. But for what she'd been through,
I think she looked good.*

Byron sat in one of the pews at the edge of the aisle, and as each
of his children came in, he would put his arm around them one at
a time and start by telling them that everything was all right. Claire
followed Brett and Diane, and Gary was the last of the three to walk
up the aisle to the front of the chapel where his mother lay.

*That whole day was really something else. Dad handled it really,
really neat. As typical Dad, he went down a couple hours before-
hand, checked the casket, made sure it was acceptable, decided that
she looked natural enough under the circumstances to have it open,
took care of whatever thoughts and feelings he had at the time, and
that was that. Then we the children showed up, and he took each
of us up to Mother's casket, and I'm sure he said different things to
each of us. He told us that he loved us and that Mother had loved
us. He explained his love for Mother, his thoughts on her last minutes and on death. There is a life after death, she is dead, it's past,
it's nothing that we're supposed to sit and ruminate about. She
lived a good full life, she wanted to be a mother and she fulfilled her
function very well. You know? I mean she felt fulfilled, she felt proud
of her children. She would probably have liked to have stayed around
a little longer, so she would be remorseful for that reason, but what
she had set out to do she had accomplished and led a full life. She
had been a good woman and had helped get them through medical
school. Then she had dedicated herself to raising her children. He
said not to grieve, that Mother had done her job here, she may not
have had complete fulfillment of her job, but she was fine "on the
other side" so to speak, that we as a family would be united again
when we all die, and that this is a passing, you know, it's just
something that happens, just to accept it and go on. Then he went
on to say that according to the medical examiner's report she had
probably died instantly in the conscious sense. He was very calm,
not necessarily measured as though he was trying to contain any
rage, no rage at all, very calm and sullen, melancholy, you know,*

in part; but here again, he had already taken care of his emotions, he was trying to help each of us.

When the actual public viewing came about, there was no viewing at all, it was more a reception, you know, as the people came by, and like I said it was almost . . . Dad was the stalwart. Everything was going to be okay. He had calmed the family and instilled his love in us so much that we were very well taken care of with ourselves and our own feelings, and we were in turn trying to convey our peace of mind to the other people who were coming to show their commiserations to us. "Hello, how are you? Yes, it was tragic. Don't worry about us, everything's okay. We're doing fine." We were consoling the other people, it wasn't the other way around. Without Dad we couldn't have done that. Maybe we could have, but not to that extent. It was very well done. I was very proud of him.

After Gary had had some time alone with his mother, he brought his camera into the chapel and took pictures of her in her casket, surrounded by flowers. At first the idea of taking the pictures hadn't seemed right to him. Then he thought that if Cortney lived, and if he ever regained consciousness, he might want these last pictures of his mother. But after taking the pictures, Gary held on to the roll of film for a long time, until finally there seemed to be no reason to have the pictures developed.

Although the family had requested that donations in Carol's name be sent to the McKay-Dee Foundation or the St. Benedict's Building Fund, over a hundred floral arrangements—pink and white carnations; red, yellow, and orange gladioli; lavender chrysanthemums; daisies; blue irises; large yellow spider mums—filled the room that Friday evening where Byron, Gary, Brett, and Claire stood in a line next to the now closed mahogany casket. The crowds that came to view Carol grew so quickly that the chapel filled, and soon, as people entered the mortuary, instead of standing in line they were seated in the next available pew, where they waited to be called forward one row at a time. Many of them waited an hour and a half to be allowed a few moments to express their sympathy to the Naisbitt family. When the Register of Friends and Family was finally closed, it bore the names of nearly thirteen hundred people.

As each of the mourners passed by the closed casket to speak quietly for a moment with the family—"Such an unnecessary loss," many of them said—the family reassured them that they were holding up fine, that a lot of their grief perhaps had been transferred to hope for Cortney. Their thoughts and feelings, their energies, now were being directed toward him. Claire was standing next to her father as the people passed slowly by, grasping her hand, kissing her cheek, many of them crying. The people and the words blurred in her mind. As she was standing there, something her father had said while they were making arrangements for the funeral came back to her.

"I hope we're not doing this again next week."

Friday afternoon Orren Walker had been released from McKay-Dee Hospital to attend the funeral of his son, Stan. The bullet wound at the back of Walker's head had proved to be superficial, and the pen that Pierre had kicked into his left ear had been safely removed. Other than circular scars at the top of his forehead and across his right shoulder, spots where the Drano had burned his skin, the state's eyewitness had nearly recovered from his injuries. Now he was being treated with high dosages of antibiotics to prevent infection at the site of the bullet wound and along the eustachian tube from his ear into his throat. All week from his hospital bed Walker had been talking with the police, going over the details of what had happened in the Hi-Fi Shop basement. When Stan was buried on Friday, Walker, with his wife and other son, and accompanied by a nurse and a police officer, attended first the funeral services then the graveside dedication. Two days later Walker would leave the hospital, soon to begin a long series of appearances in the courts as the chief witness for the prosecution.

Michelle Ansley was buried Saturday morning following services at the Lindquist chapel, where Brent Richardson eulogized his new, pretty employee who had coaxed him to dance in a high school gym only a week before. To a large gathering Brent spoke of Michelle's engagement and her wedding date of August 5, then quoted from two philosophical writings on death and the mysteries of life. When the services for Michelle had been concluded, her body was taken for interment to the same cemetery where Carol Naisbitt would be buried that afternoon.

Saturday at noon in the Lindquist chapel, Byron and his children again stood in line next to Carol's closed, flower-enshrouded casket, while people who could not attend the viewing the night before arrived early for the funeral to express their sympathy. Already, five days had passed since the murders, the mourning period having been prolonged first by the autopsy, then by the extra time needed to prepare Carol's body for viewing. Then there had been the first viewing and now the second, and the funeral was still to come. Claire wondered how much longer all of it could last. With only the four of them standing in line, her family seemed so much smaller to her. She wanted the sorrow to end, and she wanted Cortney to awaken and speak to her. Her father had told her not to worry, that they still had to work to see that Cortney recovered, but her mother was fine and now all that remained was for them to endure these last formalities.

At ten minutes to one, the organist began the prelude misic, and the last of the people in line spoke quickly to the family and found a place standing at the rear of the chapel. The pews and even the folding chairs that had been provided for extra seating were filled, and many people were standing. Just before one o'clock the funeral director, John Lindquist, drew the green accordion drape which separated the private family room, where the casket lay, from the pew-lined chapel. Behind the drape Carol's casket was to be opened for the family a final time.

In the private room with Byron and his children were the aunts, uncles, and cousins from both sides of the family. Joining the family, too, was Cortney's friend, Kelly McKenna. Kelly could hear John Lindquist on the other side of the drape requesting silence of the people in the chapel, while the family said their last farewells. Lindquist then returned to the private room and removed the lid from Carol's casket. The family gathered around the casket as Lindquist slipped the diamond ring from Carol's finger, put it into a coin envelope, and handed it to Byron. Then he replaced her small diamond earrings with plain gold studs that Claire had given him. As the earrings were being exchanged, Kelly stood to the side where he could see Mrs. Naisbitt's face. Kelly had been to funerals before, and to him dead people seemed merely to be sleeping, their faces powdered with a little makeup. But he remembered later that the feeling was different when he saw Mrs. Naisbitt lying in her casket.

"I sat with the family and everything, and boy that's when it really hits you. They had an open-coffin deal and I looked at her and I got this picture . . . Mrs. Naisbitt was a very pretty lady, but she didn't look restful to me. Her face looked like it was tied up, and you could just tell she had died a horrible death."

With the earrings in place John Lindquist turned to Claire and said softly, "Would you like to place the veil in position?"

Claire's eyes filled with tears as she tied the veil in place and her brothers leaned down to kiss their mother for the last time through the veil. Then Byron kissed Shorty good-bye, everyone bowed their heads for a brief family prayer, and the casket was closed forever. Byron had tears in his eyes as the top of the casket was lowered, but he blinked them away, and moments later when the drape separating the private room from the crowded chapel started to open, his shoulders were pulled back and his eyes were dry.

As the drape slid back, "Lara's Theme" from *Doctor Zhivago* filled the chapel. When she heard it, Claire thought: This is the beginning of the end. It will all be over with soon, just a couple more hours.

The main speaker at the funeral services was an amiable man, a doctor named Paul Southwick. Paul and his wife Beverly had been close friends with the Naisbitts for over thirty years, and in that time the two families had taken a lot of trips together, played a lot of bridge, seen a lot of movies. Memories for each of them were intertwined. As he stood at the pulpit in front of the chapel, Dr. Southwick reminded those gathered there that beautiful memories are important, and that people are the most important ingredient of beautiful memories. He said that Carol and Byron had worked to create lasting memories for their children, pleasant and meaningful experiences for them throughout their lives, and that they had done well in leaving behind these memories for the children to keep, now that Carol was gone.

Recalling some of the lighter memories he had of the Naisbitts, Dr. Southwick made people in the chapel smile when he told the story of the bowl of red punch that once overturned onto Carol's new white carpet, and Byron's comment, "We'll have to get some more punch and dye the rest of the rug." He told of Carol missing the group's New Year's Eve party that year for the first time in almost thirty years, to be with her newly adopted granddaughter, Natalie.

"She doted on her own children," he said, "and took them places and looked out for them. She was concerned about their happiness and how she could make them happier. And of course," he added, "that is what led her into the horrible thing that happened at the Hi-Fi Shop. It was her love and her concern for her children that brought her to this tragic ending of her life."

In speaking of family memories and then of Carol, Dr. Southwick had managed to keep his voice strong and clear, and his anecdotes especially had had a calming effect over his listeners. But then he turned to Cortney and the suffering the boy had endured, the horror he must have experienced, the loss his father and brothers and sister must feel, and tears came to his eyes and he was unable to continue. The Southwicks had lost a child of their own almost twelve years before when their eight-year-old daughter had tumbled over a waterfall in the mountains behind their home. Her father had found her and two other children lying at the bottom of the falls the day after Christmas. When Dr. Southwick tried to speak again, all he could say was, "I can understand their feelings."

Though he had planned to speak at greater length about Cortney, Dr. Southwick cut his remarks short, and when he found his voice again, he ended his eulogy: "I believe it's fitting for us to commemorate the life of Carol now because just within the last three or four days the trees have suddenly flourished into leaf and new blossoms have appeared, reminding us that life does come forth from what seems dead, reaffirming the Easter message that there is indeed a resurrection for all. It's reassuring to know that Carol, By, and their children someday will be reunited."

After Dr. Southwick left the pulpit, another man rose and sang "Oh, What a Day," which was followed by a short benediction. The people in the chapel still were seated and silent when the organist began the postlude with the one song Byron had requested she play in memory of Carol, "Hawaiian Wedding Song." At the song's conclusion the pallbearers stood and wheeled the casket still upon the bier past the organ, past the pulpit, and through the open doors at the front of the chapel to the waiting funeral coach. The family followed. Later, the one scene from the funeral services that would remain in the minds of many of the people seated in the chapel was the final one: Byron walking alone behind Carol's mahogany casket, and the organist playing "Goodnight, Sweetheart."

"As we were pulling into the cemetery at the top of the hill and looked back," remembered Brett, *"there was a solid train of cars for a mile and a half, clear back to the mortuary and still in the parking lot waiting to come. Just blocks and blocks and blocks of cars. It was gratifying, you know, that she had as many friends as she did."*

The city of Ogden recently had banned funeral processions, but exceptions were made for the three victims of the Hi-Fi Murders. For each funeral, police were stationed to block traffic at every intersection along Washington Boulevard, and the drivers in the processions were told to ignore the traffic lights.

Carol was to be interred in Washington Heights Memorial Park, which sat on a rise south of Ogden looking down upon the city and out upon the Wasatch mountain front spreading northward. It was a green, peaceful setting interrupted only by jets from Hill Field flying maneuvers to the south. Grass and clover surrounded the plain marble headstones set flat to the ground, and white weeping birch were interspersed with evergreens around the perimeter and in selected islands throughout the grounds. That Saturday afternoon in late April was warm and sunny.

At the entrance to the cemetery, highway patrol cars blocked northbound traffic and funneled the funeral procession through the gates. Inside, because of crank calls received by the Naisbitts (a typical circumstance in the aftermath of a major homicide), armed guards had been positioned around the grounds as a security precaution. When the family arrived in the light-blue and white limousines from the funeral home, they proceeded along the cemetery paths meandering to the east. Across the green lawn and through

the trees, they could see a large mound of fresh flowers marking
the grave of Michelle Ansley. In the grass near Carol's grave site
the press had laid their camera and sound cables and made themselves as inconspicuous as possible as they waited for the family to
arrive and the graveside dedication to begin. That night the Naisbitts would see themselves and the long procession of cars on the
evening news.

Chairs for the family had been set up near the site, and the Naisbitts sat in them, waiting for the rest of the people to arrive. It was
a long wait, much longer than the dedication itself would require.
The flowers that could fit into vans had been loaded at the mortuary
and rushed to the cemetery where they were now being stacked
around the grave site. Once inside the cemetery gates, the hundreds
of cars driven by the mourners still had to be parked tightly three
abreast along the car paths.

When at last the people had arrived and parked and gathered behind the family on the east side of the grave, the pallbearers lifted
Carol's casket from the funeral coach and carried it across the lawn,
setting it among the flowers. Then the bishop of the Naisbitt's church
ward stood before the crowd and announced that Carol's grave would
be dedicated by Byron Naisbitt's brother-in-law, Lynn Richardson.

In the Church of Jesus Christ of Latter-Day Saints, the small patch
of ground that is to be the final mortal resting place of the deceased
traditionally is dedicated as a place of peace and solitude, and perhaps a place of contemplation for the family when they come to
visit. The dedicator expresses gratitude for the life of the deceased,
and prays that the ground be safe from desecration and that the
remains be left undisturbed by the elements of the earth until the
time of resurrection. Lynn's dedication began that way, slowly and
thoughtfully.

Standing at the west end of Carol's grave and facing the family
and the hundreds of those gathered around them to the east, Lynn
prayed first for all of the spiritual things in a traditional dedication.
But then the bitterness crept into his voice, and he seemed unable
to control it. He raised his right hand to the sign of the square, an
antiquated Mormon gesture that once signified a vow or commitment. Few people had seen it used in the past twenty years, and to

those facing him now it seemed a sign of vengeance. With his arm raised at a right angle, he spoke bitterly of a society that would tolerate "this senseless killing!" Coupled with the rage in his voice, the words made several people look up suddenly. But he didn't stop there. In a voice growing in anger he described the deed as "cowardly" and the deaths as "useless," and before he could find the words to end the dedication in the name of Jesus Christ, he asked God for vengeance on the perpetrators' souls.

"I dedicated the grave," Lynn said later, "and I had so much resentment in me that I couldn't even give a decent prayer. I just kept thinking, How could anybody do such a cowardly thing! I can't even remember what I said, something about . . . I don't know, I was so hateful and resentful. Some people came up to me afterwards and said, 'We got a little afraid of what you might say.'"

The air of tension that Lynn's call for revenge had suddenly created in the mourners still lingered after he murmured the conclusion to his dedication, lowered his arm, and stepped away from the grave. Only when the bishop again stood before the crowd was the tension dispelled.

"This concludes the service," he said. "Everyone is now free to leave."

Slowly, the crowd began to disperse, and the people headed back across the lawn to their cars and eventually were directed out of the cemetery. When Byron and his children arrived back at the mortuary, he told them that from there he was driving to the hospital to see Cortney, and that when he left the hospital, there was something else he felt he had to do. "Shorty wouldn't have wanted it that way," he explained.

Weary from emotion, but relieved that the funeral finally was over, Gary, Brett, and Claire returned with family and friends to their father's house. A buffet supper had been prepared for all of them by members of their church's Relief Society.

While Byron was visiting at the hospital, Cortney thrust his tongue slightly, but otherwise did not move. Byron read a nurse's entry on the chart that Cortney was not responding to verbal commands, but Dr. Hauser had written some brief words of encouragement: from time to time Cortney seemed to be aware of his surroundings. Byron stayed with his son for a while, rubbing the boy's arms and talking to him. Then he left the ICU, went downstairs to the parking lot, got in his car, and returned alone to the cemetery.

It just bothered me. I wasn't particularly pleased about Lynn's choice of words, I guess. He had something to say about revenge, and I didn't want that for my wife's final resting place. All I wanted was just to have it dedicated so the Lord's looking after it, so Shorty would be comfortable there and rest peacefully with no bad feeling about the place. And that's all I wanted.

Except for a gardener and the bees flitting among the clover, the cemetery was deserted now and quiet. A high mound of fresh, bright flowers marked Carol's grave on the east lawn, and Byron crossed the grass to stand there, the sun at his back. With thoughts of tranquillity and love, he silently gave his own dedication, erasing the earlier words of revenge that had tainted the peaceful setting. It was a setting he would return to often. Long after the flowers had faded and been carried away, the cemetery workers would see him standing quietly in the same place, looking out over the white weeping birch and the mountains rising behind them in the distance.

You can say a lot of things about a relationship of thirty-something years.

COMA

It's just to me a time of complete anxiety. I could go along for a while and then I'd get this anxious feeling. Then I'd either have to go look at him and make sure he was still all right or else I'd have to call. So I was calling about every couple of hours. I could go a couple hours, then I'd have to check. And this would go, oh, this would go day and night for a while. I'd wake up in the night and get anxious and wonder what was going on, so I'd call the hospital. Probably didn't expect to hear anything any better, but I was glad to hear that there wasn't anything worse. Most often. Glad to hear that he was still plugging along. And when I was reassured, I'd go back to sleep.

I had a feeling of tenderness and love for him. You hate to see your son lying there all shot to hell and all burned up inside for no reason. You know. For no reason. He didn't have anyone else in the world except me and the people around him that he could bank on. And I wanted him to know that he had support. Someone was there who cared about him. When I visited, I'd bend over him and give him a kiss and tell him who it was, let him know that I was there, and let him know that everything was fine, that he was getting better, not to be worried or anxious, that everything was going to be just fine. But I didn't know if anything was getting through to him. It's a helpless feeling. I was upset, but there was nothing I could do about that. Not a thing. When you can't do anything about something, you'd better learn to live with it. And so you just wait and watch, and wait and watch. And hope everything gets better. But most days it didn't get better. Then they gradually started to square away. And then you get a little hope. And then something else happens, and that's all shattered. And then that gets a little better, and then something else happens. And so it just goes up and down, up and down. Anything he could do positive was a good day, and brought a lot of hope and happiness to see that he was progressing. And then there were bad days. You don't want to live through too many days like that. But see, it doesn't end. Because every day you walk into that hospital you're reminded that your son is absolutely critical, absolutely suffering, and there is nothing you can do for him. And this is what bothers me. This is the part I have more problems with than anything, is that . . . you . . . can . . . not . . . alleviate his suffering. You can't share it with him, you can't help him with it. He's got to do it all by himself. And I mean suffer! God! I don't know how in the hell anybody could tolerate what he had to tolerate. And what he went through no one will ever know.

So here's your bright son just getting to the point in life where he was starting to move around and starting to develop and starting to do some things that he'd been wanting to do, and somebody devastates him for no particular reason, and here he is. Here he is! What you got left. But he's still your son, and your heart aches for him, just aches for him, knowing full well that a lot of the aspirations he'd had are down the tube. And I mean down the tube. Nothing you can do about that, not one thing. It's an anguish that I don't think anybody can describe. And you finally have to get to the point that you're going to lose a son. And every day you don't lose him, there's still the fear that today you will. It's a terrible, terrible anguish. But you have to realize that there's nothing you can do about it, that you have to just take it as it comes. You have to figure that you've lost a son and anything other than that is a gift.

Just before noon on the day of his mother's viewing, Cortney had slipped his left hand down to his groin and wrapped his fingers tightly around the arterial line inserted in the femoral artery of his left thigh and with two nurses trying to hold back his hand yanked the line out of his groin. That same night he tried to pull the tracheostomy tube out of his throat. He grabbed at the IV needles in his arms and pulled at the Foley catheter that ran up his penis to drain his urine into a clear bag. The night after he tried to rip the trache out of his throat, he got his hand on the Foley and tore it apart.

Cortney's movements were not purposeful, but fitful and primitive reflexes. Except for these he hardly moved. If he opened his eyes, he would stare at the ceiling or the right wall or the left, whichever way he was positioned at the time, his eyes not focused or tracking, just open and staring, and then he would close them again and seem to go to sleep. Sometimes he would twitch a hand or a foot on command and once wiggled his toes. But even these responses often were so vague the nurse or the doctor who had witnessed them could not be sure they had actually happened.

Dr. Ken Johnson, a gastroenterologist, had been called in on the case for his experience in diagnosing and treating problems of the stomach and esophagus. Cases of lye ingestion are rare, and Johnson himself had seen only three or four, all of those in tiny children who had accidentally swallowed the caustic. "When I first saw Cortney," Johnson remembered, "he looked as close to death as . . . He was a fraction of a thread away from death. His head was bandaged, he appeared decerebrate, no purposeful movements, a lot of noises in his lungs. Every time the respirator would breathe for him, I could hear the noises coming up through the airway. I also thought he was in heart failure from the brain insult. It was stressful. Rees was upset. He said to me, 'This is one of those god-awful catastrophes and we just have to do what we can.' I know for myself I've never been so emotionally involved with a case before or since."

Cortney's injuries had led to so many complications that Johnson, Hauser, and Rees frequently found themselves at odds with each other: each time one complication was treated, it only aggravated or created others. With every complication that arose, Byron Naisbitt consulted with them or one of various other doctors brought in to examine his son. He could not walk down the hall at either of Ogden's hospitals without being stopped frequently by colleagues inquiring about Cortney and offering advice. Often he arrived in Cortney's room in the company of another physician, one of the primary doctors on Cortney's case, or another doctor he had asked to give an opinion. He made no pretense at being tactful with his colleagues. If one of them had knowledge that could benefit Cortney, he asked them for it. If the opinion of another doctor seemed viable, he discussed it with Hauser or Johnson or Rees. He was constantly monitoring Cortney's condition and the methods being used to treat him. He watched his son closely, and sometimes saw complications developing even the other doctors did not see.

"Byron's demeanor, I would say, was still basically unchanged from what it usually is," recalled Dr. Johnson. "You could tell he was uptight, he wasn't loose at all. But strong, you know. He was just his usual self, except you could tell he was a little nervous, a little hyper. He'd come in and he'd say, 'How are you, Physician?' He always calls me Physician. Then he'd say, 'Things look pretty good today?' And I'd say, 'Well . . . he's coming along a little better than he did yesterday.' He'd say: 'Well that's good. That's good. Yeah, I think he's doing better. He's going to make it. He's going to do it.' He just felt that way all the time. Always positive. And I couldn't believe he was being that positive. He was just unbelievably optimistic.

"One time, I think I saw a tear in his eye. It was right close to the second day, the first time I saw Cortney. But the moment he got over the initial shock, I think he put all of his efforts into trying to be positive. With everybody. 'He's going to make it, don't tell me he isn't going to make it. He's going to make it because I can see it.' I didn't tell him that Cortney wasn't going to make it, but the first time I saw the boy I didn't think things looked very good. And I couldn't believe that when Cortney was lying there with tubes going in every orifice and not responding at all to me, that Byron could walk in there and come out optimistic. But he would.

"There was one occasion early on when I didn't think Cort knew very much about anything, and Byron says, 'Cort, blink your eyes.' He did. I'd say, 'Cort, do this, do that.' He wouldn't do anything. One time I came in and one of the nurses said, 'Dr. Naisbitt has been here and he's been talking to Cortney.' And I said: 'What do you mean, talking to Cortney? How could he talk to Cortney?' She said, 'Well, Cort's been raising his fingers and giving him signs.' 'Oh, come on. Really? Were you there? Did you see Cortney respond?' 'Well yeah, I did.' So she came over by me and I said something to Cortney. He didn't do anything, you know. I asked him to do something again and he still wouldn't do anything. So then the nurse got her mouth down next to his ear and said: 'Cortney, now raise your finger like you did for your dad. Raise your finger and tell Dr. Johnson. Listen now, Cort, do you understand what I am trying to tell you? Raise your finger and show us.' And he raised his finger up and wiggled it just a little bit. Maybe Byron felt that he was getting through to Cortney. Maybe he had some sort of signal from the boy that I couldn't perceive."

Brett had returned to his job as an operating room technician. He was still angry that two people had been allowed to cause so much suffering, and each time he saw his brother lying in Intensive Care, he was reminded that there was nothing he could do about it. It was difficult for him to visit.

Gary and Claire spent more time with Cort than I did. I was just in and out, probably because I had my own family. And it was hard for me to go for some reason. I just couldn't stand to see him not doing anything. They didn't know what kind of brain damage he had and his blood gases were all out of whack, they were trying to get those balanced. And he looked grotesque, no color, just gray, totally lifeless. He would breathe in gasps like each was his last and his pulse hit two thirty. I didn't know how much longer his heart could beat that fast without going into fibrillation. Nobody would give even a hint of a hope for him staying alive. Hauser never had a word of encouragement, he kept saying, "Don't count on it." Cort just looked deader than a doornail and I hated seeing him in that shape, knowing there was nothing I could do.

I'd go in and hold his hand, and the tubes were running out of his body, and the respirator's sucking and blowing, you can smell the medication they're atomizing in the respirator, all the lights are flashing and the monitors are scribbling. For a nickel and a ball bat I'd have spent fifteen minutes alone with Pierre and Andrews. I couldn't understand how anyone could do that to another human being.

I didn't like going because I just hated to see him that screwed up. But Dad'd say, "We've gotta go in there and be positive, gotta talk to him, touch him." The first two weeks all the visits were the same. There was always somebody from the family there when a new one arrived. I'd go in and ask the nurse how he's doing. "Any improvement?" "No. Here's his chart." I'd look at his blood gases. "Any change?" "No change." He didn't move. He had no reflexes. "Has he said anything?" "No." "Opened his eyes?" "No." Finally, after about two weeks or more, I can't remember, he squirmed his left leg. You know, it moved an inch. That was a big deal. I wanted to see improvement, and it was so slow. It was like watching the hour hand on your watch.

After I'd looked at the chart and talked to the nurse, I'd go into his room. "Cort, this is Brett. Just came to see how you're doing. We love you. Keep trying. We're behind you." I'd touch his hand, touch his face. Then maybe let him relax for a while, let him know you're there, but try not to disturb him too much. But I'd get to fidgeting so bad in there, I just couldn't sit. Before I left, I'd give him another short pep talk. "Cort, I'm going now. I'll be back to see you tomorrow." Then give him a little kiss on the head and a hug, if you could get through the wires.

"They didn't just go in there and look," said an inhalation therapist who frequently encountered the Naisbitt family in Cortney's room. "You see so many patients' families go in and just look, with this stare about them. But they didn't. They went in and they talked to him. They would talk to him about things that were going on. They never fell apart. They just stuck together and they worked together, and there was always somebody there. Day and night, there was always somebody. Gary'd go up there and he'd stay for a while, and then he'd come down here and talk to us. He'd say: 'We're going to bring Cortney through. We don't have time right now to weep over Mom's death, we have to just pull together for Cortney.' He was really strong. I was amazed at how they all stood up through all of this, and stuck together and supported each other and supported Cortney. I saw Dr. Naisbitt talk with him. I saw the whole family doing that. I saw Claire go in several times and talk with him, you know, and he was just gone. He wasn't responding to any voice stimulus at all, and they would just sit there and talk and talk."

By the end of the first week in May, Cortney was still alive, but his progress was so gradual and filled with setbacks, it could hardly be measured. Occasionally, he would obey commands to stick out his tongue or squeeze and open his left hand. Most of the time, however, he would lie still, drooling out of the corners of his mouth, his eyes closed and a red rash, caused by the massive doses of steroids he was receiving, creeping across his chest, his back, and his face.

On May 7, Dr. Johnson took Cortney to surgery to perform an endoscopy, an inside look with a fiber-optic microscope at the damage done to Cortney's esophagus by the Drano. Johnson had waited over two weeks before looking at the inside of Cortney's esophagus, certain that most of the scarring would now be visible.

The inside of the esophagus is usually gray, but Cortney's was streaked with red. At 33 cm and again at 27 cm, Johnson saw two elongated ulcerations in the mucosa. Both were bleeding around their edges, and upon their surfaces were patches of tissue, normally moist, that had gone dry and brittle from the burning of the lye. If either of these lesions was deep, it would take little to perforate the esophagus, opening an avenue for infection to leak into and spread throughout Cortney's chest. Given his other complications, Cortney had almost no chance of surviving such an infection. Though Dr. Johnson was aware of the difficulty in calculating the depth of an esophageal burn, he thought that neither of the two lesions appeared to be deep. Only later would he discover that the encouraging appearance of Cortney's esophagus had been grossly misleading.

Byron continued to visit with Cortney early each morning, again during his lunch hour, and every evening, sometimes till long after midnight. When he visited, he would walk into Cortney's room and say, "Cortney, this is your dad." Then he would take hold of Cortney's arms and rub them or massage the boy's legs while he talked.

"It's seven thirty in the morning. You've been in the hospital a little over two weeks today. Connie the nurse is here and she's taking good care of the Duke. So you've got nothing to fret about."

As he talked, Byron sometimes would lift Cortney's legs a little and move them left or right, trying to revive the feeling of motion in his son. As always, he examined Cortney carefully, looking for signs of new complications.

"I talked to the Terrys next door and the Rubens, and they all said to give a big howdy to my sick partner. Said they can't wait for the Duke to get back in the neighborhood. Course, Kelly's been up here to see you every afternoon. And guess who called? Wolfgang! Wanted to know when you'd be ready to solo that Cessna Skyhawk again."

While Byron was touching him and talking to him, Cortney occasionally would open his eyes and stare at the ceiling or blink if his father asked him to, but mostly he lay still, his eyes closed, his mouth slacked open, his body slightly feverish. Sometimes, his father would ask: "Cortney, do you remember what happened to you? Do you remember going to the store?" After that one episode when Cortney spoke to his father during the first few days he was in the hospital, these questions never received any kind of response. Byron asked them because he was afraid that Cortney would relate his present surroundings with what had happened in the basement.

"You're in the hospital now, St. Ben's," he would say. "You were hurt at the store, but you're okay now. There's no one here to hurt you and you're safe."

Byron touched Cortney and talked to him the whole time he was in the room, but he didn't know if Cortney felt his touch or understood even a word he was saying.

While Cortney lay in coma at St. Benedict's Hospital, Pierre sat in the Weber County Jail, awaiting his trial for murder. During the time he sat there little happened. He read a few books, leafed through some hot rod and motorcycle magazines, and listened to incoming calls over the police radio down the hall. There was a jailbreak in May and six prisoners escaped, but Pierre and Andrews were not among them. One Sunday, Pierre threw a supper tray at a guard when the guard served him a fried chicken drumstick instead of the wing Pierre had requested. Later, Pierre tried to sue the sheriff for $300,000 for not allowing him to take an afternoon nap.

In those first weeks Pierre's mail was full of threats from people who wanted to do to him what he had done to his victims. The letters came from various states across the country, typical hate mail in the aftermath of a mass murder. They arrived with other typical letters from people who were praying for his soul. One elderly woman from Missouri wanted to take Pierre into her home when he was released from prison.

Pierre, Andrews, and Roberts finally were arraigned, all on charges of aggravated robbery and first-degree murder. Their lawyers then began a series of hearings to suppress evidence and to determine whether trials for the three men would be joined or separate, in Ogden or elsewhere, open or closed to the press.

Rita James had resigned as Pierre's attorney, a decision inevitable from the moment she had read of Pierre's arrest in the small-town Georgia newspaper. As she explained later, the community pressure that would have been on her, or any other local attorney defending Pierre, would not have been in his best interest. "It wasn't exactly that everybody wanted to avoid the heat," she said. "We've all had people upset at us before, but if Dale was going to have what he obviously had to have, which was really top-notch representation, then it had to be somebody who wasn't going to be subjected to that sort of heat, and that meant going to Salt Lake for lawyers." Perhaps more important, the other reason that Rita could not effectively represent Pierre was personal: Byron Naisbitt was her gynecologist.

Rita had visited Pierre at the county jail and explained to him why she could no longer serve as his attorney. He said that he wanted a private attorney and not a public defender, and Rita agreed that the magnitude of the case probably required more experience than could be found in the public defender's office. There were other reasons she felt that Pierre should seek private counsel: the head of the public defender's office in Ogden lived three doors from the Naisbitts and might be subjected to the same community pressure that had influenced Rita's resignation. Then too, while Roberts had secured a lawyer from out of state, Andrews already had agreed to be represented by a public defender. With future conflicts likely between the cases of Pierre and Andrews, ethics would make it difficult to represent both defendants out of the same office.

After her meeting with Pierre, Rita contacted a number of criminal lawyers in Salt Lake City, afterward submitting to the judge a list of those lawyers willing to represent Pierre in the Hi-Fi Murders. From the list the judge had appointed two attorneys, one of whom had tried a dozen cases of first-degree murder and had never had a jury impose the death penalty on one of his clients. The public defender's office allocated a portion of its budget to paying for Pierre's private counsel, and the Weber County commissioners agreed to negotiate additional fees and legal expenses for Pierre.

One of the first steps Pierre's new attorneys took to build their defense was to make an appointment for Pierre with a prominent Salt Lake City psychiatrist, Dr. Louis G. Moench. They wanted to know if Pierre was legally sane.

"Yes," said Dr. Moench, "I think it's probably the most gruesome crime that's ever occurred in this state, in my memory. Although I've heard of some pretty bad ones, I think it's the worst. The sadistic quality here, the unmitigated and unnecessary cruelty, the ingenuity and variety of indignities to the people, I think this is the worst.

"As a psychiatrist, I see quite a few people for the court. In this case I was appointed to examine Pierre to see if he was legally sane to stand trial. The determination of his sanity or insanity is all that was done, and that's pretty crude, really a legal exam and not a medical one. So the things that are most important about this man, about finding out why, and what his problems are, and his thinking patterns, the dynamic mechanisms, were unfortunately not part of my examination.

"He was a cooperative person at the time, reasonably placid, reasonably amiable, freely talked about some of his background and answered my questions. I had the impression that he really wasn't informing me of anything though, just going through the motions of answering questions and not helping me very much.

"He was born in Tobago, what they call Mason Hall, I assume that's a city. Was raised in Trinidad and moved to Brooklyn at the age of seventeen. There's a problem with his parents, but I didn't explore it. He said he finished three and a half years of college in Trinidad majoring in physical science, got a C-plus average, and then had three months' additional college at Long Island University. He said he and his family are active Seventh-Day Adventists, and that he attended church until his incarceration. He said he worked as an institutional aid in a children's service department in New York as a counselor for children for about a year. He didn't give any more detail on it. He said he worked as a service clerk for the phone company for three years and had a short time in a restaurant cooking during a strike by the phone company. He joined the Air Force as a volunteer in May of 1973.

"I don't think all of this time adds up correctly.

"He said he'd never been in any other legal trouble except that he was charged with car theft in January 'seventy-four and had not been tried for that. Said his home life in Trinidad was average. Spent most of his time at home. His father worked off and on. Said he didn't feel deprived. He was disciplined by whipping, but he said he deserved it. He and his family often attended church. He said on moving to New York he didn't join any street gangs, he didn't drink, he didn't take any drugs, and got along well with his siblings. I got the feeling he was presenting himself as Mr. Clean. He didn't fulfill the criteria for insanity to the extent that he couldn't stand trial. I had the impression that there hadn't been any difference between his mental state at the time of the crime and the day I saw him.

"It would have been very helpful to pursue the interview to try to find some of the dynamics involved. He did say he was injured in a motorcycle accident in about 1965 at age fifteen or sixteen. He had a head injury, said he required twenty-five stitches, spent two months in the hospital, denies any episode of coma or unconsciousness, although he said subsequently he'd had transitory blackouts lasting a few minutes several times a week. He said no one observed him in these, so he couldn't say, but he didn't think he had any convulsions or lost his urine and there was no residual amnesia. So this wouldn't be a classical seizure. This is important because some people disposed to behavior disorders have the behavior disorder instead of a convulsion. They act out during that time, and then generally have amnesia for what they've done just the same as someone else has amnesia for a seizure.

"I didn't try to elaborate on the discrepancies in his story because I didn't think he indicated any legal defense of insanity. But I

thought he was conning me. In his serial subtraction for instance—
this is pretty elementary—he kept making mistakes: a hundred mi-
nus seven equals ninety-three, eighty-six, seventy-seven, sixty-one,
fifty-four, forty-four. . . . If these were all repetitive mistakes, it
would be more consistent with brain damage. But his random errors
were not that consistent. He ought to have neurological work,
though. Legally, it wouldn't change anything, he's legally sane, but
these things show up and it's of interest.

"Usually by the time an interview is about half over, the person
will tell me pretty much the details of what happened during the
crime. But when Pierre was talking about the day of the murders,
he simply claims he doesn't remember much about it. He'd been
given some money by his friends to rent them a garage for their
van. And he said he did rent the garage. He was sitting with the
guys, as he says, while they, not he, popped pills, 'reds'—I assume
that would be Seconal, I'm not sure. He gave me the impression he
was always the innocent victim of something, that somebody else
always got him into trouble.

"They did go to the garage and then they left. They drove him to
a friend's place where they could get speed, where *they* could rather
than he, then stopped at a gas station to get gas for the van. He
went to a grocery store for Excedrin for a headache, Seven Up, and
a Coke for Andrews, one of the other defendants. Then they went
to a park, the other two smoked weed, and everything took place
from there. He wouldn't elaborate on what took place. He said that
later he was putting some stuff in the garage, apparently speakers,
and blacked out for a couple of minutes. He said he didn't know
where the speakers came from. It was my impression that he was
not telling me everything he knew. I thought he was trying to keep
control over some of his private information and wouldn't let me get
inside of it, which I'm still convinced is true.

"Basically, I think Pierre's a very inferior person, that is, he has a
tremendous sense of inferiority, and at the same time he goes
through the process of denying it. Then it becomes a sense of power.
His feelings of wanting power, I think, represent his feelings of inferiority. It's an attempt at compensation."

* * *

Cortney's weight continued to fall. On May 8 two nurses slid a metal tray beneath him and pumped it upward until Cortney's body hung free of the bed. He weighed 110 pounds. For the first two weeks after he was shot Cortney's nourishment had not been critical to his survival, but now it was becoming a serious problem. After fighting infection and trauma without benefit of food, Cortney's body was beginning to break down its own muscle tissue and feed upon itself. To avoid this, he required six thousand calories a day, a diet equivalent to that of an active lumberjack. But Cortney was not even alert enough to swallow water.

The only way the doctors could feed Cortney the quantity of food he now needed was by a relatively new and difficult to regulate procedure called hyperalimentation. Despite the difficulties, Johnson started the feedings immediately, pumping massive amounts of calories and protein directly into Cortney's veins.

On May 10, two days after Dr. Johnson started hyperalimenting Cortney, Dr. Hauser examined the boy and made the following notation on his chart:

Remains comatose (18th day) and responsive only when vigorously aroused. . . . Atrophy upper right extremity is pronounced. . . . He no longer fixes gaze on examiner even with stimulation. I feel chances of functional recovery lessen with each day of persistent coma.

The next day a nurse was taking Cortney's vital signs when she noticed a slight twitching just below Cortney's left eye. Cortney's eyes were closed, and except for the small area of twitching, his body was still. As the nurse watched his face, suddenly at the corner of each eye appeared tears which quickly overflowed and coursed down his temples into the sterile wrapping still around his head. The nurse touched him and tried to turn him gently onto his side, but at her touch Cortney's body became rigid, his thin muscles taut and vibrating.

The nurses continued talking to Cortney, but he did not utter a word, or even moan. If commanded to open his eyes, sometimes he would open them slightly. If the nurses asked him a question, with his eyes still closed he might nod his head, or even squeeze their hand weakly. Most of the time he did nothing. After he cried that day the second week in May, tears frequently came to his eyes when the nurses talked to him and reassured him that he was safe and everything would be all right. The tears were one of the few contacts they had with him.

Upon returning to school the day after her mother's funeral, Claire had broken out in a rash. In her apartment at night, when she had tried to sleep, she had shaken uncontrollably and awakened in the morning unable to pull herself out of bed. For the first few days, she had had difficulty getting dressed and driving a car. She had missed her morning classes each day, and when she finally had forced herself to attend an advanced chemistry lab, she found that she could not read simple numbers on a digital readout. But final exams covering her course work for the entire year were to begin the second week of May, and she still had to prepare for them. She kept saying to herself that her father would want it that way.

During these last two weeks of school Claire had made several trips back to Ogden to visit Cortney, and she and Scott finally had talked to her father about their engagement. When she completed her exams, she moved home with her father and Gary to begin planning her wedding and to spend as much time with Cortney as possible.

We'd go over and we'd visit every day, several times a day. Usually we'd try to work it out in shifts, so that not everybody was there all at once. Even though . . . . oh, I don't know. It was hard to sit there because you were neurotic, you wanted action now. But we did that. We'd go over and we'd just sit and we'd hold his hand and we'd talk to him and stroke his hair and tell him we loved him. We'd just tell him everything was okay. Everything's just fine and he's, he's doing okay. But he looked terrible. Just lying there so long and skinny. And he was yellow all over. And still just kinda had crusty things on him. You know, like blood and stuff, from his trache. And they were always pumping gunk out of his stomach and his lungs and everywhere else. Just dried up blood, because I'm sure he kept oozing and it'd coagulate. I remember he'd kinda convulse all the time too, you know. And when he'd get raspy, the nurses would come in and suction out his lungs. You could tell he was trying to cough. He would jiggle all over. I mean his chest would just kind of come up, like he was trying to cough, but he couldn't because he had this trache in. I remember how horrible that was. I just thought, Can't they help you cough? This is probably the way it is all the time with patients like that. But to me it just . . . I don't know.

The nurses were really nice. They'd come in and work around us, changing his bottles and all that stuff. It would be like just me and Brett maybe would go over, or else I'd go over and relieve whoever was there for a while. I guess we really were there a lot. I'd rub his arms if he was cold. It seemed like he was always cold because they had him on an ice blanket, and he was always shivering and shaking. Of course, Cortney was out of it. It seemed like an awful long time he just lay there. I don't know how long. And his eyes had this stuff on them, kind of like grease or something. I don't know what they put on them, and I don't know why they put it on. But his eyes were kind of dark and blackish, and greasy for some reason. And, like I say, he was yellow all over. He looked so sick, you just can't believe it. His hands . . . his fingernails were all really dry and corroded off. You know? I mean it was just . . . I don't know. He had stuff running off of his face, I guess where the acid, or the Drano, had burned it all to pieces. It was all crusty. It was amazing to me that he was really alive. I couldn't believe that you could look like that and still be alive. He had all these tubes and wires from every place, going down his nose, in his throat, he had them everywhere, every orifice, you know. And then his head was bandaged up. That made him look a little better, I think. Maybe not. But he just looked . . . he looked kinda like a . . . what did he look like? He looked just like a dead person. Only with all these wires and things in. 'Cause he never moved or anything. Sometimes, I remember, he would kinda move his fingers, just a little bit. This wasn't right at first. And he would wiggle his feet occasionally. I guess maybe his toes were first. This was after a long while it seemed like. And I mean everybody just went crazy. You know? "He moved!"

After less than a week of hyperalimenting Cortney intravenously, the doctors discovered that Cortney's kidneys were not "recognizing" and redirecting the nutrients where they were needed, but passing them out of his body with the excess water. He was still losing weight, and the doctors agreed that they would have to find another method of feeding him.

They now had two alternatives. They could cut a hole through Cortney's abdominal wall directly into his stomach and place a gastrostomy tube. Or they could try to take advantage of a new development in Cortney's condition: he seemed to be showing the first faint signs of stirring from coma. Even the skeptical Dr. Hauser had noted, "There very definitely appears to be attempts to follow verbal commands."

Though Cortney had not yet begun to respond to his surroundings in a purposeful way, Dr. Johnson hoped that with these apparent small gains in consciousness he might now be alert just enough to take tiny amounts of soft foods and fluids orally without choking or aspirating any of them into his lungs. For the initial feeding a nurse dripped 20 cc of water into Cortney's mouth with a special tube feeder. Twenty cubic centimeters equals a little over one-half ounce of water, and that was placed on Cortney's tongue about an eighth of an ounce at a time. At first he held the water in his mouth, refusing to swallow.

The nurses pleaded with him, "It's water, Cortney, just plain water."

Still he wouldn't swallow. The nurses talked to him and reassured him, coaxing him along until finally Cortney's face folded into a slight grimace and he spit up about half of the water. But the other half of that first sip entered Cortney's throat, and slid easily down to his stomach. More half-sips followed, and when the ordeal was over, Cortney had swallowed and kept down a quarter ounce of sterile water.

After this modest success, Dr. Johnson had the nurses every hour put drops of lukewarm broth or cool ice cream between his lips and try to persuade him to swallow. Cortney would hold the liquid in his mouth for a long time while the nurses talked to him. Sometimes he would then close his eyes, tighten the muscles of his face, and swallow. But most of the time even the meager two ounces of fluid they placed in his mouth simply dribbled down his chin. Even when it appeared that Cortney had swallowed the liquid, sometimes a nurse watching him later would see that he had only been holding it in his mouth. Then he would part his lips and let it spill out of the corners. Finally, on May 20, Dr. Hauser wrote on Cortney's chart:

> Four weeks today from injury. Recent gains in level of con-
> sciousness being maintained, but still unable to take mainte-
> nance fluid requirements by mouth. Gastrostomy should be
> planned with long-term nursing care in mind. Prognosis for
> functional recovery at this point quite grim.

The doctors had given Cortney five days to respond to the oral feedings, and now it was clear that though he seemed to be rousing slowly from coma, Cortney was not yet alert enough to swallow the fluids he needed to stay alive. Dr. Rees scheduled the operation for placement of the gastrostomy tube directly into Cortney's stomach for the following afternoon.

During the five-day period that the doctors had been trying to get Cortney to swallow, Brett had visited his younger brother one morn-ing. When he walked into Cortney's room and gave his usual greet-ing, "Hey Cort, how's it going?" Cortney had opened his eyes slightly and watched as he walked from the door of the room over to the bed rail. The nurse had noticed right away: Cortney had never "tracked" before. When he had opened his eyes in the past, they had rarely seemed to focus on anything, and never had he followed anyone moving across the room. But that morning Cortney had ac-tually watched Brett. After that episode he would sometimes follow the nurses with his eyes in jerky movements around the room, his right eye still deviating outward.

As Cortney's responses to his surroundings gradually became more frequent, his periods of restlessness seemed to intensify. With his left hand he began pulling at his hospital gown, wadding it in his gnarled fingers, sometimes gripping the bed rail on the left side of the bed and jerking himself over to that side. His left hand and leg were moving continuously, and his eyes were open much of the time. When the nurses rolled him onto his left side or his right side, immediately he would pull himself onto his back again. Frequently, the nurses noted that Cortney seemed "restless" or "in some distress" or "apprehensive." They constantly reassured him that everything was fine, that he was safe and there was nothing for him to worry about. That's when Cortney would silently begin to cry.

One night, within an hour's time, Cortney pulled the IV needle out of his right arm, then grabbed hold of the larger needle infusing into his right groin and the Foley catheter draining his urine. The nurse was able to stop him before he could pull out the Foley or the larger needle. Two days later he pulled the trache tube out of the base of his throat. The next day, he pulled at the IV in his right groin again, slipping the needle a quarter of the way out before a nurse could wrest his hand from the line. The day after that he grabbed hold of the Foley again and this time pulled it all the way out.

Cortney began pulling things out so frequently it became necessary to tether both of his hands to the bed rails. The restraints were long enough that he could still pick at his blanket and gown, but could not reach any of the tubes or needles. Though Byron knew the restraints were necessary, when he saw the anguish in Cortney's face and the boy's hands trembling at the end of the restraints, he wanted them off. He did not want his son continuing to relive those hours spent tied up on the floor of the Hi-Fi Shop basement. But Cortney had pulled out every tube in his body at least twice, and without his left hand tied it would soon be impossible to keep in any of the tubes.

Byron himself came up with a solution to the problem. After observing the incision and placement of the gastrostomy tube by Dr. Rees and Dr. Johnson on May 21, he contacted a woman named Maxine Bradshaw, president of an organization of LDS church volunteers called the Relief Society. Byron asked her if she could find volunteers who would be willing to sit with Cortney a few hours a day, to watch him and talk to him, and primarily to hold onto his hand so he would not have to be tied. The solution was an imposition to the ICU staff and annoyed some of the nurses, but it was tolerated out of respect for Dr. Naisbitt and sympathy for the situation.

The volunteers began their shifts holding Cortney's hand at seven the following morning. Since the gastrostomy tube can't be used for feedings until the wound around the tube has sealed, the doctors were especially concerned that Cortney not tug at the tube while the incision still was in this three-day healing process. Having to wait three days before they could use the tube anyhow, they couldn't afford to have Cortney yank at it and delay the feedings even longer. Cortney now weighed 101 pounds.

When Byron wasn't at the hospital with his son, he was either seeing his own patients and delivering babies at the rate of one a day, or it was late at night and he was home. Since Gary stayed at the hospital at night and Claire often spent time with her fiancé Scott, Byron was usually alone there. He had strong support from his brother and his in-laws and the community, but his life was nothing like it had been before the murders.

There's an emptiness. No matter who you talk to or what work you do or how interested you are in what's going on, there's still an emptiness. There's always something missing. Something been left out. Especially right there at first. And then as time goes on, it doesn't change. You have to make off with an entirely different kind of life. Any time you go out of the house, or go someplace, you're used to having someone with you. Used to having your meals together. Used to coming home for lunch and having someone there. And now you are doing things all by yourself. I mean there is no one there. You want something, you fix it. If you want to go someplace, you go alone. When you come home, there's no one there to greet you. You come in the house and it's empty. And you're the only one there, and it is blacker than hell. And when it's night, it's a black beast.

That probably was about as tough a part of it as anything. The house is dark and it's quiet and there's no one there. And it just gets lonely. But you know that's the way it's going to be.

*   *   *

For the next three and a half weeks the Relief Society provided a twelve-hour vigil over Cortney every day. When the last woman had completed her shift in the early evening, Byron or Gary or Brett or Claire, or frequently Uncle Lynn Richardson or Uncle Paul Naisbitt, would sit with Cortney until midnight, when nursing students from Weber State continued the vigil as volunteers until seven the following morning, when the first woman from the Relief Society arrived to begin the day again. Byron told the women: "I'm positive that Cortney can hear. I know he's not responding much, but I know he can hear. Hold his hand and keep talking to him, tell him what's going on."

One of the women talked to Cortney about sailboats and airplanes. Another knew that Cortney was interested in astronomy, so talked to him about stars and the planets. Others had children in Cortney's classes at Ogden High and told him what was happening with the class these last few days of their sophomore year. They read books to him and held pictures before his staring eyes, and when Cortney had progressed to sitting in a wheelchair in the afternoons by the window, they would talk about the city and point out landmarks. Cortney never responded to their efforts, never nodded in recognition of a picture or a building or the sound of a familiar voice. Even with his eyes often open now, he stared straight ahead seeming not to hear.

The women found it difficult to talk to Cortney for the two, sometimes three, hours they were with him each day. Though they exhausted topic after topic that might interest him, nothing they said ever changed the expression on his face. Some of them described it as a look of extreme boredom, while others said there was hatred in his eyes. But something else made the visits difficult for the women emotionally: most of them had children Cortney's age. Watching their own children grow, they also had watched Cortney through the active phases of his youth from the time he was a baby. One of them, a neighbor of the Naisbitts' with two sons of her own, had seen Cortney one evening a week before the murders. As she had driven by the Naisbitt home, Cortney had been standing alone on the front porch, the setting sun reflecting from his blond hair, making it appear gold. Cortney had smiled and waved at the woman as she passed, and she remembered thinking what an impressive young man Cortney was growing up to be and what an appealing smile he had. A month later she walked into the ICU to sit with Cortney for the first time and saw him lying comatose and skeletal, the tubes rising from his stomach, from his throat, the wires in his arms, and before she could stop herself she began to cry.

Venice Flygare, another Relief Society volunteer who sat with Cortney in the ICU, later talked about her own experiences during that three and a half weeks.

"I happened to be there I guess at the hour that By came in a lot. Because he'd come in before rounds, and then if he had a break between deliveries or surgery, he'd come in, in an operating gown, you know, just for a minute to let Cortney know he was there, and that he loved him. One day when By was there—course I had noticed this with Cortney before—he would lay with his eyes shut and then he'd kind of scowl and pull a face. And he did this once when By was there and I said, 'Do you think he's in pain?' And he said, 'He could be remembering.' That's all he said. So, I often wondered if he was remembering the torture he'd gone through. One thing that bothers me to talk about, maybe the other ladies had it, too. But you'd hold his hand, because if he got nervous like that, he'd start fighting. So, I always held onto his hand, and if he could get his fingernails under mine, he'd just dig. And I never did tell him not to, I mean I just tried to handle the situation. Or if he could get his finger under my watch, he'd twist it real tight. One day By came in when this was happening with my hand, and he tried to explain to Cortney that I wouldn't hurt him in any way and that he wasn't to hurt me.

"I felt that By was mighty strong, I don't know about inwardly, but he sure never let down one minute in front of that boy. When he came in, I asked him if he wanted me to go out. I felt like maybe they needed to be alone. But he never asked me to leave. He talked to Cortney about who was there and visited with him just like he could hear, which maybe he could. That's something we don't know. One thing I did notice, course you know what a proud man By Naisbitt is, and there were comments by the nurses that he still had this pride. Never ever did he ever look like he hadn't slept. His clothes

were pressed and clean and sharp, he looked like that every morning when he came in. Just his old self. And to think that he could
ever take the time to look and act like he did with all he had on his
mind. . . . He would come in and he would hug Cortney and rub
his face and his head and kiss him on the cheek and tell him that
he loved him. And he would talk about the things they were going
to do. They were going to take a boat and they were going to go
places. I don't know if it was to take Cortney's mind off of what he
might be remembering, but it was the plans that he was making for
what they were going to do. I think he talked about them going on
an ocean liner. It's hard for me to talk about . . . I guess this is
where I was asking if he would like me to leave. Because it was just
. . . oh, I don't know. I'd never seen a man act like that. So completely emotional. And I would think about the hurt that he was
going through with the loss of his wife, and yet he had to turn every
energy he had right to this boy. I'm sure it was a contact thing that
he felt Cortney needed, and maybe By needed it as well. I often
wondered if his feeling was the feeling that I had, that it just seemed
so futile, you know, that it was never going to do any good the way
that Cortney was."

Cortney's uncle, Lynn Richardson, often visited in the evening,
assuming the responsibility for holding Cortney's hand after the last
woman from the Relief Society had left for the day. Recently, he
had got Cortney to respond to him by saying, "Cortney, if this is
your Uncle Lynn talking to you, squeeze my hand." And Cortney
would. If his uncle told him any other name, Cortney's hand would
remain limp.

The evening of May 24, Lynn brought a deck of cards into the
room. Byron also was visiting, and Lynn began dealing hands to
Byron and himself on top of Cortney's chest. Cortney's eyes were
open, and he was staring at the ceiling. As they played cards, Lynn
and Byron talked, drawing and discarding on Cortney's chest, Cortney lying with his eyes open, staring, sometimes blinking, sometimes closing his eyes for minutes at a time. After dealing one hand
Lynn was getting ready to discard a ten, when he hesitated, fanned
the cards out evenly, and held them up in front of Cortney.

"Pick me out the ten," he said.

Cortney seemed to be looking at the cards, but he didn't move.

"Go on, Cort," urged his uncle, "I know you can do it. Pick me out the ten."

Byron was watching Cortney's eyes, and Lynn was offering encouragement, when Cortney's left hand came up slowly off the bed, trembling. He blinked several times as though a film covered his eyes, the one eye still staring off to the side. His hand seemed to take forever to reach the cards, but eventually Cortney placed his fingers on the ten and pulled it from his uncle's fist.

"You guided the cards under his hand," said Byron.

"Okay," said Lynn, pleased with Cortney's response, "let's shuffle 'em and do it again."

Lynn shuffled the cards and again fanned them out in front of Cortney.

"Show your dad here I didn't cheat, Cort. Let's do a different one this time. Why don't you get me the four?"

Cortney's shaking hand again came off the bed and drifted slowly upward. It took so long to rise to the cards Lynn had difficulty holding them still. But neither he nor Byron said anything as they watched the hand float across the top of the cards until it stopped and tugged at the only four.

Byron was always looking for signs that Cortney had retained his vision. He thought perhaps that Cortney had recognized his face a time or two in the past, but he wasn't sure. That Cortney might be able to see small numbers and intellectually distinguish one from the other was a bonus he hadn't hoped for. He praised his son and Lynn praised him too, but Cortney's blank expression never changed. Soon he closed his eyes and did not open them again for the rest of the evening.

One morning at the end of May two nurses went into Cortney's room to prepare him for what had become his daily routine of sitting in a wheelchair for an hour or two. Each day the nurses propped Cortney in the chair, wrapping a wide cloth strap around his midsection to keep him from sliding out or pitching forward. Without it he couldn't sit up. Even with the restraint he would slump to the right, his eyes gazing at the floor and his right hand gnarled and lying limp in his lap.

When the two nurses that morning clamped Cortney's tubes, pinned the Foley to his gown, and lifted his IV bottles off their hooks to hang behind the wheelchair, one of them said to him, "Are you going to walk for me today, Cortney?"

Cortney's eyes were open, but he seemed not to hear. For the past week, with Cortney becoming slightly more aware of his surroundings, the nurses had been challenging him to take a step or speak a word. While some tried a soft approach, others were more demanding. Cortney ignored all of their efforts. He had been in bed so long his muscles had atrophied to where his legs would not have supported him even to stand next to his bed. During that week the nurses had been rubbing his arms and legs, running them through passive range-of-motion exercises as he lay in bed, hoping he would soon try to take that first step since he had walked downstairs into the basement of the Hi-Fi Shop.

As Cortney was rolled onto his side and propped gently into a sitting position at the edge of the bed, the nurse said again, "Today would be a good day to try, don't you think?"

With one of them on each side supporting him under his arms, the nurses lifted Cortney from the bed, and when they had him standing, limp and weak in their arms, he did not lean toward the wheelchair as he usually had, but continued to stand, swaying within their support. His body was rubbery; if the nurses had released their grip on him, he would have sunk to the floor. But he gave no indication he wanted to sit down. He just stood there next to his bed, shaking and holding onto the nurses.

On previous mornings the nurses had dragged Cortney from his bedside to the door of his room and back again, just to revive in him the feeling of movement. When Cortney stood with support that morning and did not merely collapse toward the wheelchair waiting for him, the nurses felt he might be ready to try on his own.

"You want to try walking for me, Cortney?" said one tentatively.

She moved around behind him, while the other nurse supported him from the front. But Cortney wouldn't lift his foot. He just teetered in the grasp of the nurses. The nurse behind him placed her knee against the backside of his knee and lifted his foot gently for him. The foot came up and dangled like that of a wooden puppet on a string, and when the nurse lowered her knee, Cortney's foot flopped to the floor as though the string had been cut in two.

"Cortney, that's wonderful!" said the nurses. "Let us see you do it again."

They praised him and encouraged him, and though Cortney seemed to be concentrating on lifting his other foot, it didn't move. Again, the nurse behind him coaxed his foot off the floor with her knee, and again it flopped forward when she pulled her knee away. Cortney's face was blank, but while the nurses were again praising him, by himself he lifted the first foot far enough off the tile floor to let it slide forward an inch or two. He was still swaying between the two nurses as they held onto him, but that single, meek step was one of the few purposeful movements he had made since the murders more than five weeks before.

The nurses had waited a long time to see their energies result in even the slightest progress for Cortney. After weeks had passed and Cortney had been kept alive but still remained in coma, it had been difficult for them to maintain their morale. Now, when Cortney's father was notified and came immediately to the hospital, one of the nurses in her excitement ran up and hugged him.

As Byron listened to the nurses describe Cortney's first meager step, he remembered the strong and coordinated teen-ager his son had once been. It was painful for him now to think of Cortney struggling so pitifully to shuffle one foot forward a few inches. But Byron would have been thrilled just to know that Cortney had again been out of bed. He had waited weeks to see his son even wiggle a toe, and he wasn't concerned now how he looked moving on his feet.

The next day Cortney walked again, this time for Dr. Rees, as the doctor was making his midmorning rounds. Rees had heard reports of Cortney's ambulation the day before, but he was skeptical as to how much of the effort was Cortney's and how much was the nurses'. When he arrived, another nurse was lifting Cortney from the bed to the wheelchair.

"Will you walk for Dr. Rees, Cortney?" she said. "Let's show Dr. Rees how you can walk."

With another nurse supporting Cortney from the front, she got behind him as the other nurse had done and was about to lift his foot with her knee when Cortney lifted his own foot and shuffled it forward a few inches. Then, after hesitating a moment and rocking back and forth, Cortney dragged his other foot forward.

Rees was incredulous. "I think one of the greatest things I have ever seen was when Cortney got up and walked with support at St. Benedict's. I can't remember what day that was, but I just couldn't believe it."

Since plucking the cards from his uncle's hand, Cortney had begun to perform simple deeds that required at least a minor degree of hand-eye coordination. One afternoon he held up bright plastic toys shaped like tiny animals and examined them briefly in a vague, disinterested way. Later, he took a safety razor into his hand and with a nurse holding a mirror in front of him made short scraping motions at his face. He held the razor loosely and his hand shook, but when the nurse said, "Oh, Cortney, you forgot one over here," he seemed to comprehend and tried in his weak way to run the razor over the spot he had apparently missed.

Through the last week of May and into the first week of June, Cortney's condition improved daily. He gained ten pounds on his new gastrostomy feedings, and orally he had started taking small amounts of baby food. On sunny days the nurses would prop him on the edge of his bed, then assist him in shuffling to his wheelchair to be wheeled out onto the sun porch. His head drooped as he walked, and sometimes he had to be reminded to drag his right foot forward, but he had now progressed to taking eight steps without first being prompted by a nurse's knee.

Jackie Gelinas, the night nurse in charge of the ICU, had been involved with Cortney's care nearly every day for the past six weeks and had watched him evolve from his prolonged, deathlike coma into a state of sporadic awareness. But the more progress he had made, walking, holding a razor, drinking from a cup, the more hostile he had become.

The morning of June 5 Jackie had watched Cortney suddenly punch his father, then pound him again and again and again, while his father held him cradled in his arms.

"Go ahead, Cortney," Byron said, "hit me if you want."

All that day and into the early hours of the next, Cortney continued to be restless. He tore the covers off his bed and hit at the people who were sitting with him, until his hand had to be restrained again. Then when a nurse taped his trache, forcing him to breathe through his mouth and nose, he gagged and tensed his body, trying to cough the trache out of his throat. Finally, the nurse assigned to him for the night shift complained to Jackie that he had become so hostile she could do nothing with him. Jackie said that she would take him as her patient for the rest of the night.

Jackie let Cortney moan for a while, before walking into his room and shutting the door behind her. While Cortney coughed and hyperventilated, she quietly checked his pulse and blood pressure, and after she had recorded his vital signs on the chart, she sat down on the edge of his bed and looked at him. He glared back at her with one eye, the other staring off to the side.

"Now, Cortney," Jackie said softly, "there's nothing wrong with you, you can breathe as well as I can. I'm not taking the tape off."

Cortney strained his hand toward her, but he could raise it only a few inches from his bed before he reached the end of the strap anchoring his wrist to the bed rail.

"Do whatever you want," said Jackie. "You can even holler and yell if you want to. Go ahead, holler and yell."

When she said this, as she remembered later, "His eyes got just wild, the pupils just so big, like, 'Lady, I'd kill you if I could get out of here!' "

Then Cortney moaned loudly and at once seemed startled that any noise at all had come out. Jackie continued talking to him, and he became more and more agitated as he heard her say it was all right to scream. Each time he opened his mouth it seemed as if he couldn't believe the sound of his own voice.

"You can even talk, can't you?" Jackie goaded him. "There's nothing in the world that's keeping you from talking."

Four other nurses in the ICU were tending their patients or scanning the monitors at the nurses' desk, when they heard a hoarse outcry coming from Cortney's room. Before they could run in, they heard more yelling, and when they had crowded into the doorway, they saw Jackie sitting on the edge of the bed, a loud sort of animal growl still rising from Cortney's raw throat. At the end of the tether, his left fist shook at the nurses now gathered in the room behind Jackie.

"What are you doing to him?" one of them asked her.

Jackie kept her eyes on Cortney, who looked angry and confused.

"Do you want us to leave the room?" she said to him.

Cortney was flailing the air with his fist, as if he wanted to strike out at someone but didn't know how or even whom to strike. Then he said, "Yes!"

The word came out slowly and Cortney's voice after all those weeks of silence was like a croak, but it was clear what he had said. The nurses had thought they would never hear him speak. They had been astounded when Cortney, after so long in coma, had merely begun to open an eye or squeeze their hand when they asked him to. When he said "Yes!" that morning, even Jackie got tears in her eyes.

"Well now," she said, "what I think we're going to do is we're going to get up and walk out to the nurses' desk. Do you want me to call your dad?"

"Yes," said Cortney again.

The nurses untied Cortney's hands and, being careful to hold onto the left one, stood him at the side of his bed, where Jackie ducked under his arm to support him. With another nurse on the other side of him, she helped him shuffle slowly into the main room of the ICU and put him into a wheelchair. Then two of the nurses ran down the hall to tell the nurses at the third-floor desk that Cortney had spoken his first word.

It was not yet six o'clock, but Jackie doubted that Cortney's father would mind her calling at that early hour.

"Dr. Naisbitt usually called every morning to find out how Cortney was doing. But this particular morning I called him first, and you could just hear him fill up. You know? You could just tell that he was starting to cry."

"I'll be up as soon as I can get there," he said.

When his father arrived a short while later, Cortney was back in bed but still awake. Jackie escorted Byron into Cortney's room and Cortney looked at his father, but even after his father had hugged him and brushed the hair from his forehead, Cortney said nothing. His fist was still working at the end of the restraint.

Jackie said: "Cortney? Talk to your dad. Say 'Hi' to him."

Byron had thought he might never hear his son speak again, but at that moment Cortney parted his lips and slowly said, "Hi."

"You can do better than that for your dad," said Jackie. "Can you say 'Dad'?"

His father was watching him closely, holding onto his hand and rubbing his arm when Cortney again opened his mouth. This time, at Jackie's urging, he began stuttering, "Dad."

Byron was sitting on the left side of Cortney's bed and Jackie on the right. Though Byron turned away from her quickly and looked out the window, Jackie could see his eyes filling with tears.

"Maybe I better leave you two alone," she said.

For a while after she had left, whenever Jackie looked up from the nurses' desk, she could still see Byron through the glass front of Cortney's room holding on to his son's hand, sometimes talking to him and sometimes just staring out the far window.

"GODDAMN!"

The day after Cortney spoke his first words his trache tube was removed and his speech improved rapidly. From his initial single-word responses, he progressed to speaking crude sentences. Often he would parrot the nurses as he heard them talk in his room. If a nurse said, "Cortney, move your foot to the right," Cortney would stammer, "Move my foot to the right." Or if a nurse said, "You look good today, Cort," Cortney would say, "I look good today."

Though Cortney was still receiving regular feedings through his gastrostomy tube, he was also taking increasingly larger amounts of food orally: small bites of scrambled egg and fruit, even shredded wheat and bacon. He swallowed the solid foods more readily than liquids, still allowing liquids to dribble out the side of his mouth unless he was handed the glass to hold and tilt for himself. Holding the glass in his own hand, Cortney was drinking root beer floats, juice, and milk shakes through a straw.

On the eighth of June, Cortney was transferred from ICU 1 to ICU 7, a cubicle in the northwest corner of Intensive Care that looked out over the hospital entrance, the parking lot, and the city beyond. Several times a day the nurses would clamp Cortney's gastrostomy tube and hold his IVs head high while he shuffled from the edge of his bed to his wheelchair, his hospital gown open in back and dangling around his skinny thighs. With Cortney sitting in the wheelchair, the nurses would then position him by the window where he could see the cars driving by the hospital.

"Let's look for your dad," they would often say.

Though the vision in his good left eye was blurred, Cortney learned to recognize his father's car, and when he saw it pulling into the hospital parking lot, he would point and say, "Dad."

But despite his increasing awareness Cortney was still frequently irrational, his moods fluctuating without warning throughout the day. One nurse recorded that Cortney "was talking more, writing numbers on blackboard, answering addition, subtraction, and multiplication problems readily." A few hours later another nurse wrote that Cortney "becomes very wild at times, hitting and kicking. Has a wild look in his eyes."

When the psychiatrist, Dr. Iverson, examined Cortney again that first week of June, he made the following notation on Cortney's chart:

> Sensorium is clearing—he is quite aware of what is going on—many of his mood changes are quite voluntary and appropriate.
> . . . When he gets upset he needs personal interaction and acceptance of any feeling that comes out. These feelings should not be repressed or shut off. This expression is therapeutic and necessary.

Two days later, at noon, a nurse assisted Cortney in ambulating on the ward, then tried to feed him his lunch. Cortney had helped to feed himself at breakfast that day, but now he refused to eat anything. He appeared tired and listless and hardly responded to the nurse. Then suddenly, as the nurse spoke to him and held the spoon at his mouth, Cortney sat up in bed, his body rigid, and stared at the wall with a vacant look in his eyes. The nurse asked him what was wrong. She snapped her fingers in front of his face. But Cortney stayed locked in that upright posture for twenty seconds, staring straight ahead, the nurse still talking to him, still trying to get him to respond. Then, just as suddenly as he had sat up, Cortney said the word "Yes" and lay back on the pillow.

Iverson was certain that after seven weeks most of Cortney's memories of the murder scene had been locked deep in his mind by amnesia. But openings would remain. Something the nurse had said, or perhaps the way she had held the spoon at his mouth, somehow had hit one of these openings, and for a few moments that day Cortney had remembered.

* * *

During the second week of June, Cortney became increasingly combative, swinging at the nurses even though his hands were still tied to the bed rails. He mumbled and screamed "Goddamn!" sometimes for hours without stopping, one "Goddamn" linked to another until the word became a meaningless slur. He was so hostile that the nurses administering ointment to his rash or changing his sheets had to be careful not to approach him from his left side. Many of them had bruises on their bodies from when they had got too close or had come toward Cortney from the wrong side and he had hit them. One night he got hold of a nurse's arm and twisted it behind her back until tears came to her eyes and other nurses had to pry her loose.

When the rest of the hospital was quiet during the late night and early morning hours, Cortney's screams often could be heard echoing from the ICU down the halls of the third floor.

"He had a lot of nightmares at night," remembered John Smith, the respiratory technician who seven weeks earlier had worked to break up the bloody edema spilling from Cortney's lungs. John was still working the night shift in June when he began getting regular calls from the ICU nurses.

"I remember them calling me up to come in and wrestle him down, because he would be flailing his arms like, 'God damn it, God damn it!' You know, just flailing, just . . . almost like he was wrestling a shadow but without any real direction. He was just flailing around and hitting the bed, 'cause I remember I even had to figure like, How am I going to get in there without getting clobbered?

"We had to wrestle him down and tie him, and this was practically every night. You could hear him all over the floor, I mean booming. They'd call me, say, 'Come upstairs immediately!' and I could hear him the minute I got to the third floor. I could hear him screaming. That was when he was in ICU Seven having all those nightmares and everything. All I ever heard was 'Goddamn! Goddamn! God—' just over and over, running right together, you know, no pause. And he never opened his eyes. He always had his eyes tightly closed and his fists clinched. That's about the time I got worried we had created a monster. We were all wondering what we had done. See, I was really upset with Hauser for not going harder on him the night they were brought in. Course I was in school, I was gung ho, I was out to save everybody that came through the emergency room doors. But now I was kinda having second thoughts, like maybe I had been thinking a little too idealistically. I thought he was just going to be bananas for the rest of his life."

Upon entering his room the nurses often would find Cortney turning in his bed, pulling at his hospital gown, and swearing. If they asked him what was wrong, he would complain that his stomach hurt. Nearly every time a nurse touched him he tried to strike her or twist her arm or bend back her fingers. When he couldn't reach the IVs in his arms because of the restraints binding his wrists, he cried for the nurses to remove the needles. During occasional intervals Cortney was quiet and cooperative and spoke in appropriate, full sentences. Mostly he swore, screaming, "Goddamn!" so loudly sometimes it could be heard all over the third floor of the hospital, and sometimes muttering it over and over so softly and soothingly one nurse described it as almost a lullaby.

Much of Cortney's hostility seemed to arise from frustration: he was helpless. He had little control over his bladder or bowels, and frequently he was incontinent of urine or stools in bed. When this happened, he got angry and tearful and appeared to be embarrassed. If the nurses tried to help him or change his sheets, he would become hostile, as if he didn't want anyone to know what he had done.

On the seventeenth of June, eight weeks after the murders, Cortney was transferred out of ICU to a private room on the surgical ward down the hall. There, his combativeness grew worse. He hit the nurses and the doctors, knocked over food trays, screamed at visitors, and pulled out the lines feeding into his body as fast as the doctors could put them back in. He fought the lab technicians so hard they could not draw blood samples, and the X-ray department was lucky to get even blurred pictures of his abdomen and chest. He hit Claire, he hit his brothers, he hit his father. He jerked on the gastrostomy tube rising out of his stomach, and often three or four nurses had to hold him down for his feedings through the tube. Several times a day the nurses could hear him lying in his bed, begging for a pain shot.

"I was at the hospital every day when he went through the 'Goddamn' period," recalled Kelly. "I'd walk in there and I'd sit down

and he'd just jump right up out of bed with his eyes wide open just
. . . just gigantic, and he'd turn over and he'd 'Goddamn, Goddamn, Goddamn!' just like that. And, you know, I'd sit there and I'd
say, 'Cort, it's okay.' He'd just sit there, 'Goddamn, Goddamn!' "

One afternoon Claire was visiting Cortney in his new room, and
Cortney was sitting in his wheelchair staring out the window. Outside, it was a warm summer day, and Claire sat quietly watching
Cortney looking out at the lawns and the houses below. For a long
while neither of them had said anything.

"Whatcha thinking about?" Claire finally asked.

Cortney continued staring out the window. Then he said slowly,
"Have you ever thought somebody was after you?"

"He was still really out of it," Claire remembered later. But she
wasn't sure how she should answer him.

"You don't have to worry about anything, Cortney," she said.
"Everything's okay."

"Well, have you ever thought about it? Like someone wanted to
kill you?"

Claire's father had told her not to talk to Cortney about the murders unless Cortney himself specifically asked. He had said that they
should talk to Cortney about happy things, about flying and skiing
and family pastimes, and not mention the murders or the hospital
or the time he had spent in Intensive Care or why his mother had
never been to visit him. In the two weeks since Cortney had begun
talking, he had never asked about any of these things. Now his
conversation was suddenly leading that way, and even though Cortney seemed to remember nothing from one moment to the next,
Claire was afraid she would say something wrong.

"Oh," she said, "do you think somebody does? I haven't really
thought about it."

"Did you ever think somebody would want to do that?"

"Cortney, everybody loves you and everything's just fine. You're
doing great, don't you think?"

Cortney didn't answer. He still had not turned away from the window to look at Claire. Minutes again passed by in silence. Then
Claire said, "Do you want to talk about it anymore?"

"No," said Cortney.

*   *   *

The first three weeks that Cortney had been hyperalimented, he had gained weight, and by the middle of June he was up to 114 pounds. But then his weight began to drop sharply. Within one week 9 of the pounds that Cortney had gained were lost again, and Dr. Johnson didn't know why. He decided to withhold the feedings for two days, in that time hoping to persuade Cortney to begin swallowing enough food to avoid the feedings altogether. But the hope was short-lived. On June 21, Dr. Johnson made the following notation on Cortney's chart:

> Plans were to try to have patient take more by mouth and evaluate his capacity for oral intake. So far today he has not succeeded in eating more than part of an ice-cream cone. Intake has been inadequate for even fluid maintenance. If this continues will be forced to use gastrostomy or IV alimentation again starting tomorrow. Fever level rising—father reports patient changing area of pain complaints. I can't get response from patient to determine where most tender.
> Impression: Clinical state slowly worsening.

That same afternoon Cortney called his father on the phone and told him he would like to go for a ride in the car. Dr. Rees and Dr. Johnson authorized the trip, and Byron was at the hospital with the car at four thirty. Cortney was brought down in his wheelchair, and after a few minutes of delicate maneuvering he was in the front seat next to his father, his seat belt fastened and his IVs hanging from the coat hook.

Byron drove slowly around town for an hour, talking to Cortney about the city and pointing out landmarks such as the high school from Cortney's past. When they returned to the hospital, Dr. Wallace was on duty in the emergency room and watched them drive up to the ER doors.

"One of the sad things," Wallace remembered later, "Cortney was very confused, *very* confused. He could walk and move around a little, but he had a lot of pain, and his favorite word was Goddamn, Goddamn, Goddamn, Goddamn. He said it over and over just like that, repeatedly, twenty-four hours a day. And of course it was from confusion. I remember By coming one time—this was after Cortney was long off the critical list—and putting him in his car and taking him for a ride. They rode around for an hour or two and then By brought him back. Let's see, what is it he called Cortney? He had a pet name for him. Duke? Anyway, Cortney was so irrational, very hostile. He was always taking a poke at the nurses. So By was helping him out of the car and into his wheelchair, and he said, 'Well, Duke, I'll see ya tomorrow!' And Cortney went *pow!* smacked By right in the mouth, you know, made his lips bleed. By said, 'In spite of the fact you hit me, I'll be back tomorrow.' And Cortney was sitting there, 'Goddamn, Goddamn, Goddamn, Goddamn. . . .' It was a real . . . Even at that stage of the game, I was wondering whether or not we had done the right thing."

Cortney had become nearly impossible to manage. He had pulled out every line but the gastrostomy tube and would hit the nurses if they tried to reinsert them. Rees got an IV started in him one afternoon, only to have Cortney jerk it out an hour later. The nurses who took care of him were exhausted, some of them even hesitant to be in his room alone. When Dr. Johnson asked them how Cortney was doing, the frequent reply now was, "Not so good, Doctor, I don't think he's going to make it."

Rees wanted to take Cortney to surgery, put him under anesthesia, then slip a line in behind his neck and down into his jugular where he wouldn't pull it out. With the new line, at least they could feed him intravenously and supply him with blood, which he needed badly. Rees scheduled the OR for the morning of June 26. During the operation Johnson planned to take another inside look at Corteney's esophagus: it had been seven weeks since the first endoscopy, nine since the murders, and an update on the lesions caused by the Drano might tell him why Cortney was refusing to eat. While these procedures were to be taking place and Cortney was sedated, the lab technicians were to be ready for blood cultures, and the X-ray department was to get films of Cortney's lower bowel immediately following surgery. But on June 26 the operations were canceled. Two days later Cortney was gone from St. Benedict's.

The final entry on Cortney's hospital chart was made by Dr. Johnson:

> Plans on 26th were canceled. IV could not be kept in yesterday. Patient's fever continues and will continue unless some aggressive moves are made. Possibly even needs all medications discontinued, but I suspect bacterial source somewhere in abdominal cavity.

For several reasons the doctors had decided to transfer Cortney to Intensive Care at the other Ogden hospital, McKay-Dee. Staff fatigue among the nurses at St. Benedict's was becoming apparent; McKay-Dee had new and extensive physical therapy facilities, which Cortney would need if he was ever to become functional again; a surgical resident was on call twenty-four hours a day to assist Dr. Rees should an emergency operation on Cortney become necessary; and since Byron Naisbitt's office was in the adjoining medical building, having Cortney at McKay-Dee would be more convenient for his frequent visits. But the real reason for transferring Cortney, Dr. Rees explained later.

"The problem was he didn't have any lines. He had 'em all out. And was so aggressive that you couldn't approach him. He was screaming and swearing and abusive and all that sort of thing. I mean, somebody just tried to murder him, and who knows what was going on in his head. Maybe he thought we were just continuing the torturing events that he'd been through. So he pulled everything out. I've forgotten how many times I tried just to put an IV in his arm, or anywhere. But if I put the lines in where he could get at them, he'd have them out in five seconds. We'd restrain him, we'd give him big jolts of drugs to calm him down, but he was manic. And the problem that was really wearing on me was how to get blood into him. He got to the point where he was so combative I couldn't even get an IV into him to do that. Yet he was anemic. I tried for five days to give him some blood, and he kicked me in the face and bit me and a few other things. Wouldn't let anybody get near him. One time I was trying to put in an IV and there were two nurses trying to hold him still, and I was trying to sweet-talk him and his dad was too, and he hauled off and kicked me right in the ribs. Knocked me against the wall. It was maddening. So the only alternative I had was to put him to sleep and sneak an IV in from the back, burrow it under the skin and down into the jugular. I went to talk to the anesthesiologist about this, and he wouldn't even talk to me about it. He says, 'He has to have blood *before* we'll put him to sleep.' I was caught in this very awkward position of trying to get a line into him to get his blood back up, and the only way to do it was to put him to sleep, and Anesthesia wouldn't put him to sleep because they felt his blood was too low. But I knew there was an anesthetist at McKay that would do it for me. In my discharge summary I said we transferred him for rehab purposes, which in essence would have been true, but the real reason I transferred him was I couldn't get cooperation from the head of Anesthesia at St. Benedict's. The day we transferred him, I'm sure his father doesn't mind me saying this, he was psychotic."

NIGHTMARE

The morning after Cortney arrived at McKay-Dee Hospital he was taken to surgery, where the anesthetist put him to sleep and Dr. Rees cut into his right jugular to insert a catheter. While Cortney was still sedated, Rees and Johnson ran an endoscope down his esophagus to look at the old lesions. Seven weeks earlier, when Johnson had first seen the inside of Cortney's esophagus, he had been surprised that the lye ingestion had not caused more damage. Now that the scars had had time to deepen, Johnson expected the esophageal lining to appear more corroded than before.

"I figured, well, he's having a hard time swallowing his saliva. He's got pain, probably from strictures in the esophagus, and severe inflammation. And it's going to look worse than it did the first time because I know that's the way it is. I'd read about it and I'd seen it once. And I just knew it was going to be worse. But I didn't think it was going to be *that* bad."

Cortney's esophagus, from where it attached to the back of his throat all the way down to the lower burn ulcer, was blood red and swollen. Johnson couldn't see beyond that because scar tissue from the caustic burns had formed a castlike stricture so tight the endoscope would not pass. Cortney had been refusing to eat because everything he swallowed was backing up at the stricture. If something wasn't done soon, his esophagus could close off completely.

The doctors had only two options. One was to cut out the stricture and transplant a section of intestine to bridge the gap. But this was major surgery, and Rees was certain that given Cortney's metabolic state, if they put him on the operating table now he would die.

The other alternative was a relatively simple procedure called dilatation, where a mercury-filled tube tapered to a point at one end is fed down the patient's throat and worked gently back and forth to open the stricture. But there is a danger too in attempting to dilate the esophagus: the scar tissue forming the stricture is thin and brittle, and there is always the possibility that the tube will break through. A single pinhole in Cortney's esophagus would allow air to leak into his chest, collapse his lungs, and a massive infection would follow as saliva leaked in with the air. And the leak couldn't be stopped. No surgical procedure would plug it up, and the esophagus couldn't be cut out because Cortney would never survive such an operation.

Despite the danger of perforation, if Cortney was ever going to swallow again, the doctors had to try to dilate him now. Waiting any longer would only allow the stricture to tighten and make future attempts to dilate him even more dangerous.

With Johnson assisting and Cortney lying on his side still sedated, Rees selected one of the thin rubber tubes, called bougies, and carefully fed the tapered end down Cortney's throat. As the tip of the bougie approached the stricture, Rees could feel it beginning to bind up. He pressed the bougie gently into the small opening, trying to stretch it wider, but Johnson could see he was having trouble.

"What's it like?" asked Johnson.

"It's tight," said Rees. "It's really tight."

Rees pulled the bougie out slowly, got a smaller size, and again inserted the tip of it into Cortney's mouth. When the tip reached the stricture, Rees tried working it back and forth. But this time it seemed even tighter than before. Again, he carefully withdrew the bougie and reached for a third, even smaller. After it too became bound in the scar tissue, Rees decided to quit. They couldn't afford to have the stricture tighten any more, but as tight as it already was, Rees couldn't take any further chances of punching a hole through the esophagus.

Cortney was wheeled out of surgery and taken to the recovery room for observation as he came out of the anesthesia. During the procedures he had undergone, his vital signs had remained stable and his low blood count had not proved critical. Already he was receiving fresh blood through the new catheter in his jugular vein.

With Cortney in Recovery, Johnson and Rees went to see other patients in the hospital.

Johnson was on a stairwell between floors a short while later when he heard the hospital operator paging Dr. Rees. Taking note of the page, but thinking little of it, Johnson proceeded to the next floor where he was to examine a patient. During the examination he heard the operator paging Rees again. This time Rees was told to report to Recovery immediately. Upon hearing the second page, Johnson left his patient, went out to the nurses' desk, and called down to Recovery to see if anything was wrong.

Rees had arrived only moments before and already was examining Cortney. The nurse had reported to him that shortly after the two doctors had sent Cortney to the recovery room, his blood pressure had dropped and his pulse suddenly had increased. He had turned cold and clammy. At that point the nurse had had Dr. Rees paged.

Rees went to the phone to talk briefly with Johnson.

"He's still in recovery and he doesn't look good," he said. "He's trying to get shocky."

"Oh, God," said Johnson, knowing what was coming next.

Then Rees said, "I think we perforated him."

Cortney was rushed to X-ray, and from the moment he saw the first picture, Rees knew that the esophagus was lost. On the film a small, light-gray mass was forming in the left chest adjacent to the stricture. It was air already beginning to leak through the perforation.

How rapidly the air pocket in Cortney's chest expanded over the next twelve to twenty-four hours would indicate the size of the perforation. For now, there was little to do but monitor the leak and be prepared to go into Cortney's chest with tubes should the air increase and an infection start to form.

While the doctors watched the progression of Cortney's esophageal leak on X ray, Cortney was in Intensive Care, lying in a fetal position on an ice blanket, shivering and delirious from a fever that remained between 102 and 103 degrees. He couldn't stand to be touched. If the nurses tried to move him or roll him over, he would slap weakly at their hands or grab for the bed rail so he couldn't be turned. He could communicate when he wanted to, but most of the time he was withdrawn.

"He was like a pitiful animal suffering," said one of the nurses. "When he was alone in the room, he would cry out these terrible, hurt-animal sounds. And yet you could go in and say, 'What's the matter, Cortney?' and chances are you'd get no response at all from him. No response at all."

Cortney weighed 106 pounds. Despite frequent injections of Valium, Demerol, and morphine he was restless, sweaty, his breathing quick and shallow. He knew his name was Cortney, but he told a nurse he was only fifteen. When the nurse asked him where he was, Cortney had no idea.

A few hours after the first set of X rays was taken, a second set showed a continuing leakage of air into Cortney's chest. Air still had not penetrated the lung vicinity, but a thickish fluid was beginning to form immediately adjacent to the lung. Then hours later the third set of X rays came back, and the situation in Cortney's chest had changed dramatically.

The small pocket of fluid that had shown up on the second film had rapidly expanded, invading the lung cavity and filling the region at the base of Cortney's lung. Ahead of it, pressing upward, was an even larger mass of air.

The pockets of fluid and air continued to grow until, thirty-six hours later, Cortney's left chest on film was totally opaque, a solid block of gray. The perforation had not sealed off, and the resulting air and fluid in Cortney's chest had pressed into the pleural cavity, finally collapsing his lung.

Rees took Cortney back to surgery and inserted two tubes through his rib cage, one in his lower chest for draining off the fluid, and one in his upper chest for drawing out the air. The tubes were attached to a pressure pump, but the air and fluid could not be sucked out as fast as they were building in Cortney's chest. The following day Cortney's lung, like a deflated balloon on the end of a stick, shriveled even further back toward the bronchus, and the space created filled with the incoming fluid.

With his lung collapsed, Cortney went into respiratory distress and couldn't breathe without an oxygen mask. As the air was drawn out of his chest, his lung partially reinflated, but the dense fluid there now was keeping the lung collapsed. And though the lower tube drained quarts of the fluid, the tissues inflamed by the infection continued to manufacture even more. The serum itself was almost like pudding, so thick it began to clog the chest tube. In three days the tube sealed off completely and Rees made plans to remove it, and insert a new tube on the morning of July 4. The night before Rees could replace the old tube Cortney himself reached up and pulled it out of his chest.

Since the first night at St. Benedict's, nearly two and a half months earlier, the visits to see his brother had never been easy for Brett. Now they became even more difficult.

I had been in hospitals a million times and seen people suffer, but to watch Cort suffer like that was tough. I was familiar with the chest tubes because I had been working in the open-heart room, and I knew what they were pulling out. It depressed me to go in there. He was never feeling good, never comfortable, always in pain and messed up and plugged in and unplugged, and I really felt bad for him. I was always interested in the charts to see what I could dig out of those, almost like he was a patient, not my brother, because if I looked at him like he was my brother, if every time I walked in there I dwelled on that part, I would have gone crazy. I always treated him like Cort. I always came in and gave him a hug and a kiss and that sort of thing, held his hand for a while and sat there, but in my mind I had to almost look at everything clinically. It was just hard to see little brother laying there all shot to pieces and hurt.

He'd been through ten weeks of stuff that would've killed the majority of people. Yet he was making this progress, and we were really getting enthusiastic. And then all of a sudden, everything turned around again. You felt like, The poor little bugger just can't make it anymore. Something is going to snap, and his whole system's going to collapse and he's going to die. He was always flirting with death, and that was hard to cope with.

We tried to continue our lives, but it was always there. You go to a show, before you go in, you call the hospital. You come out, you call the hospital. When you're working, something will pop up and remind you, and the thoughts come back. I wonder what's happened? I wonder if his temperature finally dropped or if they finally got his lung clear, if they finally got it reinflated again? Just all the time, thoughts.

I was busy with the family and the baby growing up, and I'm sure I put in the least amount of time at the hospital. But even when I'd get up there, I'd feel myself kind of drifting back into it and really worrying about things, getting all these emotions built up, and it'd screw me up for the whole day, trying to get all that sorted out and put back in my mind, so I could go on with other things. That's what made it hard for me to see Cort. I think Gary spent a fair amount of time over there, and Claire was with him an awful lot. Dad was back in the grind, but he spent all his time at the hospital. I think he got a little bit down about this time, because it got really critical again, and the question he had to ask himself was, How much more can Cort take before he just gives up?

While Cortney lay feverish and breathing off a respirator, Claire hung posters around his room, bright cheerful posters, some of them with pictures of airplanes. She brought him funny get-well cards and read them to him and held them up before his eyes so he could see. She talked to him about flying and tried to make him comfortable and did little things for him that the nurses couldn't do. She held his hand and whispered encouragment. With a hole in Cortney's esophagus, his lung collapsed, and infection building in his chest, Claire was doing the only thing she could think of to do: try to give Cortney something to live for, so he wouldn't give up.

"That was the hardest part," she remembered later, *"when he got better and brought hope. And then suddenly got worse."*

Claire had her lows and her doubts, said Gary, *but she was supportive during that time to try to help Dad. Her thing was, Don't bug me with the details, tell me he's getting better if he is, and if he's going to relapse a bit, fine, I'll try to keep hanging on. Claire really doesn't want to know what all the possible complications*

*might be. She wants to know that he's okay and that he's going to
get better. If you leave it at that, she'll go with the peaks and the
valleys. She's strong that way.*

*I was getting impatient for Cort to pull through, but I didn't feel
the emotional intensity that I had when he was at St. Benedict's.
Whether I had grown accustomed to that intensity level or what, I
don't know. You don't go through something like that without becoming emotionally exhausted, but as the level raises, you get used
to it, almost callous. Back at St. Benedict's we kind of got our hopes
up, and then all of a sudden we're right back where we started from
with this setback. I was already worn down, but Cort was still with
us, so I was encouraged. I had some doubts, I had some worries, I
vacillated back and forth, but still I'd come back to the old feeling I
had gotten long ago, that he'd make it. And that's what I kept trying
to tell the rest of the family.*

*Dad was always very optimistic. I'm sure inside he was just ripped
apart, but when Cort was making a recovery there for a while, he
was very optimistic. Then when Cort had this relapse, Dad got a
bit depressed. I think it was more emotional exhaustion than anything. He was just getting worn out. I was low before but I kind of
gained momentum, so I was hitting a peak through that time, even
with the setbacks. A couple of times I actually stepped in and sort
of switched roles with Dad, my hope taking over and his waning
for a while. He was getting kind of desperate. He had the bishop
come in and give Cort another blessing. He was groping, he was
reaching out, looking for anything he could get, any kind of help. I
remember one night in the hall outside the ICU, he said to the bishop,
"I think I'm going to lose my son."*

One afternoon Gary visited Cortney at the hospital, then returned
home to find his father standing alone in the backyard. He was
hosing off the porch, absentmindedly spraying leaves and twigs across the concrete. To Gary he looked tired and depressed.

Gary walked onto the patio, cracking a standard joke between the
two of them.

"I keep telling you, you can't make this stuff grow."

His father looked up. "How's Cortney?" he asked.

Gary reported what the nurses had told him and what he had read on the chart: Cortney seemed slightly more aware of his surroundings, but the massive infection in his chest kept him feverish and gasping for air. His heart pounded as if it would break through his ribs. With little change, the story was the same they had been hearing for a week now.

Byron listened quietly, nodding as Gary spoke. Then for the first time since the murders, Gary thought he saw his father's mask of composure drop away. It was in his face and his voice and his words: he did not understand how anyone could survive even the complications Cortney had experienced at St. Benedict's. For Cortney now to get a perforated esophagus, massive chest infections, a collapsed lung, high fevers . . .

"You just can't take that kind of punishment that long," he said. "I have hope and I feel he's going to make it, but I just don't see how."

On July 4, Rees had placed the new tube in Cortney's chest, slightly lower than the first, and for the next ten days the fluid had drained. But for all the fluid that was being pulled from the cavity, the X rays of Cortney's left chest remained essentially unchanged. Without the oxygen mask over his face Cortney could hardly breathe.

As Cortney lay in his bed, feverish and sweating, the tube in his chest dripped a thick, dark-colored serum filled with small clots of blood. From the gastrostomy tube in his stomach drained a viscous substance in varying shades of yellow-green. He cried for pain shots, and whined when the nurses tried to move him. He could not stand to be touched.

"Cortney was using all his energy just to survive," said one nurse. "I remember he didn't have any fat, and you looked at that thin chest and that heart was just going just like this, and it looked like it was going to come right out of his chest."

With his esophagus punctured, Cortney's only form of nourishment was the formula being fed into his gastrostomy and his jugular IV. But these highly concentrated mixtures were creating a rich sugar environment in Cortney's body, a ripe medium for further infection. They also made Cortney's stools liquid, and he was incontinent in bed four or five times a day. The liquid stools caused him to chafe and develop sores on his buttocks and groin, openings in the skin for bacteria that once inside would spread rapidly despite the high doses of antibiotics Cortney was receiving.

Besides his buttocks and groin, open sores were developing across his collarbones and ribs, his shoulder blades, elbows and knees, points where the skin had stretched thin and was beginning to tear. Cortney had become so emaciated that there was no fatty, protective tissue over these bony prominences, and the skin breaking down was creating even more avenues for infection to enter.

With every system in his body already stretched beyond its limits, Cortney did not have the defenses left to fight off another infection. He was so close to death already that the nurses were surprised when they returned for their shifts each day and found him still alive.

"They'd take him into surgery to drain an abscess or something," one of them remembered, "and he'd have a big fever and come back from surgery blue, not breathing very well, and we'd keep thinking, Cortney won't be here in the morning."

It gets intense, you know. It gets really intense and you have to realize that you may not end up with a son. Cortney was sick as a dog all the time down there. Rapid pulse, tremendous infections, and high fever. He was just sick unto death all the time. And so I just had to realize that he may not make it. And if he didn't, then every day was a gift. Every day that he was alive and getting better or at least holding his own, or was just alive even, was a gift. Just an absolute gift. And these feelings don't change. Every day you look at your son and you hope, Well, today he's going to get better. And you walk in there and my Lord, his temp's off the chart and his pulse is off the chart. And he's laying there gasping and he's got all these tubes and junk in him. I mean it's a hell of a feeling. Just a feeling you can't describe. And you're helpless. There's not a thing you can do about it. You know that the people taking care of him are doing everything in their power. And you know very well that if any more could be done for Cortney, you could call on somebody

*with more expertise and they'd do it. But we had everybody with
all the expertise around already working on him. So you have to
just rely on their judgment and their professionalism to get your
son through his crisis. That's all there is to it. And the feelings that
go along with that are indescribable. They just are indescribable.*

*So the feelings, sure they get bad, but then you get hope that the
next day's going to be better. And then the hope makes you feel
better and so you get to feeling like you can go another day, and
he'll go another day. And if he goes another day, with his problems,
we sure to hell ought to be able to go another day with what little
piddly problems we have. We didn't have any problems. Cortney had
all the problems. We just had to wait.*

Feverish and irrational, Cortney often talked nonsense, sometimes at night in his sleep, but mostly during the day when he was
awake. With his eyes open and a confused frown on his face, he
would tilt his head and say things like, "The gas cap is off," or "This
is a nice seven forty-seven." Frightened and sobbing, he once
screamed that the finnan haddies were coming to get him, and when
the nurse promised she wouldn't allow anyone suspicious into his
room, Cortney said to her, "But you don't know, they're masters of
disguise."

There was a difference between Cortney talking nonsense and
Cortney having nightmares—actual dreams in which he relived the
scene at the Hi-Fi Shop. On July 9, early in the morning when it
was still dark, Cortney became restless in his sleep, jerking his arms
and legs about the bed. The nurse thought he appeared frightened.
Then Cortney started talking as though there were someone else in
the room besides the nurse.

"Those two men," he whispered, "don't let them take me downstairs." Then he yelled, "Don't put me on the floor!"

He thrashed in his bed, twisting his arms and legs in the sheets.
Then he stopped and looked at the nurse.

"When they put me on the floor, something exploded!"

Cortney often had nightmares where he groaned and turned in
his bed but said nothing. Only occasionally did he speak out. Ladora

Davidson took care of Cortney frequently and remembered only once hearing him talk in his sleep.

"It was in the middle of the day," she said, "and he woke up screaming: 'They're coming down the steps! They're going to get me!' And then the next thing he said was 'Oh, my God! My mother, my mother!' He'd wake up many times, very sweaty, and I'd say, 'Cortney, what were you dreaming?' And he'd say: 'I don't know. I've been running.'"

The perforation had not sealed, and the tissues inflamed by the infection still leaking into Cortney's chest continued to manufacture the thick fluid that was pressing against his lung. He complained constantly of pain in his left chest, and the gastrostomy feedings nauseated him so badly he gagged and vomited nearly every shift. He cursed the nurses, screamed for pain shots, and fought being moved for anything. Then on the twenty-fourth of July the nurses heard a new complaint from Cortney, one that only the nurses at St. Benedict's had heard before: he had suddenly developed a sharp pain down in his belly. An abdominal infection that had flared briefly and mysteriously at St. Benedict's weeks before seemed to be coming back, and Dr. O. E. Grua, an abdominal surgeon, was called in immediately to examine Cortney.

This time Cortney was able to localize the pain: abdominal cramping on the lower right. The symptoms seemed to be the same as the ones he had exhibited before, when his abdomen eventually had grown distended and firm and the bowel sounds had stopped. X rays were taken, but the site at the lower end of Cortney's stomach, where Dr. Grua suspected a possible leak, seemed to be intact. The day following the X rays Cortney continued his usual complaints of nausea and pain in his left chest, but the pain in his abdomen that had suddenly flared again just as suddenly seemed to go away.

For the next two weeks Cortney slowly improved. Scar tissue was finally beginning to seal the perforation in his esophagus, and the fluid stopped forming in his chest, allowing his lung to begin the slow process of reinflating. A physical therapist began working with his limbs. Cortney was gradually becoming more alert, talking more, and once even attempted to smile for a nurse.

Then on August 6 he renewed his complaints of abdominal pain. He said he had a stomachache. Three days later a nurse noted that Cortney was experiencing "stomach distress." In a series of barium X rays taken the afternoon of August 11, Cortney's bowel was filmed and showed up even more obstructed than it had been at St. Benedict's. The inflammation had come on so much faster than before, the symptoms so much more acute, that when he saw the results of the X rays, Dr. Grua scheduled an emergency exploratory for that night.

Before he was taken to surgery, Cortney said to a nurse, "My stomach's so bad." A short while later his father accompanied him into the operating room and watched as Dr. Grua cut him open, probed his abdominal cavity with his fingers, then pulled out his intestines and examined them as he would a ticker tape.

I don't think anybody will ever know what torment my son had to go through, physically and mentally. I don't think anybody's ever going to know that. Lord, they talk about stress. When you're all burned out inside, and your head is all shot up, and your body, every system has been damaged, I don't know how in the hell anybody can figure that that's not stressful.

I had a feeling that very first night that Cortney was going to make it. I came home and I said a little prayer, and I had a feeling from that minute on. And I just went along with that right from scratch. I didn't know how far he was going to go, but I knew within myself that he was going to be all right. And that he wasn't going to die.

Then they took him to surgery at the McKay that time to dilate his esophagus and they perforated it, went right through it, and from then on there was no more esophagus, it was all hyperalimentation. And with hyperalimentation, they were feeding him all this sugar. When Grua cut him open, they did a biopsy on his liver and it was fatty-degenerated, it couldn't hack all the sugar. And his guts were inflamed and they got adherent and massed together. And they were taking quarts of stuff out of his chest just so he could breathe. He was one sick cracker. He had high fevers every day. Tachycardia off the chart. Short of breath. Sicker than hell. And

*getting all these damned medications in tremendous doses, and just
sick. I mean sick! Hell, he was sick like that for six weeks.*

*See, when you got your lung down and you're just short of breath
anyway, you can't breathe, you've got infection all over hell, your
heart's doing about two or three times normal speed, and this goes
on day in and day out, and your fever's going up and up and down
and up, where do you run out of reserve? I'm telling you, all his
systems had been just all shot to hell, and I don't understand. Any
one of the things he had could have killed him. Any one of them.
Anytime in there he could've gone any minute. It just was one thing
after another, and I didn't see how anybody could keep up under
that kind of program for week after week, month after month. I
thought he was going . . . if he was going to die, that's when I
thought he was going to die.*

Cortney's intestines were red from inflammation, and his colon
had stuck to his liver. The liver was enlarged and mushy. The ap-
pendix too was inflamed and twisted backward. The lower stomach
valve that Grua had suspected as the source of a possible leak was
intact but appeared weakened.

Throughout the procedure the anesthetist had difficulty getting
enough oxygen to Cortney, and then Cortney's blood gases suddenly went out of balance. Byron rushed over to the anesthetist several times, checking the ventilator and the blood gases.

"Is he pink?" he kept asking. "Is he pink?"

When Dr. Grua completed the two-hour exploratory, pointing out
his findings to Byron, he stuffed Cortney's reddened intestines back
through the incision. Then he oversewed the weakened area at the
lower end of the stomach and prepared to close. There was nothing
else he could do except rest the intestines, increase antibiotic cov-
erage as he had done before, and wait. When Cortney left the operating room, he was still on high oxygen.

For days after the exploratory Cortney lay motionless on his back,
the deep abdominal incision held together by two large, white bone
buttons sewn to the skin of his belly. Beneath the buttons his intestines remained silent day after day, paralyzed by the inflammation.
His temperature rose again to over 103 degrees and he was put

back on the cooling mattress, shivering and sweating at the same time, as the nurses tried to control his fever. His heart pounded 170 times a minute, and the doctors could not slow it down even with carotid massage. He couldn't be fed orally because of his damaged esophagus. He could take nothing through his gastrostomy tube because of the inflammation in his intestines. The only way the doctors could feed him was to hyperaliment him intravenously, and even that had to be moderated to avoid the further degeneration of his liver. Since his arrival at McKay-Dee seven weeks earlier, his weight had increased to 132 pounds, but now it started dropping rapidly.

With heavy doses of antibiotics, painkillers, and tranquilizers being pumped into him, Cortney was lethargic and unresponsive. Still, he begged for more pain shots, and would beg again and again only minutes after they were given. He pleaded so frequently for shots to deaden the pain or help him sleep that the nurses had to say no, then try to console him and comfort him until it was time for his scheduled injections. As they spoke to him, Cortney would scream, "I hurt! I hurt all over!"

Cortney lay in bed, drifting in and out of awareness for five days before the fever finally began to break on August 16. Then his bowel sounds slowly began to return, and the inflammation in his belly appeared at last to be subsiding. By the seventeenth his temperature had dropped to below 100 degrees and he seemed more coherent. On that day Cortney said to a nurse, "What is this illness I have?"

Two days after he asked about his illness, Cortney wanted to know why he was in the hospital. He continued to be belligerent and uncooperative, but now that his fever was down, he began verbalizing more, having short conversations with the nurses. Prior to his exploratory he had also been speaking more to the nurses, the day before his operation he had even been able to arrange his thought processes well enough to give a simple explanation of the workings of the calculator his father had brought him from home. But awakening from coma is a confused, gradual process, with drugs and high fever adding to the confusion. Despite his signs of increasing consciousness the nurses had never felt that Cortney was truly coherent when he spoke to them. Now, for the first time, they sensed that he sometimes was actually aware of what he was saying. One afternoon he said to one of them, "I wish I could wake up and find this is just a bad dream."

Claire had been to southern California for a few days in July and brought Cortney some Mickey Mouse ears and a T-shirt from Disneyland. By then Cortney had been in the ICU so long and had collected so many things while there that his room had begun to take on the comfortable ambience of his bedroom at home. Hanging from the ceiling was an orange, radio-controlled airplane with a six-foot wingspan, given to him by his next-door neighbors. Smaller model airplanes hung from the bar above his bed. He had a portable stereo with headphones in a corner of the room, and on a bedside table sat a terrarium filled with plants and a tiny ceramic deer. The ICU housekeeper had taken Cortney's poster of a 747 cockpit down to the hospital engineers and had them cut a board to tack it on, so it could be stood up in front of Cortney like a real cockpit with all of the dials and gauges. There were posters on the walls that Claire had hung, puzzles that Cortney now sometimes dawdled with, and his chess set and calculator sitting nearby. Hanging next to his bed was a ribbon of brown-check material with a typed card above it that read:

Cortney Naisbitt—Monday, April 22, 1974—Wolfgang Lange

Although Cortney was apparently more conscious now, he still paid little attention to what was happening around him. It seemed that the more aware of his surroundings he became, the more depressed and discouraged he felt. When he walked, he had to be reminded to stand up straight and sometimes even to move his right foot forward. He wanted a nurse with him constantly and cried when he was alone even for a few moments. Though he could communicate in simple sentences when he wanted to, most of the time he appeared tired and despondent.

"He had a little cassette and he played the Kingston Trio," remembered one of the nurses. "He liked that. And he'd play, I think it was 'Fiddler on the Roof.' The tape was kind of old and it didn't sound too good in one part, but he wanted to listen to that over and over. Those and his calculator were about the only things he showed any interest in. His friend Kelly came around when he was here, but a lot of times Cortney would just not visit. I think it was because he was just so sick. And he wasn't always rational. He was always sort of semiconscious. He'd swear and rebel at everything, but mainly he was just a poor, whimpering, crying individual that still wasn't with reality a lot of the time."

Byron's office was in the medical building adjacent to the hospital, and with Cortney now becoming more aware, the frequency of his father's visits was even greater than in the past.

When he was in the McKay, why I'd run in and see him in the mornings when I'd make rounds, see if everything was all right. Then I'd call him from the office just to see if everything was okay. And if I had to go to the hospital, I'd run in and see him. And at lunch I'd run up and say hi. And after work I'd run in again and say hello. All through the day I'd just check in every time that I was over there. I'd run in to see him. And if I hadn't been there for a while I'd get to wondering about him, so I'd call. Just so that he knew that someone was looking after him and he wasn't alone, that someone was there. That was the whole point. So he wouldn't feel like he was just dumped in there and left.

I'd just talk to him, you know, find out how he was doing and what was going on, and what he did through the day. And try to bring new stuff so that he could have something there for him. He had his airplanes in his room and his calculator and things, all this sort of thing for him. Just try to make him comfy. Sometimes he wouldn't say much, and sometimes I wouldn't say a great deal. I'd just come into the room and I'd just sit. I don't think you have to converse. You just have to know that someone is around when you need them is all.

The doctors who had tipped the balance back in Cortney's favor with every new complication that arose often wondered if their continuous mending of Cortney's body would ever be justified by the return of Cortney's intellect. Over the weeks, as he had awakened gradually from the coma, his behavior had remained that of a child much younger than his chronological age. He would cry and call the nurses names and yell that they were trying to hurt him because they didn't like him. "But even then," said one nurse, "there would be flashes of a very bright boy. He might act like a four-year-old, but he could do things on his calculator that were intellectually beyond where he was emotionally."

Before the murders Cortney had had a fascination with calculators and computers, and one day near the end of July his father had brought a small calculator to the hospital. Then when his family had visited, they had set up simple problems for him to solve. At first, with the calculator cupped tightly in the rigid fingers of his right hand, Cortney had merely punched at the numbers they told him to. But gradually he had become capable of setting up the problems himself; he learned to use the functions correctly and often arrived at the right answer. As time went on, the problems had become more complex.

Dr. Johnson walked into Cortney's room one day to examine him and saw the calculator lying on the bed next to Cortney.

"I said, 'What's that for?' " remembered Johnson. "And one of the nurses said, 'Well, that's for Cortney, his father brought it for him.' And I said, 'What do you mean?' 'Well, Cortney is working some problems.' And I said, 'Uh, what kind of problems does Cort do?' 'Oh, he's doing algebra and trigonometry and some kind of advanced stuff. I don't know, they bring him in problems and he works them on the calculator.' I thought that was a bit unusual. I had wondered if he was ever going to be able to go to school and participate in things, especially when he went berserk and was acting so childish, pulling out his tubes and giving Rees a karate kick. I thought we might have a kid that just had no control at all over his emotions. But when I saw that calculator and he showed me his work, about that time I thought that he was for sure going to be okay."

One of Cortney's regular visitors was a lively and amiable man of seventy-five, a Catholic priest named Father Louis Kern. Father Kern had met Carol Naisbitt and her children one day years before on the ski slopes and occasionally thereafter had seen them skiing. After the murders he had been one of Cortney's first visitors, and since then he had looked in on Cortney nearly every day.

"When I read about the accident and learned it was this lovely lady and her son, well, I went up to the hospital, and I asked the dad, I said: 'Dr. Byron, you know I'm a Catholic priest, but I feel a great interest in this boy in there, and I just love him as a human being. Can I give him a blessing?' And he said: 'Father, he needs all the help he can get. You bet your life you can.' So Cortney was unconscious and I went out to see him every night at St. Benedict's, and made a little kind of what we call a novena for him, Saint Jude, the Saint of the Impossible. [Chuckle] Because it was pretty hopeless to start out with.

"Then I had to leave for Europe, and just as soon as I came back, I went out to see him, and they told me that he was at the McKay Hospital. So I went every night to visit him there, and really he was a fitting son of that noble father. I really thought the boy was remarkable, and he [chuckle] he was human. Every now and then he'd use some good old forceful adjectives. I got kind of a kick out of it, because I remember that that was a sign that he was getting well. I don't know when I've had an experience that impressed me so much, actually. When I'd leave, I'd give him a normal Catholic priest good-bye there, and I'd say, 'Well, God love you now.' And one day he said, surprised me, first word I ever heard him speak really, he said, 'God love you too, Father.' "

Father Kern visited Cortney in the evenings, and the first thing he would do upon entering the room was drop to the floor for ten quick push-ups.

"If I can do this," he would say to Cortney, "then so can you." Then he would stand up and say, "Now come on, give me a good handshake," and he would grab hold of Cortney's tightly gnarled right hand, spread the fingers apart, and place them in his.

"Well now, that's good, that's good. Now, I have some problems, Cort, will you help me?" Father Kern taught Spanish and French at a Catholic school in Ogden, and at night he often had to grade papers. "Will you use your machine to help me figure out these grades?"

"He had a little computer there," remembered Father Kern, "and he was fooling around with it, and so he'd help me figure my grades. And it was fine. He forgot everything else but helping me."

As psychiatrists had expected, Cortney's memory of the murders appeared to have been erased by amnesia. Now, unable to remember what had happened to him, yet becoming more aware of his surroundings, he would be confused at what he saw and felt, and he would ask questions. And someone at some time would have to tell him why he was in the hospital and how he had been hurt. Someone would have to explain to him why his mother never came to visit. But how would they know when Cortney was ready to hear?

"It was told to the family," said Dr. Iverson, "and should have been suggested to the doctors and nurses and everybody else to leave the accident alone for many months until he had a chance to recuperate physically, and integrate in other areas emotionally and intellectually. Then maybe he could be approached. Otherwise, I thought it would be too traumatic to him. I thought that when he had worked through the loss enough, he would start talking about it. And if they brought it up before then, it could possibly cause him to regress emotionally. If *he* brought it up, it would indicate that he was prepared to talk about it."

Cortney had begun asking questions about himself and the hospital often, but he seemed uninterested in the answers. It was as though he would forget his question as soon as he had asked it. While Claire was visiting him one day, Cortney asked her, "Why am I in the hospital?"

"You've had an accident," said Claire.

Cortney did not ask how the accident had occurred or what his injuries were. He seemed not to want to know any more.

After his first shallow probing with questions about his surroundings, Cortney finally asked about his mother, as he awakened one morning the latter part of August.

"I just told him his mother couldn't be there right at that time," remembered the nurse, "and he said, 'Why?' His dad had said that if he asked just to tell him his mother was sick. Because he wanted to tell Cortney."

When the nurses would tell him his mother was sick, Cortney wouldn't pursue the matter. Even his family's noncommittal replies, such as, "Mother loves you, but she can't be here," brought no response from him.

In August, Claire's wedding announcement appeared in the *Ogden Standard-Examiner*.

You know how you have your little picture in the paper? And they tell about your engagement and when you're going to get married and all this stuff? Well, that was in the paper, and I brought the paper clipping to the hospital. And it said, you know, "daughter of the late Carol Naisbitt," or something like that. And I didn't know whether Dad wanted him to read it or not. But he said, "Yeah, give it to him to read." So Cortney read it, and he just said, "Oh, that's really nice." And he was really excited about Scott, and all that. And he wanted to see my ring and the whole bit. But he didn't say anything. He read it a couple of times very carefully. A couple or three times, very carefully. But he didn't say anything. We were hoping he would ask about it, because the trials were coming up before too long, and he had been watching TV. He watched TV all the time, and he knew all about what was going on, on TV, you know. So here he is, it's going to be flashed across television, and Dad didn't want him to learn from the TV. But he didn't want to just tell him, either. Because he wanted him to face it. Dr. Iverson was the one that kind of advised Dad. He said: "Until he asks about his mother specifically, we're not gonna say anything about it. Because he knows that he might not be ready to face it. When he asks about it, he'll be ready." So we were all just going, Oh, please ask us about it.

Nearly two weeks had passed since Cortney's fever had subsided after the exploratory. His condition, though still fragile, had continued to improve, and he was stronger than he had been since he had arrived at McKay-Dee two months earlier. On occasional afternoons toward the end of August, Byron began taking him out of the hospital for short visits home.

The first time we took him out of the McKay, the one I recollect, we put him in the car and took him home, and he had all his bottles and tubes and stuff still in him. It took him a while to get in and out of the car. You gotta remember he was so damn weak he couldn't do anything at this point. Just to get in the house was a major effort. And to get out of the car, or do anything at all, you know, just to move, was an effort.

At first we would have to take him in in a chair, and then pretty soon he got so he could just walk just a little bit and he'd walk in from the car. He'd go up the front walk, through the front door and then he just lay there on the couch. I'm not sure if he was aware he was home. But it was nice for us to have him home, and he gradually got more and more used to that, and it was great for everybody. I don't know if it was really great for him, but it was great for us. It was a feeling that he was making some progress. After being in the condition that he was in for such a long time, it was great to see him move around a little bit. Made me feel like he was getting better quicker. I knew basically that he wasn't getting better quicker, but it made me feel like he was.

Then we started taking him up to the fish hatchery up here in the valley. He used to like to go up there and fish when he was a little kid. So we would haul him up there in a wheelchair and push him down to the creek, dangle him a pole. He would have trouble throwing the pole out. He hadn't practiced a lot using his left hand, and his right hand wasn't worth a pinch. But he'd catch a few fish. Kind of. If it looked like he was losing them, why we'd help him a little bit. So, I don't know. We would just talk a lot. Claire went up a couple of times and Gary went up once. We would go up and sit there and fish for a while. He wasn't . . . I'm not sure he was right with the program even at that point. He didn't, you know, notice the surroundings much, but he did seem to enjoy just sitting there and fishing.

Up Ogden Canyon and north into Nordic valley is an old dairy farm backed up against the mountains. Behind the dairy barns in a meadow of short green grass meanders a deep, slow stretch of creek stocked with hatchery trout. The farmers once allowed people to fish there and charged them a small fee for the fish they caught.

Labor Day morning, the second of September, Byron, Gary, and

Claire picked Cortney up at the hospital at eleven o'clock. After maneuvering Cortney into the front seat of the car and hanging his IV bottle from the clothes hook, Gary and Claire climbed into the backseat and Byron drove up Ogden Canyon to the fish hatchery. As early as it was, leaves on some of the trees in the surrounding Wasatch mountains already were beginning to turn.

Cortney's blond hair had darkened during his long stay in the hospital. He was pale, his complexion marred by patches of tiny reddish bumps. On his chin was a bit of a goatee, a thin moustache on his upper lip, and soft, wispy hair covering both cheeks. That day he was wearing a yellow Windbreaker and a white tennis hat.

When the Naisbitts arrived at the hatchery, Byron and Gary got Cortney out of the car and put him in his wheelchair, while Claire unhooked his IV bottle and hung it on the stainless steel rod rising behind him. With Cortney settled in the chair, they wheeled him down to the creek and Cortney took hold of a cane pole with his left hand, using his tightly cupped right hand as a fulcrum. Gary baited his hook and helped him swing the line out into the creek.

Before long Cortney had hooked a fish and pulled it out of the water by himself. The fish was flapping at the end of the line, and Gary helped Cortney maneuver it back over the grass. Then Gary grabbed the line and handed the part just above the hook to Cortney, who took it in his left hand. As Claire held onto the cane pole, Gary snapped their picture, Cortney sitting in the wheelchair holding up his fish and trying to smile.

The hook baited again, Cortney swung his line a little way into the creek and waited, poised in his wheelchair for another bite.

"I wish Mom was here," he said.

Byron, Gary, and Claire were standing around him, watching the end of his line. They looked at each other but said nothing, and then Cortney was again occupied by the nibbling of a fish at his hook.

After having more sharp tugs on his line, and eventually pulling another fish from the water, Cortney told his father he was tired and ready to go back. He seemed happy with the day's outing.

On the drive back down the winding canyon road, Byron drove slowly because of the Labor Day traffic and the shallow ruts that jarred Cortney's gastrostomy tube, hurting his stomach. Gary and

Claire talked to Cortney about the fish he had caught, but Cortney didn't say much until they were halfway down the canyon. Then, staring ahead through the windshield, he suddenly asked of no one in particular, "Where's Mom? How come she never comes to see me?"

His father said, "Well, she's just not here. Can we leave it at that?"

Cortney said, "No."

The other three were silent wondering if Cortney would ask again.

Byron was prepared to tell Cortney about his mother and the murders, as soon as he was certain that Cortney was ready to hear. Even though Cortney seemed to be pursuing the matter for the first time, Byron wanted to be sure. Then Cortney asked again and his father said, "Cortney, your mother was in the same accident as you, and she's not as well off as you are."

"Well, if she can't come and see me," said Cortney, "can I go and see her?"

It's difficult to tell your son that's been all shot to hell, and who's been sick and needs his mother, and needs the love and affection that she can give him, the attention and strength . . . it's difficult to tell him that he's not going to have that.

They had reached the mouth of the canyon, where a reception center and parking lot sat hidden in the trees on the south side. Byron pulled into the deserted parking lot, stopped the car, and turned off the engine.

Then he said to Cortney, "You really don't remember, do you, son?"

Cortney shook his head, looking at his father and waiting.

"Your mother's dead, Cortney."

For a moment Cortney just stared at his father. "Oh, no," he said finally. "No she isn't."

"She really is," said his father, "and we have to face the fact that she's gone."

"No she isn't," he cried. "She isn't gone."

Tears started down Cortney's cheeks, and his father wrapped his arms around him and let him cry.

I think he knew that his mother was dead. I never lied to him. He was going to have to know and he was going to have to face that fact, and he was going to have to live with that fact. You can't change it. I told him that on the day this all happened that his mother was shot and had the same thing happen to her that had happened to him. And I told him that he was young and strong and was able to live through it, and his mother was older and she didn't have the strength to live through it. And that they had taken her life.

Cortney cried for a long time in his father's arms, as his father held him and rocked him gently.

"Do you know what's happened to you," said his father, "why you're in the hospital and so sick?"

Cortney shook his head.

"Do you want to hear about it?"

Though he was still crying, Cortney nodded.

His father told him that on the way home from his flying lesson back in April he had stopped to pick up some pictures and had been trapped by two men downtown. His mother had come looking for him, and she too had been captured by the two men. Then the men had forced them to drink something caustic and had shot them. That was why he was sick and had been in the hospital so long, and why his mother had never been to visit him.

Claire was sitting in the backseat next to Gary, crying.

We all were crying. Cortney cried and cried, and Dad just held him and tried to comfort him, and he said that even though Mother wasn't there, we were all together, and we had each other. He said, "It's too bad you have to ever even know, but you'll have to know sometime." And he said: "Go ahead and cry, we've all been through it. It happened months ago, and now it's your turn."

PIERRE

Dale Pierre's birthplace, the isle of Tobago, lies in the azure waters of the Caribbean due east of Venezuela. Twenty miles to the southwest of Tobago is Trinidad, where Pierre spent most of his childhood. These southernmost islands in the West Indies, once under the British crown, now comprise a country named simply Trinidad and Tobago.

In southern Trinidad, between the city of San Fernando on the west and the cane fields to the east, is the community of Pleasantville, where Pierre lived from the age of five to the age of seventeen with his mother and father, and eventually a brother and six sisters, in a modest cinder-block house. The house was pink with a yellow gallery and rows of white ventilation brick above the jalousied windows. In front was a matching pink and white brick fence, and in the backyard, high above the house, coconut palms drooped and banana fronds fluttered just above the roofline. It was the largest house on the block and filled with furniture built by his father, a quiet man with a reputation as one of the finest wood craftsmen in San Fernando.

A short distance from the pink house, along roads running through cane fields, was the local government school, where Pierre was taught by a man named Cecil Colthrust. Pierre's favorite teacher, Colthrust had a deep, authoritative voice, and an unusual awareness of each child in his class. One afternoon after the murders he was standing in the breezeway on the second story of the small school, remembering Pierre as a young student, one of the brightest he had taught.

"I had Dale for two years," he said, "from about age nine to eleven, preparing him for the Common Entrance Examination for college [the equivalent of junior high and high school in the United States]. He was in the top three in his class all the time, very consistent in a class of fifty. Both mother and father were active members of the PTA, and I visited their home on more than one occasion. We just chat and chat and chat, not necessarily about the children, just talk, friendly with it sort of. It would be unfair for me to say that things were lacking at home for I saw no evidence of ill treatment. I think he had an ideal home background, an ideal set of parents, you know. They lacked nothing. They were very religious people, Seventh-Day Adventists. Very, very religious. His father used to be a very good joiner, and then he did this what we call sideline also as a joiner at night and on weekends. I would have this opinion of him, that he was a father who meant well for his children. They had a nice home because he built a lot of the things for his home."

In his early years in school Pierre not only was a good student, he was a fast runner as well, and represented Pleasantville as a sprinter in the hundred-yard flat race. "But whenever he won," remembered Colthrust, "he would gloat that he was the greatest. I mean, he would walk in the corridor and do things that he must be observed. You must see him. He could be loud, classes might be in progress, he might call out to somebody, so then the teacher say, 'Boy, what is your name?' 'I'm Dale Pierre!' 'Oh, you are the fella who won the . . .' 'Yes'm.' You know, that attitude. He would project himself, he must be known.

"Now if he lost, well then, he would look for some sort of an excuse to show why he lost. He would not accept it and say, 'Well, look, I have lost and this is it.' I remember once in his best subject, math, he didn't get the mark that was expected of him, and he just figured, well, the teacher must have favored some other student to allow the student to make a higher mark than he made, which wasn't so, it was just through sheer carelessness on his part. But he doesn't lose of his own, must have been somebody else's fault, never his. And this is Dale. Somebody else must have caused him to be on the losing end.

"Even at play he had sort of a controlled temper. He would get highly offended and you could see it, but when he realized that authority would be down his throat eventually, he would become sort of subdued. It was inborn. You couldn't call him a bully, but if given the opportunity he could have been."

Colthrust had read of Pierre's involvement in the Hi-Fi Murders in a local newspaper called *The Bomb*. When he also learned of Pierre's previous arrests for stealing the Corvette and the Rivieras, and the manner in which he was soon caught after returning to the scene of the crime, Colthrust shook his head. "A hell of a fella! You mean that he would say this and do this and do that and then go back and . . . It really ties up then. Yes, I'm seeing it now. You see, now that this has happened and I could take my mind back and certain little things that he would do, certain of his mannerisms, let's say his general deportment, this idea of wanting to be observed, wanting people to know, 'Well I am this, I am that,' it sort of ties up now. He has matured, his fanciful ideas. I wonder what he wanted to establish? Really. He's the greatest?"

One Saturday morning a man named Ben James was drinking beer in a Pleasantville rumshop, only a block from the pink house where Pierre had lived as a child. From the time the Pierres had moved into their new pink house until they had immigrated to the United States twelve years later, Ben James had lived next door. That morning at the rumshop, Ben was telling a small audience about the son of his former neighbors.

"From the time that child go to school," Ben said of Pierre, "he was a worthless fella. And the parents, they was very disappoint of his doing during his growing up days. I don't know what is the cause, or what happen, but they had plenty worries in his growing up.

"I could carry you home now and show you coconut tree where when he start to grow up, I say to him, 'Boy, don't pick the coconuts!' He didn't care what I say. He pick the coconut and drop it down the fence! The only difference myself and the Pierres have is when Dale come picking the coconut. We never had nothing else between us, so I can't say anything of difference toward the father and mother.

"I could tell you, before we came to live Pleasantville I have known the father. I give him job to do for me which still in the house. I'm living there now, and if you going in the drawing room you see a table there, the father make it for me. The bed in the back room, the father make it for me. We have certain thing in the passageway, father make it for me. There's not no maybe about that, he is a good joiner. He had a good reputation, you understand. I mean, I'm giving a mon what he is. He's a very good joiner and a fella who keeps up to his character. Sticks to his words, even in his movement and so on. He's a very good fella, a good citizen. His wife also. She was working in hospital as ward assistant.

"But Dale have differences in his growing up. He run away, and sometime he sleep in my gallery or neighbor gallery, and he didn't care one thing about it! So he was very worthless. I don't know for what reason, you understand. I tell you as a tis. Whenever he stay out, I don't know what is the cause. Sometime they beat him, but I wouldn't say that they was severe in correcting him. They correct him in a way that he should go the right way.

"Well, the time come up which they had some improvement. They went to the States, and there they make their home. Why you think they carry the boy there? That he should have a better future! The parents did all they could for him, they do all within their power to do good for him. I know that because we living neighbor, and I will tell you they didn't relax of giving him his future benefits.

"Now since then, Mrs. Pierre come back here many time, Trinidad, and I never see her a tall. But still, if I could disclose our relationship, her family and I, it would be very difficult. So I wouldn't disclose that. . . .

"Mmmmmm, well, as neighbors we talk. I and the wife have more discussion than the mon. You see, because a morning I was home and she disclose this thing to me. I was never interested to find it out, because although we becomes friends, I don't want to know her past. Right? But it happen 1959 or '58, somewhere around there. She tell me and I just accept it like that. So you see, this thing, I don't want to disclose it because . . .

"Um, which I want to say is this. She had a brother in Tobago who kill their sister."

* * *

Pierre was born on a rise known as Jigger Hill on January 21, 1953. Jigger Hill was at the center of his grandfather's small cocoa plantation in the lush central highlands near Mason Hall, Tobago. When Pierre was three years old, he and his family moved across the channel to Trinidad, eventually settling in Pleasantville. They had been gone from Jigger Hill for three years when Pierre's uncle murdered his own sister in the same two-room shanty where Pierre was born.

Pierre's uncle was named Lennox; at nineteen he was the youngest in a family of three boys and four girls. In 1959 he was living on Jigger Hill with his ailing father and his sister Merle, who was seven months pregnant. One day an ongoing feud over Lennox's refusal to help harvest the cocoa crop or assist with household chores erupted into a fight, and Merle told him he was no longer welcome in the house. Her father sided with her. Furious, Lennox boarded the inter-island ferry to Trinidad, swearing he would return just to kill Merle. Weeks later, on June 12, he did return, and when night came, he stole up on the quiet, dark house on Jigger Hill, a flashlight in one hand and a machete in the other.

Merle's body was discovered hours later by her brother-in-law, his flashlight illuminating the most macabre scene he had ever witnessed. Merle was lying between the drawing room and the bedroom, the blood-spattered nightshirt rising over the mound of her belly, and irregular red puddles congealing on the floor around her. Behind the white mound Merle's head was cocked askew and twisted backward, little more than her windpipe joining it to her body.

After hiding in a mango tree all night, Lennox was captured at gunpoint the following morning as he approached a water truck parked on a dirt road. He made no attempt to escape, dropping the murder weapon still in his hand at the command of the arresting constable.

Lennox was incarcerated in the Scarborough jail until the next scheduled assizes were held in Tobago some months later. When his estranged mother went to her other sons and daughters asking for money to hire a lawyer to defend him, Pierre's mother refused.

"I give not'ing a tall," she said. "Lennox has bring a disgrace on de family, an' I not encouragin' any wrong t'ing."

When his case eventually came to trial, Lennox was represented by a lawyer, a Trinidadian white. The most damaging testimony against him came from his usually taciturn father, who said on the witness stand that Lennox had come crashing through the house like a tractor. He described how Lennox had chopped the pregnant Merle in the neck with the machete, then had come searching through the brush where the old man had escaped with a grand-daughter and was hiding. Lennox was found guilty of first-degree murder, and was transferred to the main prison at Port of Spain, Trinidad. While his appeal was pending, his mother would visit him, bringing him oranges and mangoes. One day she asked him why he had killed his sister.

"She get to high talkin'," he replied, "an' so it happen."

A few months later Lennox was taken to the gallows and hanged.

When Pierre was growing up in Pleasantville, across the street from his house was a lamppost that served as the "liming" spot, or meeting place, for the neighborhood boys. Pierre was rarely permitted out of his front yard, and the boys who gathered at the liming spot often saw him peering at them over the pink fence. The Pierres would not allow their son out of the yard, because the core of the element that gathered across the street was a family of brothers and their friends known locally as "badknobs."

"They would not have been a good example for Dale to follow," said Pierre's teacher, Cecil Colthrust. "If he was prohibited from playing with them or associating with them, I think it would have been for his own good, because they came here and they gave us no end of trouble. They were always involved in all sorts of things, fighting, petty thefts. I wouldn't have wanted my boy to go there. I would keep him in. And if I found him disobeying me, I would give him a heavy scolding and then maybe a good licking when he deserves it. Dale's father was trying to do the best for his boy, discouraging him from going out and idling at the corner there."

Pierre resented the restrictions imposed by his parents, and as he got older, he began sneaking across the street to lime with the boys. When he got caught, his parents would give him "a good licking." Children in Trinidad often were disciplined by what was termed a licking or thrashing, what amounted to a hard spanking with a belt.

Pierre's mother administered most of the lickings he got, but he never seemed to resent her or her actions.

"Even though my mother did beat me with any and everything and very severely at that," he later wrote,

> it was not a constant thing. I had periods of up to six months without a beating. My adoration for my mother stems from the fact that in spite of everything, she did all she could to encourage me to seek an education. She also gave me more liberty as far as visiting some of my more acceptable friends. All in all I can safely say that when bad came to worse I could always count on her support.

Though Pierre professed to adore his mother, he detested his father, a quiet, hardworking man whom Pierre seemed to resent precisely for those qualities. He once described his father as "a classic workaholic," and in a letter wrote this paragraph about their relationship:

> The conflict between my father and myself was mostly one of personality. I am not the type who is likely to get caluses on his hands from hard work. I am the type of personality you're likely to find in an office on the 50th floor of the Rockerfeller Building, dressed in a conservatively modern 3 piece suit, drives a Mercedes 450 SLC or more likely a Dino Ferrari and lives in a Park Ave. penthouse, and here lies the basis of our conflict.

Since his teenage years, Pierre had had a thin scar on the left side of his head that ran from the forehead back, creating a natural part in his hair. When he was examined for legal sanity after the murders, he told the psychiatrist that he had injured his head in a motorcycle accident when he was fifteen or sixteen and had spent two months in the hospital recovering. He said that after being released from the hospital, he had blacked out several times a week, implying that he suffered from seizures.

Pierre had never been in a motorcycle accident.

One Sunday morning after church when he was thirteen, Pierre was standing in front of the chapel with a small group of boys who were taking turns riding a bicycle. When it came Pierre's turn, he steered the bicycle into a lamppost.

Though he was bleeding from a cut on his head, Pierre never lost consciousness. His parents had him taken to Casualty at nearby San Fernando General Hospital, where a young Canada-trained physician, Dr. Edmund Chamely, put twenty stitches in the eight-inch laceration. After sewing up the wound, Dr. Chamely examined Pierre's eyes for signs of brain compression or swelling, and tested his reflexes and his motor and cranial nerves. His examination revealed that Pierre had not suffered a concussion, and X rays showed that there was no skull fracture. When questioned later about the incident, Dr. Chamely pulled Pierre's medical file and wrote the following notes on the injury:

> Fell off bicycle—3/6/66
> No concussion. Suffered laceration 8″ to left scalp with blood loss. When examined on the ward, there were no neurological abnormalities. Patient was in no distress. Sensorium was clear. Recovery was uneventful.

Pierre was kept on the general surgical ward overnight for observation and was released the following day.

Recalling parts of his Trinidad childhood in a letter, Pierre once claimed that as a young child he was "dumb" and that his teachers complained to his mother

> on how playful I was and was not learning anything. Then one day my mother took it upon herself and she decided that I would learn something. So with a strap in her hand and my school books I was called to the table every night to read, memorize poetry and do arithmetic and any failures were met repeatedly with the strap. After a few months I had moved from the bottom of the class to around 5th place in the end-of-term tests. From then on there was no turning back. I will be forever

thankful to my teachers and my mother to this day for the education that I now possess.

Pierre never made it past the tenth grade. After passing the island's Government Common Entrance Exam, he entered St. Benedict's College, a private school, at the age of eleven. With a passing mark being 45 percent, Pierre ended his first term at St. Benedict's with a 49. His second term he scored 39.5. After finishing with an average of 31.5 in his third term, his mother removed him from the school in January of 1966 and enrolled him at Southern Academy, a government school supported and run by the Seventh-Day Adventist Church. In his first term at Southern, Pierre's grades were only average, dropping each term after that. In July 1967 his mother received a rare letter from the principal:

> It is with much regret that I must bring this matter to your notice. The complaint has come to my office that Dale has grown extremely talkative and lazy and that he has refused to do Geometry and Latin. I sincerely hope that you will have a serious chat with him and that he would have mended his ways and resolved to fit into our programme here at Southern Academy by the time School re-opens in September.

When school reopened in September, Pierre flunked six of his eight subjects and that was his last term at Southern. But his poor grades were not the reason he was expelled from the academy. One of Pierre's teachers, Bernice James, said: "I don't remember too much about Dale. I can remember that he had a fiery temper, and this could get you into trouble obviously. I also remember his name being called in connection with the theft of something at some time. That much I remember, but I can remember nothing else about the incident."

A recommendation form later sent to the school by a potential employer was returned with a notation penned by another of Pierre's teachers: "Was ~~guilty~~ suspected of dishonest conduct."

Frank Providence attended Southern Academy at the same time as Pierre and agreed with other students that while in school Pierre had stolen money, books, and a cassette player. Providence described Pierre as "a fella didn't talk much. Use to keep to himself. You might be around and he might be around, but he just there. He was a kinda background mon. Always here and there, kinda lurking." Providence added that if someone else had something that Pierre wanted, he would either talk them out of it, or take it from them. " 'Where you get that?' " he imitated Pierre. " 'Look nice.' If you turn your back, next thing you know, your thing missing."

At the age of fifteen, having completed the equivalent of the tenth grade with substandard marks, Pierre left school never to return.

After being expelled from Southern Academy at the age of fifteen, Pierre became an apprentice at the huge Texaco oil refinery north of San Fernando. In the company's long history not a single apprentice had ever been dismissed. Two months after he began work Pierre was caught stealing from another apprentice and was suspended for one week. In a report of the incident a supervisor wrote that Pierre "has shown signs of being sorry for what he has done and promised that such a thing will never happen to him again."

Three months later, after five more apprentices had reported having money stolen, Pierre was again caught. An apprentice had complained that his wallet was missing, and during the ensuing shakedown, Pierre had tried to return the wallet without anyone seeing him. In a detailed statement to his supervisors Pierre denied having stolen the wallet, claiming he actually had "hidden" it. He didn't say why he would want to "hide" the wallet of another apprentice.

Having already been suspended for a similar offense, Pierre was dismissed from the Texaco apprentice program. After he was gone, there were no more reports of theft.

Explaining his dismissal from Texaco in a letter years later, Pierre did not mention hiding the wallet:

> One payday after I had cashed my check I took the liberty of strolling around the immediate downtown area. While I was there my wallet was lifted but I never missed it until I got back to the work area. When I did miss my wallet I got very an-

noyed. So while we were at PT I saw the perfect opportunity to recover my loss and I seized it. There were no witnesses neither was any evidence found on me but none the less the circumstantial evidence weighed very heavily against me and I was released from my apprenticeship. My parents were very embarrassed and took it very hard; especially my mother, but I never told them what had actually happened. Personally I felt terrible about the whole thing and sort of secluded myself for a while. I have a terrible ego as far as my image is concerned.

When Pierre was six or seven years old, he had stolen from a neighbor's porch a small cage containing a yellow and black songbird called a semp. Another neighbor had seen Pierre take the bird and notified the owner, Mr. Patterson, an older man who refused to confront the small boy or his parents about the incident.

"It was only a bird," he later explained, "and he was such a little child to me. I would never do such a thing. But that Dale was a scampish fella."

Now that Pierre was sixteen, no longer in school, no longer an apprentice at Texaco, he spent his days at home, playing cards with the boys who "limed" under the lamppost across the street. His father had warned him not to associate with the boys who gathered there, but Pierre ignored his father. One afternoon, returning from work early, Pierre's father caught him playing cards and chased him until Pierre jumped a fence and ran away to his great-aunt's house. There he remained for months, paying only occasional visits to his family, usually during the day when his parents were not at home.

One morning Pierre returned to Pleasantville, broke into the Samuel house across the street, picked the lock on the Samuels' dressing table, and stole a white hand-purse from the drawer. The purse held eighty-eight dollars, money Mr. Samuel was saving for the payments on his new taxi. When one of the Samuel boys recalled having seen Pierre in their yard that day, and two neighborhood boys saw Pierre the following day in San Fernando buying new clothes at a department store, Mrs. Samuel went to the aunt's home and found Pierre.

"I said to him, 'Dale, I guess you know what brought me here.' And he said, 'No.' I said, 'Yes, you know, you know what brought me here.' And I said, 'Why did you take the money, why did you go into my house and take the money?' He tried to put up a little defense by saying it wasn't so, but that is all. So I say: 'Why did you do a thing like that? If this thing had reach the police, maybe you would not have been able to go to the States with your mom. You are a nice boy, Dale. Remember your sisters, they are all trying to reach somewhere. You must behave yourself and don't do things like that.' "

Mrs. Pierre reimbursed Mrs. Samuel the eighty-eight dollars.

Pierre later wrote his own version of the incident:

> I came home one day to check things out. On this particular day I took the shortcut from the bypass through the Samuel's backyard and went home to pay my visit as I intended. After visiting, where one of my sisters implored me to return home, I left and went back to my aunt's. About the very next day Mrs. Samuel came down there and accused me of stealing eighty dollars from her house. The allegation was so damned preposterous that I was infuriated. The house showed no signs of breaking and entering and neither was the place where the money was supposed to have been kept. You would not believe the hate and revulsion I felt for Mrs. Samuel as I watched the fat bitch sitting there with a straight face lying on me."

The next day another neighbor's entire record collection, stolen the week before, was found at Pierre's aunt's house.

Carol Smith, a pleasant girl with a round body and a plump face, lived across the street and down four or five houses from the Pierres. While Pierre lived in Trinidad, his only relationship with a girl was a platonic association with Carol. After learning of the murders, Carol talked about Pierre as a teen-ager just prior to his leaving for the United States.

"The first day I didn't really see the papers, a friend told me about it. Then I sat down for about four days reading this thing over and over and over and over to make sure it was really Dale. They say that when you reach the States, and you bunch up with certain people you done get bad. I said, 'Well, he done had his bad ways already, so it just kinda bring it out more then.' You see, he was always a wicked fella. Like if you pitching marble, he will take all the marble and run home. Or if you buy something new? He will take it and run home. Or else throw it away, or hide it. And he is a very good liar, too. They say he used to handle a lot of money, and a tape recorder and thing, but I don't know about that.

"The boys across the street was a kinda influence over Dale, too. Because, you see, he liked what they were doing. He wanted to be a top mon, too. He might not be in the thing itself, but when those boys come and say, 'Well, we rob a store,' he will want to get in the action. You know? He will question them, what they did, how they enter, and then now you find, well, he will go and sit down and think about what they tell him. He will try to have an imagination of the store and how they did the job.

"He and his father really didn't used to pull either, because Dale was just kinda a boastful fella then, if you understand. He brag and want to be a big mon. And his father was very quiet. He never interfere with anybody. But Dale had a kinda big shot alive about him then. No matter what it was, he wanted to be top mon. He wanted to have a big house, with everything in it. A big car. He wanted to have the biggest car Trinidad could ever have. Everybody must look up to Dale then, and when Dale coming down the road they must hol' up and look at Dale passing.

"When he learned he was going away to the States, he made big plans. He said he was glad to be leaving, and when he come back all of us would be surprised. He would be somebody in high society, somebody we would read about, and when he come back people would say: 'Hello, Dale. How's it goin'?' "

During the months preceding his family's departure for the United States in June 1970, Pierre kept mostly to himself. "I stayed to myself because I preferred it that way," he later wrote,

> and partly because of Mrs. Samuel's accusations. I felt that Mr. and Mrs. Samuel were trying to get me into trouble, so I stayed away from anyone and everyone that was a potential threat.

People on the block, especially the Samuels, were devious, underhanded snakes as far as I was concerned. That fear was further compounded by the embarrassment I felt about the Texaco incident. At this time there was so much going through my mind I doubt I could remember it all. My main thought was to make a big success of myself when I came to the U.S. just so that I would be able to go back there and flaunt it in their faces. Nothing would please me more than to see the look of pain and disgust on the Samuels' faces should I turn out to be successful, and as I lay in that backroom all I thought about was how and in what ways I was going to achieve my goal. I was thinking whether or not I was going to get caught up with the hippies and lose sight of my goals; whether or not I was going to end up like Sam Cooke—being shot because of involvement with a white woman. I was also wondering whether or not being transplanted into a society as free and as loose as America was described to me to be, would cause me to degenerate and become a bum. As these many thoughts raced through my head I would repeat to myself: I won't let it happen. I will be successful. I will not lose sight of my goals.

The idea of moving to New York caused me more excitement than I was capable of keeping under wraps. As you may well imagine the one thing I looked forward to mostly was to make Mrs. Samuel green in the face. Even as I hung around the house keeping myself out of sight I would get a morose feeling at times which I would quickly dispel simply by thinking about my planned success and the Samuels' ultimate jealousy. My thoughts, whether of the deepest or shallowest nature, consisted of nothing but plans for *vindictive success* [Pierre's italics]. The only fear I can recall having was that maybe I would be kidnapped or killed by some crazy.

I don't remember the exact date but it is either June or July 7, 1970. It was about 3 o'clock pm and I remember that it was very hot. My cousins were there and so were some of the family friends and two of my friends from down the street. I am still in Trinidad. I am all packed and ready to leave for America. All the neighbors are peering out of their windows as pictures were taken of myself with my cousins and with various members of the family and of the house. We then packed into the two cars that were to take the selected few to the airport—Piarco International Airport. I am supposed to board a PanAm 707 on a non-stop flight to LaGuardia Airport in New York City. My baggage was checked in, my passport and Visa cleared, and I bid my last farewell to everyone and everyone is wishing me a safe flight. I then boarded my flight, when it was called for the third time, which was to bring me to New York.

As I sat in my window seat on the left side of the aircraft, I could see my family and friends still waving to me. I could remember thinking about getting to meet the hippie girls we heard so much about in Trinidad. I was thinking about all the money I was going to be making and that I was going to buy a sports car. Then the aircraft took off and I almost cried.

When I arrived in New York, around 7pm, as I stepped out of the aircraft the first thing I noticed was the chilly wind blowing. I was already looking for snow when I saw the frost come out of my mouth when I laughed. The very next thing to confront me was the size of the airport. I cannot exactly remember my reactions but I stood there looking at everything. I remember getting my baggage and heading for a telephone where I made my call to the number I had and was able to get in touch with my father's roommate, because my father was not expecting me. There was some question as to my coming before the rest of the family.

By the time I got to Brooklyn it was dark and I felt completely lost and disoriented by the complexity of everything. I can remember thinking what if the driver just took my money and dumped me off anywhere he felt. That fear was short lived because I soon arrived at the address. I finally met my father's roommate—it seemed as though he was looking out the window for me. He told me that I would have to spend the night at his apartment until he could check with some people to locate my father. He told me that my father had moved to a larger apartment as he was expecting us to come soon.

I can still remember my first day in the USA—when I opened

the refrigerator the foods—especially the fruit—looked different—the pops were in cans insted of bottles like I was used to. I can remember turning on the radio and the very first things I heard was the news, as for music the very first song I heard was "Band of Gold" by Freda Payne. The radio station I was tuned in to was WABC—New York. I spent most of that day looking out the window at the people and cars as they passed by. I had thought about going for a walk but quickly discounted that idea for fear that I may get lost or kidnapped or something.

Finally my father's friend came home from work and informed me that he had located my father. He also asked me whether I had gone out to check out the "chicks," whereupon I asked him if he was raising chickens. He broke out laughing and I couldn't understand why. I asked what he was laughing at and he said he was talking about the girls not chickens. So I told him I did not go out and why I did not. He assured me that there was nothing to be afraid of in that neighborhood and that most of the residents there were West Indian anyway. So I packed my suitcase and we left to find my father. My father's friend elected to give me a mini tour of the general area first to check out the chicks as he said.

We found my father's new apartment which was in total disarray as he was painting and decorating. The apartment was finally readied and my mother, sisters and brother arrived about two weeks later. Our house was one in a lower middle class neighborhood. However, seeing the interior of our house you'd never believe it's the home of a lower middle class family. My mother and father was always very particular about the conditions in which their children lived. I will tell you that my home was a very cheery place to live as far as environment is concerned. The neighborhood itself was not that spectacular. It was not very clean but it was a lot safer than most. It was a good place to live.

It was now time for those in the family who could to find jobs. As for my employers there were three. The Dept. of Social Services, the New York Telephone Co., and a fast-food outlet called Nathan's. The job with the New York Department of Social Services I can't remember too well. It was the first job I had when I came to this country. I don't remember too much about the job except that I hated it. I think I had a janitor job there. I'm not sure.

At the telephone company I was a service clerk and I wanted to be a switchman—so I was not happy at that job. As for Nathan's, the fast-food outlet, I worked there for about 3 weeks because I was on strike at the telephone company. I worked the deep fryer and the ice-cream machine while I was there. I left the job because I felt humiliated in some way. It was more an embarrassment than anything else. I did not like the idea of being a servant to anyone, and that's exactly what I was as a short-order cook. I hated the job so badly that I decided to break the picket lines and go back to work. I was not a union member anyway. During this time I was constantly hoping for something better. I thought that my education demanded a better job than I had at the telephone company. I wanted to do something more important. I have always had a vision of myself as an important person very well-off socially and financially; and well-liked by all who knew me.

It may come as a surprise but I was never the friendly type. And I certainly was never outgoing or very sociable. All the friends I had could possibly be counted on my fingers. My activities were limited to the Park Circle Roller Skating Rink, and the Brooklyn Public Library at the corner of Eastern Parkway and Flatbush Avenue. I also spent a lot of time at the movies—I may even go so far as to say that I was a "film nut."

I ran around with some guys who could be characterized as "boys around town." They were the regular know-it-all types. My sexual escapades—up until I met these guys—were nil, and as such I was mocked and jeered for a while. I have never and will never be party to a "gang-bang." I think that sort of behaviour is deplorable and certainly tells much about the moral character and social dignity of the participants. But I was more-or-less forced into my first sexual encounter. I think the girl's name was Lisa.

I started to learn to drive because the urge to buy a car was becoming greater. It had now been about two years since I came to the country. I had to take the practical part of my driver's test twice before I passed and got my driver's license. I bought myself a car—two as a matter of fact. The first one was a 1963 Pontiac Bonneville—I had an accident because there was no brake fluid in the cylinders. That was no big loss because the car only cost me $150 plus registration and insurance. About 8 months later I found a super bargain in Pennsylvania. A 1969 Road Runner with a 383 high performance engine and a 4 speed transmission. It cost me all of $800. I later crashed the Road Runner while drag racing one Sunday night. It got away from me at about 110 mph. Nothing happened to me and then I got bored. Then I decided to join the Air Force for two reasons. The first was that promotion in the telephone company wasn't about to come my way. Secondly I thought it would be nice to become a pilot.

I entered active service with the United States Air Force in the first week of May 1973, and I was instantly disillusioned. Before I knew it I was on my way to Lackland Air Force Base for bootcamp. Lackland is in San Antonio. My head was shorn of all hair, even though I was promised that this would not be the case. I happen to be extremely self-conscious about my physical appearance—I was devastated by this incident.

The 6 weeks of bootcamp I spent at Lackland AFB wasn't so bad after all. But none-the-less I was dissatisfied because I found out I was not going to be a pilot but a helicopter mechanic. I then inquired how I could become a pilot. After being told of the 4 years of college plus 6 years mandatory Air Force enlistment—10 years was too long and I again became restless.

While in San Antonio I managed to fall in love with a Mexican divorcee. I had planned to get married to her but I got cold feet and chickened out. I was then sent to Sheppard AFB in Wichita Falls, Texas for my tech school training. There I met and subsequently fell in love, again, with an Oriental girl. She was Japanese American. I was going to ask her to marry me but I couldn't after what happened in San Antonio. I believe her name was Lisa.

My tech school training was now completed and I graduated. I was assigned for OJT training at Hill AFB in Utah. OJT means on the job training. I was trying to exchange or sell my Hill

Field orders but nobody wanted it so I was stuck with it and destiny.

I came to Hill AFB in Sept. or October 1973. At Hill the routine was the same as tech school except that I ran my own life here. In my spare time I did not do much except play pool, visit the Airmen's Club occasionally and read a lot. I did not indulge in any social events except to go to the movies. This is something that anyone in the Air Force who knew me can tell you. A lot of people on the base knew me but I don't think that any of them can be classified as friends. I don't remember how Andrews and I became friends or to be associated with each other but I'm willing to bet that it was because of music. That is the only thing we seem to have a common interest in.

To explain my priorities and likes—let's put it this way. I have always been obsessed with the idea of living easy. I have always wanted to improve my social stature, my intellectual ability and my financial position, but it has been my experience that most of the black servicemen seem to be content with their station in life. Their excuse for their passivity was always that "you can't go far in this white man's world." I feel otherwise. It has also seemed to me that the average black serviceman likes to dress outlandishly—or in a scrappy manner; I try to keep myself presentable at all times. I dress conservative-mod, and I pick clothes with colours that compliment my skin colour. The guys with whom I was most familiar, including Andrews and Roberts, thought it hep to be one of the boys—doing a lot of drugs, boasting and chasing every available female in Utah, and being in the know as to what the latest top 10 songs were—on the Soul Charts. I got into photography, read a lot, played tennis and went to the movies a lot. I also prefer jazz to soul. They never spoke to me much about their parties because I was never interested, and besides I did not hang out with them. On one or two occasions Andrews told me about "dope parties" that he went to. I guess that's why he overturned his van twice while speeding and once borrowed somebody's car and wrecked it on the way back from a party. I was usually in bed by midnight. I spent a lot of time by myself because my priorities and likes differed drastically from what was considered hep by fellow servicemen. I couldn't dance, never smoked and as a result, never met or became popular with the town's girls.

As an airman I was trained to be a helicopter mechanic. I worked on H-53 helicopters, the biggest helicopter I ever saw. But I was extremely dissatisfied with my position and as a result I was less than the model airman. I decided I didn't like Utah or the Air Force anymore so I filed for an early discharge. I understand that it was approved by my immediate commanding officer and was supposed to be on the way to the base commander for final approval when I became involved with this case.

As I look back on everything I believe everything that happened to me was supposed to happen. Maybe there is a lesson in it somewhere I am supposed to learn.

RECOVERY

That Labor Day afternoon, when Cortney's family told him about the death of his mother, Cortney wanted to hear more about her funeral. His father said that of course Cortney had been sick in the hospital and couldn't go, but that there had been lots of people and pretty flowers, and the police had stopped traffic and given his mother a special escort to the cemetery. Crying, Cortney asked to see his mother's grave. The four of them had then driven to the cemetery on the rise south of town, where Cortney stared for a while at the bronze plaque engraved with his mother's name and the date of her death. Then his family had returned him to the ICU, Cortney seated in the wheelchair, still wearing his white tennis hat and still crying. When his family had gone, the nurse helped change his clothes and put him back to bed.

"Cortney," she said, "what's wrong?"

"They told me what happened to my mom," he said. Then his face reddened and his lips began to quiver. "They killed my mom, and I hope they get killed, too."

For the rest of the evening Cortney was upset, an angry look often crossing his face until he finally fell asleep. When nurse Judy Baxter arrived for the midnight shift, Cortney was still asleep and remained sleeping till the early hours of the morning when she walked into his room again.

"I don't remember why I went in the room," she said later, "but he was awake and I asked him how the fishing had been. I think they went out to the fish hatchery. It had been fun for him, and he was very glad to have gotten out of the hospital. He was so sick of it at that point. And I asked him how things had been with his family, and he said, 'They told me that my mom's dead. Is that really true?' And I said, 'Cortney, yes. When you were shot, your mother was with you. She died that night.'

"He didn't say anything. He sat there. I was sitting on the side of his bed, and I remember holding his hand, and then he just started to cry. No sound, just tears and tears. He'd cried before, an angry kind of spoiled cry, but this was quiet, no sound, tears rolling down his cheeks, and just looking at me. And then he said something like: 'Why? Why does this happen?' And then he said, 'Is that why she doesn't come to see me?' And then we talked about it for a few minutes. Then he said, 'Did she die that night?' and I said it again, yes, it had killed her right away, and she had not had to go through a lot of pain or any of the operations and hard times that Cortney had had to go through. That night was tearful. We talked about his mother for a while, and then he said: 'They told me my mom is dead. Is that really true?' And then we went through it all again."

After Cortney had been told many times of his mother's death and had begun to accept that she was gone, hardly a shift went by that he did not say to one of the nurses in his slow speech, "Tell me about my mother." Then he would say, "I miss my mother, I really miss my mother."

"After he was aware that his mother was dead," said one of the nurses, "Cortney went through a grief period and he cried buckets of tears. He'd get to thinking about his mother, and tears would well up and he'd just sob and talk about her. Sometimes he'd call out: 'Momma! Momma!' you know, just crying in his sleep. It'd about break your heart, but when he'd wake up there was no comment at all. It was like as soon as he became conscious he'd block it off and that was it."

Cortney's trips out of the hospital became more frequent now, especially for Sunday dinner when Gary, Claire, and sometimes Brett, Diane and baby Natalie, came to the house. Everyone would visit with Cortney; then while they ate, he would lie on the couch with his two IVs hanging from the steel tripod. Cortney's meal was served when his father measured out the formula and injected it with a syringe into his gastrostomy tube.

At first Cortney had seemed to look forward to his time away from the hospital, but after a few weeks passed, he appeared to be more uncomfortable each time he was brought home.

After he had been out of the hospital for a little while the first times, why he was anxious to get back in the hospital, he felt more secure there than anyplace else. I'd bring him home for weekends. Not even that . . . I'd pick him up on Saturday morning and take him back on Saturday night, and then I'd pick him up on Sunday morning and take him back Sunday night. And I'd bring him home in the evenings sometimes after work. We'd just sit and watch TV or whatever he wanted to do. Sometimes we took him for a little ride, but it would tire him right out. And he wouldn't be really interested in what was going on around him at all because of his own problems, you know. When I took him back Sunday night, he was glad to be in his own hospital bed. He was frightened more than anything, I think. I think he was frightened to be home, because he had gotten used to all the security of the hospital and everybody running in and out every few minutes. He was more comfortable there, and I guess I wouldn't blame him. That's where he had everything at his fingertips and knew that he was safe.

Cortney's progress in the hospital continued slowly but steadily. When his eyes were examined, he was unable to count fingers held before his wandering right eye, but at least the eye was projecting light. He still experienced periods of nausea and vomiting, but the perforation in his esophagus had sealed completely and he could swallow small amounts of juice, broth, and water. His weight had climbed back into the low 130s.

As Cortney grew more alert, he also became more cognizant of his handicaps and pain. He learned that he was helpless. When the speech therapist placed a pen in his right hand, he could not move it without help from his left. If he felt the need to urinate or defecate, he had to ask a nurse either to bring him the bedpan or help him hobble to the toilet in his room. He could do nothing on his own. All of his muscles had atrophied and contracted. Whenever the physical therapist came to stretch them with range-of-motion exercises, the pain was so bad Cortney fought even being touched.

On the twenty-fourth of September, five months after the murders, Cortney was finally transferred out of ICU to an acute care ward. When he left, the nurses talked about his chances of survival.

"You don't take odds on anybody around here that's real ill like that," said Annette Wilson. "Cortney was just too sick, there was just too much involved, and too many times he looked like he was going to die anytime. This was in September even. Some days it looked like we were making progress, other times it looked like we were just going downhill. Even when we released him, knowing he had an esophagus that was full of holes and a lot of other problems, most people here didn't think that he would make it, that with these other surgeries and everything he had ahead of him he wouldn't survive. Everybody said, 'Well, he's not going to live very long.' "

The day after Cortney arrived on the acute care ward, he was given a tub bath, his hair was shampooed, and his father picked him up at five in the afternoon. A surprise party had been planned for him at home, and his father wanted him to look his best. It was Cortney's seventeenth birthday.

For the party eight of Cortney's friends gathered at a neighbor's house, then went as a group down to the Naisbitts' and rang the doorbell. While they were waiting for Cortney to come to the door, they unrolled a big banner that said "Happy Birthday Cortney!"

Dr. Naisbitt opened the door, winked at the kids, and said loudly, "Just a minute!" When the door opened again, Cortney was shuffling forward, his right hand tucked into his chest and his head bent low. Behind him his father was carrying the tripod which held two bottles with lines disappearing into Cortney's pants and up the back of his shirt. When Cortney finally reached the door, all of his friends yelled, "Happy birthday!"

Chris Southwick was standing in the back of the group, holding up one end of the banner. When he and Cortney were younger, they looked so much alike and were together so often they had frequently been mistaken for twins. But Chris had not seen Cortney in five months, since the day Cortney was shot.

"I felt bad that I hadn't visited him at the hospital," Chris said later, "but I couldn't bring myself to do it. I think it was a fear of how he might look and how he might be. You know? I just had a fear of that. And also, I wanted to remember Cortney as he had been. I didn't want to see him all chewed up or shot up. I wanted to remember him and the times we had spent together when he was well and happy."

Now, Cortney stood right in front of Chris, and Chris finally had to look at him. Cortney was skinny and gaunt, his hair had turned brown, and his skin was pallid with an unnatural sheen to it. His face and neck appeared bloated, and his mouth seemed small and pursed. His right eye stared off to the side. Just above the top button of his shirt, a thick red scar showed at the base of his neck.

"It wasn't Cortney," said Chris. "Not the Cortney I remembered. I didn't even recognize him, he looked so different. He was so much littler, and he was just so . . . so different looking. And it shocked me, you know. It hit me for the first time what he'd been through, and it really, really hit me hard. I couldn't believe it. I remember him standing there, and he said, 'Hi, Chris.'"

"Why don't you invite them in?" Byron said to Cortney.

Cortney shuffled backward out of the way, and Chris, Kelly, and the rest of his friends walked past him back to the den. In a few minutes Cortney joined them, his father following slowly behind with the tripod.

In the den Cortney sat at one end of the couch, propped up on pillows, and listened to the stories of what his friends had done over the summer; and about life at school, now that they had entered their junior year. When they asked him questions about the hospital, Cortney answered slowly, often licking his lips, sometimes trying to smile. But his attempt to smile looked more like a frown, wrinkles creasing his forehead and his mouth slightly open in a circle. He once tried to hold a glass of Coke in his hand, but he shook so badly he had to set it down.

Asa, a Japanese woman who had worked for the Naisbitts part-time since Cortney was ten years old, had prepared a big chow mein dinner for everyone except Cortney. While Cortney's friends ate chow mein, Byron made jokes about the special dinner he had fixed for the birthday boy: a liquid formula to pour down the rubber tube sticking out of Cortney's stomach.

After dinner Cortney got some help opening his presents, and Claire brought out the cake she had baked for him: an airplane in white icing, with yellow Life Savers for windows. Everyone had a piece of cake, and either shot pool for a while or talked to Cortney and looked at his presents. Then they thanked Dr. Naisbitt, Claire, and Asa for the party, said good-bye to Cortney, and went home to get ready for school the next day. When they had gone, Byron drove Cortney back to the hospital.

On October 2, Claire and Scott were married in the Mormon temple in Salt Lake City, Claire wearing the same dress her mother had worn when she and Byron were married in the same temple thirty-two years before. The wedding ceremony was in the morning, with the reception held later in the evening at the Ogden Golf and Country Club. With the help of her father, Claire had planned everything: the decorations and flowers with accents of peach and green, a buffet for the seven hundred guests, a band playing dance music. But it was not as much fun as she had once envisioned it would be.

It would have been more fun if Mother had been there. She would have loved to address the invitations and make sure everything was done just right. Looking for the wedding dress and all that stuff. You know, she always kept asking me all the time: "Are you and Scott getting married? Do you think you will? Well, what does he say? Does he say nice things to you?" She always liked to know every detail. And I'd just go, "Oh, yes, Mother, he says nice things to me." When we were buying furniture and stuff, she'd say, "Well, do you think Scott would like this?" And I'd say, "Yeah, yeah, I think he'd like that okay." And she'd say, "Well, if you don't think he'd like it, maybe you shouldn't get it." She'd say stuff like that. And this was a year before. No, a year and a half! We'd only been going out for a year. So she'd say stuff like that, and we'd kinda chuckle about it. And she'd say: "Of course, we don't really know if anything will ever happen. And probably nothing ever will." Then

*she'd say, "But if it does." And I'd say, "Yeah, Mom, I know, if it
does." So anyway Scott told me not to tell her that we were going
to get engaged. He said, "No, let's make it a big surprise." So I just
said, "Okay." But I always wanted to tell her.*

*I think Scott and I had started talking about it like in February.
And then while Mom and Dad were in Hong Kong . . . did we get
the diamond then? I think that Brett had just found the diamond.
And Scott decided to go ahead and get it. But he said: "Now, don't
tell 'em. Don't tell 'em yet." And I said, "Okay." I wasn't going to
tell anybody for a while. Because we hadn't decided what we were
going to do yet. And Scott hadn't decided when he was going to give
it to me. We didn't have the ring anyway. Just the diamond. Mom
kept asking me but I hadn't told her anything. And here she and I
had gone and done all these things years before, china, crystal, furniture, getting all these things together. It was just really crazy.
And the thing is, I know this is what she wanted all her life: to
have the excitement of getting all set and ready to go for the big
day. But I never told her. And then she wasn't there.*

Claire was in the receiving line with Scott, greeting the guests
when Cortney appeared at the doorway in his wheelchair, his two
brothers standing behind him. That day he had had the last of the
needles removed from his arms, and he was dressed like one of the
wedding ushers.

*We went up and got him dressed for Claire's wedding and took
him down to the country club, Gary and I did. Put him in his tux,
boutonniere, and a fluffy shirt and cummerbund. He was pretty
sore all over, had no stamina. Just was all he could do to get up
and get his clothes on and go down and sit in the chair. It was kind
of a struggle getting him dressed. His belly hurt and he had the
gastrostomy tube poking out just below his sternum with a little
clip on the end. We tucked it in, but it was still poking out a little.
Of course he couldn't eat anything. Could hardly get ice down. I
think that's about all he could handle. Anyway, getting him dressed,
everything hurt him and he still couldn't walk very well. He spent
most of the time sitting down and wanting to go home early.*

*But having him there was kind of a big deal to Claire, you know.
They had a line that stretched on forever, and Claire left the line
and everything stopped and everyone talked to him. Kind of a big*

deal. And then we just sat him down and let him enjoy it. I don't think he did, too much. I think he was hurting too bad. He just sat in the chair kind of humped over.

Course, Claire was beaming from ear to ear, and Dad was beaming. It was a nice affair, but I think there were still some bad thoughts about it. It was kind of tragic that Mother wasn't there. Mother liked to entertain. Everything had to be just perfect. Not that the affair would have been any different. But she would have been out buzzing around and going a mile a minute, and making sure everything was just so. And it would have been. She would have had it scheduled right down to the last second or the last chicken wing or whatever. She would have really enjoyed that.

In early October Cortney was transferred again, this time to the rehabilitation wing, where doctors started him on a program to teach him again how to care for himself: how to dress himself; how to feed himself; how to get in and out of bed; how to get through the day physically with help from no one. But Cortney had been in Intensive Care so long he had come to rely on the nurses for everything, and no one seemed able to motivate him to learn otherwise. He would shave his face or bathe not because it made him feel better, but because a nurse would badger him if he didn't. Often it required three nurses an entire hour just to coax him out of bed. He preferred to lie there all day, watching television and napping. Sometimes, when he was supposed to be in a session working hard with a therapist, he would simply walk away and wander down the halls or over to the nurses's desk, where he would sit in a chair wanting to be mothered.

As far back as St. Benedict's, a physical therapist had been taking Cortney's limbs through passive range-of-motion exercises to keep his muscles from becoming too contracted. But Cortney was so opposed to even being touched that a consistent therapy program had not been maintained. Now, he couldn't raise his right arm above his head, extend his right elbow, or straighten his right knee. His right hand was virtually useless. Underlying his problem with contractures from being immobilized so long was the partial paralysis of his right side resulting from the gunshot wound in his head.

While on the rehab wing Cortney became the patient of physical therapist Steve Spencer, whose job was to stretch and strengthen Cortney's muscles, teach him to walk again, and eventually to develop more dexterity in his hands.

"God, I saw that kid for the first time," remembered Spencer, "and I thought he was on death's door. He knew that, and his dad knew that, everybody knew that. While we were treating him, he could have developed an infection and died on us any time. So we were being real careful with him. But wow! Was he ever a tyrant! Wild, yelling 'GOD DAMN IT! Get out of here! GOD . . .' That's the word he'd say over and over, he'd say that word probably five hundred times during the course of a half hour while I was working with him. He was really out of touch with reality. He'd go into these fits of rage, flailing and fighting around almost as if someone was trying to apprehend him and bodily drag him to his death. He'd literally pull us around the department, and we'd be holding onto him, one of us on each side, and he'd just be screaming 'GOD DAMN IT!' the whole time. I broke horses that were more cooperative than Cortney. I was bent over stretching on his leg one time, and he reached out and slapped me on the side of the head. I came up madder than a hornet. 'You touch me again and I will smash your face on the wall!' And he tried to slap me again. He just didn't understand what was going on.

"Cortney wouldn't cooperate, he wouldn't get out of bed and go eat his breakfast in the dining room. Part of his therapy was to get him going on his own, get him to accept that the nurses are not going to wait on him hand and foot, and that he's going to get up, get dressed and go into the dining room, have his dinner and participate in physical therapy. Boy, he wouldn't do that at all. Nothing ever worked. You'd say, 'I want you to go down and work real hard,' and it was always, 'Let's play with my computer,' or 'Let's talk about school.' I couldn't ever get him to understand that if he didn't exercise it every day, three times a day, that that hand would get worse, that it would get stiffer, less functional, more contracted.

"He was scared to death, though. He was depressed to think that he couldn't see. I think he was fearful of a lot of things, and in spite of all that, he coped with it the best that he could. He didn't cope with it maybe as good as I wanted him to, but he hurt like crazy for a long time. He had this tube sticking out of his stomach. He couldn't even swallow anything. He drooled and had a lot of distasteful acid and stuff regurgitating up into his mouth all the time, and he was sick. He contracted a couple of infections. So throughout all of this it wasn't that he was real healthy and just being an obstinate brat, he was sick and weak. Some days he'd come in here, and I'd swear the guy was going to . . . . He just really looked bad. And in spite of all of that he kept coming in and doing what his dad wanted him to, so I feel that he was making a pretty maximal effort as far as he could see. The only thing that I wish I could have done with Cortney is motivate him.

"There were times when he was very mellow. After he'd gone for his walk and he was back in bed, he kinda liked you to stay around. He'd say, 'Don't leave, just stay and talk to me or play with my computer or listen to my records.' He was lonesome. He understood that he had a lot of disability, and he was scared. He had to adjust to the fact that his mom was dead, and he couldn't see out of his right eye, and he couldn't use his right arm. It's a miracle that guy lived. I thought it was great, I thought it was fantastic the recovery Cortney made. To think how damaged he was, shot right in the head at point-blank range. I just can't believe shooting in the head with a twenty-five. Of course, the acid in the esophagus came closer to killing him than the shot in the head. Yeah, Cortney had to overcome a lot of things that I'm sure I didn't even perceive."

After a change of venue to Farmington, Utah, in Davis County, twenty miles south of Ogden, the trial of the Hi-Fi Murders began October 15 and lasted for one month. The jury selection alone required nearly two weeks. When defense attorneys attempted to force Cortney to appear as a witness, Dr. Iverson testified that Cortney was a victim of retrograde amnesia and could remember nothing about the incident. He said that he had never seen and probably never would see a patient who had gone through that kind of trauma. He added that it was doubtful Cortney would ever recover.

Lighted by a soft fluorescence, the ivory walls of the courtroom were wainscoted in dark paneling, and a copper clock imbedded in one wall silently kept time. The prosecutor, Robert Newey, was composed and methodical, speaking in a soft voice as he developed chains of evidence with over three hundred exhibits and sixty witnesses. At one point the entire forward area of the courtroom was filled with the 120 items that had been taken from the Hi-Fi Shop, twenty-four thousand dollars' worth of receivers, turntables, amplifiers, and speakers recovered from Pierre's rented garage.

Newey or the four defense attorneys sometimes would raise objections, and once a shouting match erupted when Newey's assistant allegedly caught Roberts's attorney coaching his alibi witnesses as they testified from the stand. But mostly the atmosphere of the courtroom was subdued. At lunch one day, halfway through the trial, a juror unfolded his napkin to find a crude drawing of a gallows and the inscription, "Hang those niggers." When polled by the judge, the jurors stated that the incident had not influenced them, and a motion for mistrial by all defense attorneys was denied.

Day after day, as Newey called to the stand officers who had collected the evidence at the scene, technical experts who had examined and photographed the evidence, and witnesses who had seen Pierre or Andrews or Roberts near the Hi-Fi Shop the night of the murders, the three defendants sat quietly with their attorneys. Pierre was at the defense table a few feet from Newey, most days dressed in a loose-fitting black and white shirt with large, billowy sleeves.

As the trial proceeded, Pierre took notes, making what appeared to be ink blots or doodles in the margins, notations he later claimed were actually a special code to remind him of important points to be brought up on appeal. Between periods of writing he often looked up to stare at members of the eleven-man, one-woman jury, as though he were taking notes on them, but his note taking consisted merely of a summary of the facts as he heard them come from the witness stand. Other than claiming to perceive an obvious prejudice in nearly all of the 140 prospective jurors questioned by the court, and noting that there were no blacks on the jury, Pierre made almost no comment on his thoughts or what was happening around him. At the bottom of one page he berated a police officer: "Today I've seen something that really hurt me, a patrolman brought in a woman with her baby on her shoulders and booked her into jail for a traffic ticket. I don't care what the circumstances were but any officer who can bring a woman and her baby to jail and book her 'for a ticket' has got to be a dog, I mean a real dog."

Pierre had two attorneys, Gil Athay and Robert Van Sciver, but Van Sciver had laryngitis during most of the trial, and Athay conducted Pierre's defense.

"We had to go basically on an identity defense," said Athay. "Orren Walker's testimony and his description of Dale Pierre just wasn't enough, in my opinion, to put him there. His initial description was a guy, you know, five foot ten. Pierre is five five. Walker never recognized the scar on the forehead. And nobody ever talked about a foreign accent or having difficulty understanding the guy. And that's what we flew with. That's all we could do. We looked at all other aspects. We ran the possible psychiatric defense, but to no avail. I think in this kind of a case you've got to run a psychiatric evaluation. I mean, you've got heinous facts, you've got a girl raped, you've got people with caustic soda poured down their throats, you got people strangled, you got pens kicked in the ear, you got all the ugly elements. And Pierre comes across as very quiet, mellow, somewhat of a loner, but never had any prior history of violence other than . . . I have to concede the 'other than' is the airman who was found stabbed in the eye with an ice pick or whatever, but that was such a nebulous tie-in. He did well in school. I think he liked school. He won some inter-island competition at the age of seven, some educational testing program, I don't know what it was. But he was something of an honor student in Trinidad at the age of seven. Everything he told me about the place was a pleasant experience. He liked Trinidad. He liked being there. He was accepted. He wasn't the minority, he wasn't an outcast, he wasn't different. He denied being in any trouble while he was down there. You know, of any kind. He was a very religious young kid. And that was pretty much the way his life was. You know, he was the choirboy, the kid who sang in the Sunday choir."

On the witness stand nearly two weeks into the trial, Orren Walker relived the details of what transpired in the Hi-Fi Shop basement from the time he arrived at eight o'clock. With his arm outstretched, he pointed at Pierre sitting at the defense table and said that he was the man who had met him with a gun at the top of the stairs. He pointed at Andrews and identified him as the man who had held the revolver on him from the bottom. For one whole day and part of another he told and retold of Carol Naisbitt's arrival, the Drano, the shootings, the rape of Michelle, and how he had played dead as Pierre had tried to strangle him with electrical cord, then had kicked a ball-point pen three times into his ear. He showed the jury the scar on his shoulder where the Drano dripping from his mouth had burned the skin. Another scar on his forehead had been treated with plastic surgery. As he spoke of his son, Walker cried but refused to leave the stand.

Byron Naisbitt also took the stand to testify as to the injuries sustained by his son.

"I can't even remember Naisbitt's testimony in detail," Pierre said later. "It made me mad the way he was obviously playing the jury for sympathy. In his voice and characterizations. It was obviously rehearsed. He'd stop and take a big swallow in the middle of a sentence and bow his head. I think he talked about his son couldn't eat or something, and he'd pause on just the right words while he was talking. Two or three of the jurors were looking at me hard like they were going to kick my ass or something. It was obviously rehearsed, you could tell it. Any novice in the courtroom could tell. I thought it was gross myself. But then I was on that Valium, and I had an I-don't-give-a-damn attitude. That's the way I felt. I thought it was disgusting, the details he was going into.

"The part that really made me sick where I had to get another Valium was the pictures of the place. I felt faint. They had about forty or fifty pictures in color of burns on people's faces, and where the Drano came down on their shoulders. And the girl was naked and they showed a close-up of the bullet in her, I think. I can't remember exactly where it was at. It was generally gross. They had pictures of the whole room down there. The court broke about then for lunch. I told Athay I was sick and he asked for the doctor."

Friday evening, November 15, the jury heard the last of the summations from the attorneys and the instructions from the judge. At

six forty-five they were adjourned to have dinner and begin delib-
erations. The courtroom cleared, and the prisoners were escorted
back to their cells under armed guard.

Most of the major participants in the trial stayed the night in the
courtroom. Deloy White, the detective from the Ogden Police in
charge of the investigation, had his coat off, the butt of his revolver
sticking out from under his armpit. Newey was in his vest and shirt
sleeves. At the defense table Andrews's attorney, John Caine, played
hearts with Pierre, Andrews, and a reporter from *The Salt Lake
Tribune,* the game watched closely by security guards with their
sleeves rolled up. In a small room next to the courtroom, Detective
White, Orren Walker's son Lynn, the assistant prosecutor, and a
television news reporter were engaged in another game of hearts.
Roberts was giggling with his wife in the front spectator row. His
wife was smoking a Tiparillo. The court reporter was reading a book.

At five o'clock in the morning the jury returned with a verdict.
Pierre was found guilty on all five counts, three for first-degree murder, two for aggravated robbery. For Andrews the verdict was the
same. On Roberts, the jury hung on the three counts of murder,
but he was convicted on the two counts of robbery. The jury was
polled to assure that this was the true and correct verdict of each
juror; then the second phase of the trial, the penalty phase, was
discussed by the judge and attorneys. Under the new Utah death
penalty statute, if the defendant is found guilty of first-degree murder during the guilt phase, then a separate hearing is held to determine whether the defendant is to serve a life sentence for his crime
or be executed. The penalty phase was set for the following
Wednesday, November 20.

In the penalty phase of a trial for first-degree murder in Utah, the
strict rules of evidence are relaxed and the judge will allow the jury
to hear any argument he deems relevant to the sentence of the defendant. Most information presented can be divided into two cate-
gories: the character and background of the defendant, and whether
the interest of society is best served by the defendant spending a
lifetime in prison or giving up his life before a firing squad.

Throughout Utah's history 140 persons had been found guilty of first-degree murder. Of these 79 had been given a sentence of life imprisonment, 61 had received the death penalty, and 31 had actually been executed. The last execution had taken place on March 30, 1960.

On Wednesday morning, November 20, the courtroom was not as crowded as it had been during previous weeks of the trial. Pierre, Andrews, and their attorneys once again occupied the defense tables; Roberts and his attorney were now gone. Throughout the day Newey reiterated the heinousness of the murders and referred to the precise language of the Utah death penalty statute, which gave power to the jury to sentence the perpetrators to execution. Newey said that only a sentence of death would be commensurate with the crime these two men had committed. Refuting Newey's contentions, defense attorneys called to the stand sociologists, criminologists, psychologists, and clergymen armed with statistics and Bible quotes to prove that a lifetime in prison was just recompense for the acts of Pierre and Andrews, and in the best interest of society.

When defense witnesses sought to prove that the death penalty was not a deterrent to violent crime, they quoted from studies in which one state with a death penalty was found to have a greater homicide rate than a contiguous state without a death penalty. A doctor of criminology stated that the death penalty leads to sensationalism, an incentive for some murderers. The Protestant chaplain at the Utah State Prison talked of the concept of vengeance as found in the Bible.

Testifying for the prosecution, a clinical psychologist from the prison stated that during the preceding eight years ten persons serving life sentences for first-degree murder had been released. The ten men had served an average of just over thirteen years. The longest time served had been seventeen years, and the shortest, nine years and one month. Of the ten released, three had again committed murder.

During his closing argument Pierre's attorney described to the jury what would happen on the day of execution if they imposed the death penalty on his client: the sun rising, the chains rattling, the defendant drugged and crying, being dragged to the chair where he would be tied down, a heart sewn to the front of his shirt, the six rifles that would be aimed at the heart.

Newey was the last to address the jury. He spoke of the three young people who had pleaded for their lives that night in the basement, of Mr. Walker being asked to execute his own son by administering the Drano, the retching and vomiting that had followed the brown bag with the bottle around the room, the bullets fired into the victims' heads one at a time, many seconds or even minutes between each shot, the rape of Michelle. Execution for the perpetrators of that crime, said Newey, would be quick and painless, not the prolonged torture the victims had suffered.

"How humane was their executioner?" he asked the jury.

Though the trial had lasted for a month, the penalty phase had taken but one day, and the day was over. Now the courtroom was empty, and the jurors were sequestered at dinner, after which they would begin their deliberation on whether Pierre and Andrews would be executed. After the jury had left the courtroom and Pierre had been returned to his cell, Athay and Van Sciver visited him, joking with him, telling him that he'd probably still make it as the first black president of the Mormon Church. Pierre grunted. At seven o'clock the two attorneys left for dinner.

Talking to an acquaintance in his cell after his attorneys had departed, Pierre paced from the riveted yellow door with the meal slot back to the riveted yellow wall with the lone light bulb, a distance of about four steps. He liked to affect an air of intelligence and dignity.

"I like to consider myself as knowledgeable," he said. "I like to know a little bit of everything. I often feel that I am white, but I don't feel bad being black. I consider myself superior to most blacks. I don't trust them. They're boisterous, not well-mannered, and they have habits like smoking and blaspheming that I was not brought up with. And I don't get all dressed up and go flashing around like other blacks. I got my own unique way of carrying myself."

Pierre was obviously strong through his chest, arms, and shoulders, but not physically intimidating. For a short man, he was hefty, weighing 145; seven months in jail had dropped those pounds into a potbelly. As he strutted in black pants and a white T-shirt from one end of his cell to the other, he pontificated on various subjects, covering his mouth and saying, "Sorry," each time he coughed or cleared his throat.

Pierre said that he hadn't shot any of the people in the Hi-Fi Shop, because while the crime was being committed he was back at the base watching a movie called *Blackbelt Jones*.

"I still don't know where that shop is," he said.

A trusty approached the door to Pierre's cell and placed a simmering cup of coffee on the narrow shelf just below the slot. Pierre picked up the cup, looked into it, and set it back on the shelf.

"Hey!" he yelled through the slot. "More cream!"

His pacing continued.

"I intend to sue later," he said. "For now, I'm just going to lie low, then come back and prove my innocence. I wanted to take the stand to clear myself, but I feel I can beat it on appeal, and then everybody will get off. I think that three, maybe four years from now the state's witnesses will forget what actually happened, maybe some will die, and the state will not be able to put on a good case against me then."

Pierre explained that the only reason he did not take the stand on his own behalf was because to clear himself he would have had to implicate the others who actually had been responsible for the murders, and such testimony was prohibited by the Bible.

"The Bible specifically prohibits testifying against someone where they will lose their life," he said.

Since he had begun talking, Pierre had been holding a prisoner's three-inch toothbrush in his hand, raking absentmindedly at his sparse sideburns and moustache. Now he stopped and rummaged through a cardboard box at the rear of his cell, pulling out a white Bible with a faded red ribbon. He flipped through the Bible, saying he was looking for Numbers 35:30. When he couldn't find it, he placed the Bible back in the cardboard box.

The passage Pierre was looking for reads, "Whoso killeth any person, the murderer shall be put to death by the mouth of witnesses: but one witness shall not testify against any person to cause him to die." The chapter continues, "Moreover, ye shall take no satisfaction for the life of a murderer, which is guilty of death: but he shall be surely put to death."

"I can only speculate, mon," said Pierre, "but I figure five years before I am free. In that time I want to get a degree so I can be a linguist. I already speak a little Spanish and some French."

He paused for a moment, continuing to step off the four paces in the cell. Then he said: "When I get out, I'm going to change my name. But don't tell anybody that. Then maybe I will buy a little chicken ranch somewhere in California and go into the egg business."

At nine fifteen there was a knuckle rap at the door and the jailer said, "Pierre, get ready."

The jury had decided how Pierre should pay for his crime. Now the bailiff was notifying all parties to assemble in the courtroom to hear the decision.

As Pierre was waiting for the jailer to open the door, he predicted that he would get the death penalty and that Andrews would be given a life sentence.

Back in the courtroom the judge read the decision of the jury. Pierre was sentenced to die three times for the three lives he had taken. Andrews also was sentenced to die. They were the first men sentenced to die under Utah's new death penalty statute.

The announcement of the jury's decision took but a few minutes. The courtroom was soon cleared again, and in the hall outside, reporters were interviewing the various participants in the trial. Their hands shackled to their waists, Pierre and Andrews were escorted by a squad of police back to their cells. Once they were locked up again, the jail was quiet. In the morning the two condemned murderers would be transported to the Utah State Prison to await their sentence. Alone in his cell, Andrews lay on his bunk sobbing. Across from the jailer's desk, Pierre peered out from the small slot in his cell door. He was eating a bag of potato chips.

RETURN

The day Pierre was sentenced to die was Cortney's first day out of the hospital. When he walked, he could take but a single step, then bounce slightly as he dragged his right foot forward. His right eye still stared blindly off to the side, and his right hand tucked tightly into his chest. Cortney's only nourishment was either formula or food liquified in a blender and poured down his gastrostomy tube.

Byron was advised by psychiatrists that for Cortney's own good he should be placed in a special treatment center where he would receive intensive therapy for his physical and emotional disabilities. But Byron decided against that. *I babied him quite a little bit, probably more than I really should have. Just mothered him, and put up with his immaturity and stuff like that. I figured he'd had enough stress and I wasn't going to push him that hard. He'd get over it sooner or later. I don't think the psychiatrists agreed with that, but I'm not concerned what the hell they think. They felt that he'd be better quicker if we moved him right out of this house and down to an intensive rehabilitation center. And he loves his house. This is where he was most comfortable. They felt that being around here alone, with no mother, would bring back all this stuff and he'd get depressed and fool around. But they don't know him. They don't know him a bit. What makes him tick. They wanted to take him out of all this, take him away from me and just put him where he was on his own and had to start from scratch. Which probably was a good idea, but I'm not sure that would have been the best for him, and it sure as hell wouldn't have been the best for me. After watch-*

ing him through all that, I wasn't about to ship him out. So right or wrong, he stayed right here.

On weekends Byron would take Cortney up to the family cabin in Big Cottonwood Canyon. They would build a fire in the fireplace, and Byron would try to get Cortney out for short hikes. Mostly, they stayed inside and played chess, or Cortney would punch at his calculator and they would talk. One weekend at Thanksgiving they went pheasant hunting in Idaho with Cortney's cousins. Cortney was so weak he couldn't walk the grain fields, so his father propped him on the hood of a car with a 20-gauge shotgun in his hand, and told him to watch for birds that the rest of the party flushed up. In the evenings back home they watched TV together until Cortney fell asleep.

While his father was at work during the day, Cortney sat on a couch in the corner of the den that soon became known as Cortney's Corner. He slept and watched TV and did little else. Asa looked after him and made sure he was comfortable. A tutor from the school board's home and hospital program came each day for an hour to instruct him in English and history, but Cortney never read any of his assignments, and finally the tutor decided to read the chapters aloud to him during her visits and hope that Cortney would listen. Even when Kelly and Chris and other friends visited in the afternoons, Cortney usually just sat and listened to them talk about what was happening at school.

Cortney missed being in the hospital. He had no nurses to ring for when he needed something, no one to talk to whenever he felt like talking. There were relatives and family friends and Asa, but Cortney had no one to rely on to do everything for him, as he had had in the hospital. He even had to learn to feed himself: to work the clamps in his gastrostomy, to measure the ingredients for the formula and then to fill and to place the syringe in the tube. Claire helped him at first but tried to make him do as much as possible.

Dad kept trying to tell us: "Don't do it for him, because he's going to have to learn to do it himself. He's going to have to be self-sufficient."

Despite his weak condition and forgetfulness, Cortney decided in early January that he wanted to return to Ogden High, almost nine months after the murders. The decision seemed unrealistic to his father, but none of the doctors could tell him what Cortney was capable or not capable of doing. If Cortney felt that he was ready to return to school, his father had to let him try.

Though Cortney had missed the last month of his sophomore year the previous spring, he had been passed to his junior year with his class. But even Cortney conceded that he did not have the stamina to attempt a full schedule of classes, so it was arranged that he would attend two hours a day, the two hours to be in the morning on one day and in the afternoon the next. Every day at home he would continue to be tutored for one hour.

Prior to the murders Cortney was not well-known among Ogden High's fifteen hundred students. His brothers had played football and wrestled, and Claire had been a class officer and cheerleader, but Cortney was more of a loner, friendly and easy to approach but socially awkward. Other than being on the swim team, he associated little with groups, his constant companion and trademark being the small calculator he wore clipped to his belt.

"Before the accident we'd go to his house," remembered Chris. " 'Hey Cort, let's go to the Circle for a burger,' or 'Let's go to a show,' but Cortney just wasn't the kinda guy that liked to do those things. He enjoyed staying home and working on his airplanes or inventing something. Cortney was really a smart guy in those things, in scientific things and electronic things. He really got deep into that kinda stuff."

Perhaps because they had not known him before, some students did not recognize Cortney his first day back at school. When they did discover who he was, many of them had ambivalent feelings about seeing him in the hallways. They were surprised to know that he was even out of coma, and yet they were shocked at how sick he still looked. He was gray and gaunt, his body bent forward, his eyes wide and glassy. He seemed distant. Often he failed to respond when someone spoke to him, and sometimes didn't recognize students who had been friends before.

"Haunted," said one student, "that's the best way to describe Cortney then. Haunted."

The gastrostomy tube remained in his stomach, hardly concealed beneath his clothes. It still was the only way he could eat. If he talked, his speech was slow, and frequently he would pause to lick his lips. Walking upstairs, he grasped the railing with his left hand, stepped up with his left foot, then swung the right one up next to it, one step at a time. His right eye stared away from those students who tried to talk to him.

Most of the students had read of the murders and the arrests the previous spring, and they had followed the trial in the fall. They knew as well as Cortney, maybe better, what had transpired in the basement of the Hi-Fi Shop. When Cortney finally returned to school, his survival of all they had read about made him something of a hero. Despite his appearance they went up to him and talked with him, encouraged him and supported him. They tried to make him feel missed and welcome again. But much of their feeling was pity.

"Some people would go out of their way just to talk to him and be nice to him," remembered Kelly, "and Cort noticed that. In ways he liked getting the attention, but in other ways he didn't like how people that had never really known him before and stuff would put on an act, like they'd been buddy-buddy with him since he's been born, you know. Some of the girls would do that. I noticed girls that'd sit there and they'd go, 'Hiiii, Corrrtney,' real slow like he can't hear or anything. Cort knew. Cort knew pretty good what was going on."

Cortney had been attending school two hours each day for nearly a week when the news media called his father. A reporter from the Associated Press wanted an interview and a television news crew asked permission to film and talk with Cortney at the high school.

They had some pictures of him going back to school and one of his teachers on TV. I guess they had a camera take him walking up the steps or something. But we didn't do too much of that. I thought that everyone should know that he was getting better enough to at least attempt to go back to school, because everybody had so many different ideas as to what his problems were. People were really concerned about him. I used to get calls and letters and people would ask other people close to me, you know. So I talked it over with the family and it was thought that it might be a wise idea to let it be known just what his progress had been up to that point. So they did a little article in the paper and put him on TV going to school.

Cortney told the reporters he was a junior and planned to graduate with his class, the class of 1976. "I'm getting along just fine," he was quoted as saying, "and my friends think it is just great."

But Cortney did not have the stamina to be back in school even part-time, and usually reported to the sick room before he had completed his two hours of class. He was unsteady and forgot things moments after his teachers had explained them. He read slowly with his one good eye, and had difficulty comprehending what he had read. Once he had appeared on television and had his picture in the paper, his attendance at school became random. After the third week of January he was not seen at all. He had to be taken to Salt Lake City where he would spend nearly another month in the hospital.

Cortney's only hope of ever swallowing food again was an esophageal reconstruction: rare and complex surgery requiring a team of doctors and lasting nearly eight hours. The results are not always satisfactory.

To select a physician to try the operation, Byron had gone to LDS Hospital in Salt Lake City and pulled charts until he had found the thoracic surgeon with the most experience in esophageal replacements. In the Salt Lake area Dr. Stephen Richards had performed eleven, a total of twenty-five if his experience in residency and VA hospitals was included. All of Richards's patients were now eating, at least soft foods.

Cortney's situation was the most complex Richards had ever seen: a total of five strictures in the esophagus, and the surrounding organs stuck to one another. But he consented to try the operation, and Cortney was admitted to LDS Hospital on January 22, 1975. Two days later he was taken to surgery, where Richards and two other surgeons cut out the old esophagus, edged it aside, and brought a severed length of colon up beneath Cortney's breastbone. This segment of colon was then attached just below Cortney's throat and again to the short piece of esophagus remaining at the entrance to his stomach.

"This kind of reconstruction is not as good as a person's esophagus," explained Dr. Richards. "You have to understand that. But it is a way that people can eat and get themselves nourished. The colon replacement loses its capacity to contract, so all it is really is just a gravity tube. People who have this kind of an operation have to sit upright when they eat so their food will go down."

At the end of Cortney's three-and-a-half-week convalescence following the operation, he refused to leave the hospital. He did not want to return home, and begged his father to let him stay with the nurses. When he was finally taken home, he threatened to pull out his gastrostomy tube so his father would have to take him back.

Each time I'd take him back to the hospital for surgery, I'd have kind of a problem with him for two or three weeks. Till he got settled and adjusted back at home. And the one time, for hell's sakes, I thought I was never going to get him back out of the hospital. He just refused to come home. That was after his big one. He didn't want to leave that hospital, boy, and that's all there was to it. He was really having a time adjusting.

He said why should he have to be like this, and said that maybe he'd have been better off if he'd died and that kind of stuff. He didn't have anyone here really to love and look after him day and night, and he missed the people he had gotten acquainted with down at the hospital. He didn't have everybody jumping through a hoop and physicians running back and forth and nurses jumping here and there. He didn't have that much security. And he didn't have a mother, and he wanted a mother. He was having a little problem psychologically getting adjusted, and so naturally he felt that he was alone, and that this was damned more than he could handle. I just didn't listen to it, and didn't tolerate it and pointed out to him that, hell, he was in lots better shape than a lot of people, and that he could handle it, and that he would handle it, and that he had it, and that he just as well face that he had it, that it wasn't going to go away. And I didn't tolerate listening to that nonsense.

So he decided he wanted to be adopted out. He was here and he was still sick and he was upset, and he was frightened. He wanted a mother and I didn't have a mother here for him, so he wanted to be adopted out where there was a mother. It was just a phase he went through. He was feeling sorry for himself and it was bad and he wanted to be adopted where there was a mother because he wasn't getting any motherly love. I just wouldn't listen to it. I said: "All right, you make all your arrangements if you want. Go find out what you think." So hell almighty, he called up all the agencies and was going the whole damn course. Trying to find himself a mother. He told some society that he wanted to get out of my house, that he was being mistreated and the whole bit. I had the agencies calling me, "Doctor, do you realize what's going on?" "I sure the hell do, I encouraged him." They asked me if I was having some problems. And I said that I wasn't having any problems, Cortney was having some problems.

I just had to be firm enough to point out to Cortney that he did not have a mother and there was not going to be a mother and that he just as well face that fact and learn to live with it. I think he was going through all kinds of changes at that time. Lord, he was trying to find out if he was an individual at all, or alive or dead or what, or whether he could function, and I suspect that this was part of his finding out that he could make it on his own.

Cortney remained psychologically dependent on hospitals for a long while. Between February 15, when he was discharged, and April 10, when his father took him on a cruise of the Mediterranean, he had to be returned to the hospital four times to have his new esophagus dilated. For each dilatation he was in the hospital a day or two, and each time he fought going home.

In April, after Cortney's fourth return to the hospital for dilatation, he and his father flew to the Canary Islands where they boarded the ocean liner *Golden Odyssey* and sailed up the coast of Morocco to Spain and through the Strait of Gibraltar. Cortney was tired for most of the trip, usually remaining on board for the ports of call. He enjoyed driving around Gibraltar, but got sick again during an outing on Malta. He made friends with some of the crew members who showed him the wheelhouse and the engine rooms of the ship, which seemed to interest him more than going ashore. Before the cruise was over, Cortney was embarrassed twice at dinner when he regurgitated his food onto the table.

Upon returning from the cruise, Cortney went back into the hospital again, this time to have his neck opened and the stricture in his throat repaired surgically.

When he was released from the hospital, once again he refused to leave and became so combative, so adamant in his refusal, that Dr. Richards himself had to deal with the problem of getting Cortney out of the hospital.

"I even have it written here: 'Cortney said that he had no desire to return home. He only wants to stay in the hospital. It was necessary, after some discussion and the inability of any of the persons attending him to convince him that he should be going home, to take him bodily and carry him out of the hospital.' He just refused to leave. In fact, he hung onto the door frames when we were taking him out.

"I've operated on people with gunshot wounds in the chest, I've operated on people who have stab wounds in the chest, but nothing drawn out as long as this. I don't think I've ever operated on anybody who's had that much problem, that kind of violent insult. And that much emotional deficit."

After he was returned home, Cortney tried once more to get back into the hospital by claiming that he had strictured again and could not swallow. However, instead of admitting him Dr. Richards saw Cortney in the emergency room as an outpatient. On X-ray Cortney's esophagus appeared as wide as when he had left the hospital nine days earlier. Richards refused to dilate him again. He told Byron that even if Cortney experienced an actual narrowing in his esophagus, as long as he could swallow enough liquid to keep himself alive, what scar tissue remained eventually would relax and Cortney would be able to swallow almost anything.

That summer Byron often took Cortney sailing on Bear Lake or up to the cabin at Solitude. Gradually, Cortney got away from his dependency on hospitals and nurses, though he still visited the ICU at McKay-Dee two or three times a week. When he visited, he would sit down next to one of the older nurses who had taken care of him and lay his head on her shoulder. Once he showed them how he could tie his own shoe. The nurses would give him a kiss on the cheek and a hug, talk with him a few minutes about what he'd been doing, and then Cortney would leave, driving off in the little green Mazda automatic his father had bought him to encourage his independence.

* * *

On August 11, 1975, nearly a year and four months after his first solo flight, Cortney phoned Wolfgang. Since the previous October he had been calling his old flight instructor once or twice a week, first from the hospital, then from his home between operations. Each time he wanted to know what chapters he should be studying in his flight manual. But when he called this time, Cortney had a different request: he wanted Wolfgang to take him flying again.

When Cortney arrived at the airport though, things were different than the last time they had flown together. His personality had changed: He was quieter and he had difficulty remembering what he was talking about. To Wolfgang he seemed hesitant and apprehensive. "He just wasn't the same happy Cortney that I knew before," Wolfgang said later.

Wolfgang piloted the plane through takeoff, turning the controls over to Cortney after they were in the air and flying level. But when Cortney reached over to set the trim, his trembling right hand wouldn't move fast enough. Wolfgang had to set the trim for him. When it came time for Cortney to set the trim again, he was concentrating so hard on uncurling his right arm and hand toward the trim wheel he let the nose drop and they suddenly lost altitude. At the same time, one wing began to dip and Wolfgang had to grab the controls to keep them from going into a spin.

"He decided he didn't want to fly anymore," said Wolfgang, "and he started sweating. I asked him, 'You sick?' He said, 'No, I'm just a little nervous.' That was a complete change. I said, 'Do you want to go back to the airport?' He said, 'Yeah, I want to go back.'"

Wolfgang told Cortney not to worry. "It'll get a little bit better and we'll go up again. When you're ready, just call me."

A few months later Cortney did call and Wolfgang took him up one more time, but it was obvious that Cortney no longer knew how to fly. Even when he was able to get the radio mike into his hand and switch to the right frequency, he couldn't remember what to say. After that second flight, Cortney never again flew with Wolfgang. Occasionally Wolf would still see him out at the airport, and Cortney would say to him, "You gonna take me up again?" And Wolf would say, "Yeah, I'll take you back up. We'll go schedule the airplane." But then Cortney would say that he had to check with his dad first, or that maybe he should wait awhile, till he got a little stronger. Sometimes in the afternoon, Wolfgang would see him sitting alone behind the small hangars, just watching the airplanes. Cortney never again learned to fly.

In the fall Cortney returned to Ogden High, where he was again the object of much attention. The students talked with him in the halls, encouraged him in the classroom. They made him feel welcome and special, and Cortney enjoyed his popularity. The previous spring, while he was still undergoing operations in Salt Lake City, many of them had written in his yearbook that he was an inspiration. Returning to school after so long in the hospital, Cortney had an identity: he was a survivor of the Hi-Fi Murders.

"When he first came back," said one of his teachers, "he was like a hero returning."

Cortney could be seen in the halls, carrying his books under his left arm, his right hand held above his stomach and shaking. He still had a noticeable limp, but his posture was a little straighter, his speech a little clearer now. An ophthalmologist had cut and re-aligned the muscles of his right eye, and the right eye had properly fused with the left. With the aid of thin corrective lenses for near-sightedness, Cortney's vision had returned to normal. Around school, he wore smoke-tinted glasses—even indoors.

When other students approached Cortney between classes to ask how he was getting along, he would slowly say, "Just fine." But he couldn't walk up and down the stairs, from one class to another, as fast as other students. He couldn't eat the same food because the top of his new esophagus was still no bigger than his little finger. Even a spoonful of soup had to be lifted slowly with his left hand, slid into the left side of his mouth, then swung around to the front and up. Since there was no valve at the entrance to his stomach, acid frequently rose into his new esophagus, burning it and sometimes entering his lungs. Every day Cortney had to take tablets of Maalox to neutralize the acid.

In class Cortney could work trigonometry problems on the blackboard that dazzled other students, but he couldn't explain verbally what he had done. The thoughts and the ideas seemed to be inside his head, but he lacked the motor skills to express himself. Often, words and facts heard only moments before got lost in the gaps of his memory, and then there seemed to be nothing, not even the thought that something was missing. Frequently Cortney asked questions his teachers had answered only minutes before. At first the teachers and the other students were patient with him. But then, Kelly remembered, "Most of the teachers would just say, 'Well, why don't we wait till after class, Cortney, then we'll get out what you have to talk about.'"

The hero's welcome that Cortney received from the students ended after a few weeks. Now when he asked questions that the teacher had just answered, they rolled their eyes or shuffled their feet. Or laughed.

"They were a little cruel to him," one teacher observed, "to let him know that his period of grace was over."

The reality was that the students couldn't continue to make exceptions for Cortney. At some point they had to begin treating him as they would any other student. Their laughter meant that Cortney no longer was someone special, no longer a survivor of the Hi-Fi Murders. He was just one of them.

Cortney went through his senior year mostly alone. He saw friends at school and talked with them, but his life outside the classroom was spent at home. Chris was playing football, and Kelly worked in a grocery store thirty-five hours a week. Another friend, Dave Whiteley, who shared Cortney's interest in computers and electronics, had a girl friend now and spent most of his time with her. Once, Dave and his girl friend took Cortney to a pond to run Dave's radio-controlled boat, but Cortney didn't show much interest. He seemed tired. Dave had other things besides his girl friend that occupied his time, too. He and Cortney had started taking flying lessons at the same time during their sophomore year, and Dave was now a licensed pilot.

Friends sometimes called on Cortney at home, and he went bowling a few times and to an occasional movie, but he missed the football games and the school dances, the winter parties and basketball season. He didn't have the stamina to sit in crowded bleachers, and he had trouble swallowing a hot dog and a Coke. When he phoned friends just to talk, he often called them back a few minutes after hanging up, as if he had never made the first call.

Even at school Cortney got tired during the day, frustrated and impatient with his frequent losses of memory. Sometimes he would walk out of class and wander around the halls or call his father, who would encourage him to return to class. On some days Cortney reported to the school sick room until time to go home, or until his make-up classes began in the afternoon after school. Cortney was taking additional courses because he wanted to graduate with his class, and the combined credits from his sophomore year and from summer school and tutoring sessions gave him only half the number required by the state for graduation. If he wanted to graduate with the class of 1976, Cortney had to earn in his senior year one half of the 15 credits most students earned in three years of high school.

Trying to fulfill the requirements for graduation, Cortney had signed up for German, college algebra and trig, physics, computer science, swimming, and electronics. Two days a week, after school let out at two forty-five, he attended make-up or "extended day" classes in English and American history until five o'clock. On most nights Cortney was in bed asleep by eight.

As the year progressed, Cortney walked a little straighter, spoke a little faster, forgot less. But the changes came so slowly that people around him hardly noticed. And some things didn't change at all. He still cared little about his appearance, leaving his hair unwashed, his face unshaved, sometimes forgetting to brush his teeth. The few times he tried to get a date, the girls he asked wouldn't go out with him. For the senior prom he called nearly every girl he knew, but most of them were going steady and all of them already had dates. That night Cortney stayed home alone.

Cortney never complained about his handicaps or having to stay home. Most of the time he seemed almost content to stay at home and rest, and study when he could, because though he was gradually becoming stronger and more agile, he still tired easily. His only motivation was to try to graduate with his friends, yet he was so weak even that seemed at times unlikely. He was barely keeping up with all of the courses he had to pass before he would be allowed to graduate with the Class of '76.

*   *   *

In the late afternoon of May 27 the 492 members of Ogden High's class of 1976 assembled in the fieldhouse at the Weber State College stadium. Outside, on the 50-yard line, a large stage had been erected with high backdrops of red and white. In keeping with the theme of the country's Bicentennial celebration, thirty American flags lined the stage.

The stadium sat at the foot of the mountains with the red-white-and-blue stage facing the west bleachers. As the graduates gathered in the fieldhouse, the bleachers filled with over two thousand parents, grandparents, brothers, sisters, and friends. Cortney's family arrived early: his father, his two brothers and Diane, Claire and Scott. Two newspapers and the Associated Press already had published stories on Cortney's pending graduation, and television camera crews were now positioning themselves in front of the stage to film Cortney walking across to receive his diploma.

The evening was warm and mild. At seven o'clock the Ogden High School Orchestra played "Pomp and Circumstance" as the members of the graduating class began filing into their reserved section of the bleachers, half coming in slowly from the north entrance, the other half from the south. Byron picked out Cortney immediately from among the black robes. He was limping, but his limp had more of a bounce than usual, his tassle jumping at the side of his face. In over two years his father had not seen Cortney so animated.

After the class was seated, the program went quickly: beginning with the Invocation, followed by the student speakers and the commencement address. When finally the time came for handing out the diplomas, Principal Claire Fisher rose and asked the audience to hold their applause until the last student had been called. At that time the graduates would be presented as a group and the people in the stands could applaud the class of 1976.

On cue, the first row of thirty graduates then stood and began the walk across the cinder track to the edge of the stage, where they waited for their names to be announced. When a name was read over the loudspeaker, the graduate climbed the steps to the stage and proceeded across the stage in front of the crowded bleachers to shake hands with the principal and other dignitaries.

Well over half of the class had received their diplomas when Cortney rose with his row and walked down the stadium steps, taking them one at a time, limping noticeably on his right leg, but still seeming to bounce. When he got to the bottom of the stadium, he proceeded across the ramp to the stage and waited for his name to be called.

"Byron Cortney Naisbitt."

The applause started with the 491 members of his class. As Cortney limped across the stage dragging his right foot and trying to uncurl his right hand, the class suddenly stood and continued clapping, and their applause was joined by the families in the bleachers and the people onstage. Everyone in the stadium had risen and was clapping, and the television cameras were following Cortney across the stage as he made his way slowly toward the principal, who was waiting to shake his hand.

After they read my name, my dad said that everyone in the bleachers stood up and started clapping. I didn't see it because I was concentrating so hard on trying to get my hand open.

EPILOGUE

Over eight years have passed since the murders. The Hi-Fi Shop is gone, bulldozed flat to make room for a new downtown shopping mall. Even the old red brick building that once was St. Benedict's Hospital sits on the east bench in darkness, the hospital now located in a new and larger facility miles away. In the spring of 1978, Byron Naisbitt married an obstetric nurse, a woman with a masters in nursing and seven children of her own. Gary too has remarried; his new wife is a bank executive with two sons from a former marriage. At present Gary is enrolled in a doctoral program in chemistry at Brigham Young University. Claire's husband Scott completed his residency in obstetrics in 1979, and the couple moved to Ogden where Scott is now a practicing physician in obstetrics and gynecology. They are the parents of three little girls, the eldest of whom has just turned six. Brett is now the vice-president of an investment and development firm, and he and Diane have adopted two more babies, both of them boys. Natalie had her eighth birthday in November of 1981.

Brett: *Natalie has a picture of Mother in her room, and she loves to hear the story of when she was adopted. Part of the story is Mother coming over every five minutes. She wanted us to be alone, Diane and I, when we got the baby, but the lawyer said he'd be there at three or something. So at three-oh-five Mother showed up. "He's not here Mother, but come on in and wait with us." "No, no, no, no," she'd say, "this is your minute." So, she'd take off. She must have gone around the block and just sat there and paced or something. You know. Five minutes later she was back. That went on for about twenty minutes. She just couldn't control herself. Finally, the lawyer showed up about three thirty. By then she had been back and forth and back and forth. So Natalie loves to hear that story about once a month. And she likes to hear how Grandma helped Di change her diapers for the first time and all that other stuff. "Tell me about when I was adopted." She could recite it by heart.*

As she grew up, we'd tell her the story about her adoption, and she'd say, "Where is Grandma?" "Well, Grandma's dead." "Oh, really? I won't see her?" "No, you won't see her." Slowly we told her little bits and pieces of the story. So she knows how Grandma died. She knows that they were in a holdup situation. That some bad men came in with guns and hauled them off and made them drink some terrible stuff and then shot them and killed them. She just slowly accepted that that's what happened to Grandma and there are bad people and things can be bad out there, it's not all good. She doesn't think that everybody's out to get her, but she knows what happened to Grandma.

Mother would have really enjoyed the grandkids, too. And that's too bad, because she would have made things fun for them, and done things for them, and it's a shame she's not going to get that. Because the only grandchild she had at that point was Natalie. All of five months.

Things didn't really settle down a whole lot until after the trial. Until I knew that those guys had been convicted. I didn't go to the trials because I didn't want to get into all that. I think if I had gone down there and listened to the testimony, just knowing what I know about the facts, I think I would have been just fit to be tied. But I recovered quickly. I've been getting on with my life and doing the things I have to do, and I don't get myself bogged down thinking, "When are they going to get those guys, when are they going to get them?" I'm just not going to sit here and waste my time, because it's not going to change anything. It has dragged on and dragged on, but they're going to get it when they're going to get it. It's just frustrating that they haven't gotten it yet. If that makes any sense at all.

You've got to block it out of your mind. But it still comes up. Like when I'm introduced to people. "Naisbitt, Naisbitt. Is your mother the one . . . ? Is your brother the one . . . ?" And it's been over eight years. People still know me by that. I don't think it's gone away in anybody's mind.

"Yeah, that was my mother and my brother." And they ask me, "When are they going to execute those guys?" And I say, "I don't know, your guess is as good as mine." Almost without fail, everybody comes up with that question. Even now, I'll bet that happens once a month. Back then it was a lot more. But between those times, I try not to live with it. You learn to accept it, you know. I had to learn to accept it eight years ago.

There are still things that pop up, like going to the cabin at Solitude. You get flashes up there. I do anyway, because Mother liked the cabin. I can still picture her standing on the bar waiting for the mice to go away. She hated mice and when she saw them it was bar time. We'd go skiing and we'd come back and she'd be up on the bar, mice buzzing around. Maybe she hadn't seen a mouse for an hour, but she's still on the bar. I picture that a lot, just lots of little odds and ends, some of the things that she really liked and enjoyed. There were mannerisms too that Mother had that were kind of unique to her. I mean she'd do funny things. She'd do a funny walk, and click her tongue, that was one. Those things bring back memories and you have to put them out of your mind.

I'm sure if she'd just gotten sick and died or something it would have been different. We'd probably have had more feelings like Diane had when her mother died. "Well, gee, Mother would have really liked to do this, or seen this, or gotten such a kick out of the kids." But in our case you have to put a lot of that on the shelf because of the circumstances of the way Mother left us. It's just different. When you think about Mother, you always get the flashback of that night. How grotesque it was. I think that takes away a lot of the tendency to daydream about things. Because it doesn't always come back quite as fun as maybe Diane pictures her mother. When I think of my mother, sometime in that daydream I always flash back to her getting shot in the Hi-Fi Shop.

I don't know how Gary or Claire or Cort do it, but I don't like to remember her and think about her being down there. Yet it's too big of a thing just to block out. Regardless how old I get, when I have to think about Mother, I'm going to also have to think about the way she died. And I don't think I'll ever get over that.

* * *

A convicted murderer condemned to death in the state of Utah will have his case taken through at least eight major levels of appellate review, nine if the final authority of the Board of Pardons is considered. In addition the defendant can bring numerous interim actions outside the established appellate process, each requiring briefs and argument before one or more courts.

The first appeal to follow conviction and sentence in the trial court goes automatically to the Utah Supreme Court. If the defendant loses there, then a petition for certiorari is filed with the United States Supreme Court. Assuming the Supreme Court refuses to hear the case, the defendant then may come back to the state district courts, and begin with the state postconviction remedies. If the petition is denied at this third level, an appeal is filed again with the Utah Supreme Court. Once the Utah Supreme Court has heard the case for the second time and still has refused to overturn the conviction, remand the case for a new trial, or impose a life sentence instead of the death penalty, the case goes again to the United States Supreme Court. Upon the second denial by the United States Supreme Court, the case then enters the federal system, going to the Federal District Court, District of Utah on a writ of habeas corpus. If the writ is denied at this first level in the federal judicial system, it advances to the Tenth Circuit Court of Appeals in Denver. From there the case will make its way for the third and final time to the United States Supreme Court. The three-member Board of Pardons, appointed by the governor, then has the power to commute the sentence to life.

By the time a petition is filed with a court, and briefs are written and submitted, and the court has either refused to hear further arguments, or has set a date, heard arguments, and rendered a decision, a year to a year and a half will pass. At each level of appeal a stay of execution is virtually automatic until the court renders a decision, and once that decision is rendered, assuming it goes against the defendant, an execution date is again set, to be vacated later when the next court agrees to hear the petitioner's appeal and the execution is again stayed. Each time the execution date is rescheduled, court is reconvened, and the defendant is brought under guard from the state prison to the county in which he was convicted to appear again before the sentencing judge.

Nearly eight years after they were convicted of murdering three people and sentenced to die, Dale Pierre and William Andrews are still in maximum security at Utah State Prison. The date for their execution has been set five times, and though they once came within two days of facing a firing squad, their sentence has yet to be carried out. Twice their appeal has been argued before the Utah Supreme Court and twice it has been denied. Twice their petition for review has gone to the United States Supreme Court, and twice it too has been denied. Their appeal is currently being held in suspension at the sixth level in the appellate process, before the Federal District Court in Salt Lake City, while a separate appeal on their behalf is taken to the Utah Supreme Court. If their sentence is ultimately carried out, at least twelve years will have elapsed since they committed their crimes.

Claire: *I don't talk about it really very much now. People don't ask me. Well, even if they do, I don't tell 'em. Most of the time they just say, "Well, how are things?" And I say, "Oh, just fine." Because they are, basically. I mean, there are problems, but there's nothing they can do about it. It's just not something they need to hear. Who wants to sit around listening to that stuff. So you just say, "Well, they're just fine." And really they are. You think of Cortney's progression, what he's come from and where he is. And it's just a miracle. That he's even here. I know that. But he's got a long ways to go. And you just hope that he gets there. Because it's gonna be real hard on him if he doesn't. It's going to be harder on him than anybody. I don't even know if he can see that yet.*

Maybe I should take it more personally. But I don't think I would be revengeful. I don't think I'd ever feel like, "Well, I'm glad they finally got it," or something like that. Because I don't think I really feel like that at all. I just feel terrible that anybody would bring that upon themselves. And I think it's their own decision. I'm sure his family must feel just terrible, too. I'm sure they are real sad. They must hurt.

I probably think about it every day. I just think about my mom or what we could be doing, or think about Cort, or something, you know, some part of it. I'm not basically a morbid person, I don't think. But, you just do. Someday maybe I won't. I mean there's nothing you can do about it. I don't think bad things. Like sometimes, it's so funny, I think, Oh, my mom and I'll go do that. And then I think, oh. No, maybe we won't. You know what I mean? Like I still think she's around. Lots of times I'll think that. It just seems like she's just downtown sometimes. I guess it doesn't seem like that that much anymore. But for the longest time I just thought: Well, my mom's not here 'cause she's downtown. She'll be home for dinner. Isn't that crazy? I guess it's just because that's what you're used to. But even after you know it and you accept it, you're just so accustomed to things that this is your first reaction. It'd catch me off guard, you know? Like I say, I don't do it as much anymore. But still I think about all the things we could do. Then I think about doing them with the girls and how fun that will be. That will be fun. We always go places together. Go play in the snow, go to the zoo, and stuff like that. So it'll be fun. It would have been more fun if she was there, too. She could help me out, take the girls, and we'd all go together. She really would have gotten a big kick out of that. But some other time.

The Hi-Fi Murder Trial, though probably the most sensational criminal prosecution in Utah's history, was not by most standards an expensive trial. The jury was not sequestered in a hotel, and rarely did they eat more than lunch at public expense. The $15,000 charged to the county by Pierre's attorneys for fees and expenses was "perhaps the lowest fee in the state's history for a case of this magnitude," according to the judge who presided at the trial.

The transcript of the Hi-Fi Murder Trial ran forty-four hundred pages and cost $16,480.20. Jury fees for the trial were $5,953.80, and the jurors' meals another $819.95. Witness fees came to $826.80. Weber County received a bill for $4,837.36 from the Sheriff's Department in Davis County (where the trial was held) for providing security for the defendants at the trial. The Weber County attorney and the bailiff were reimbursed $221.80 for travel expenses to and from Davis County. Pierre's defense attorneys received a flat sum of

$15,000 for fees and expenses. Miscellaneous expenses for over-head and indirect support costs for the trial were an additional $10,215.

The total cost directly attributable to the Hi-Fi Trial was $54,354.91.

Other expenses were not directly attributable to the Hi-Fi Trial, but involved the time and resources of institutions supported by public funds. The Weber County public defender's budget for 1974 was $60,000, $12,000 of which went to John Caine, Andrews's at-torney. For six months a large portion of Caine's time was devoted to preparing for and trying the case on behalf of his client. Judge Wahlquist's salary was $36,000 a year; a little over six weeks of that year was spent presiding over the hearings and trial of the Hi-Fi murderers. He estimated the costs of his time and travel at $4,968. The use of equipment and the number of man-hours times an av-erage hourly wage for police officers involved in arresting the de-fendants and conducting the follow-up investigation came to $30,000, an approximation which Police Chief Jacobsen estimated was within ten percent of the actual cost. The Weber County Sher-iff's Department listed expenses of $3,724.22, the majority of which went to housing the three prisoners for seven months at $4.50 per day, the flat rate paid by the government for holding a federal pris-oner in a county jail in 1974. County attorney, Robert Newey, pro-vided a figure of $15,494.84 for pretrial preparation, his assistants, an investigator, and approximately one-third of his $17,500 salary for that year. So the additional costs proportionately attributable to the Hi-Fi Trial were approximately $60,187.06.

While Pierre, Andrews, and Roberts sit in prison, their appeals continue, and though Pierre's attorney has received no additional monies for taking the case through the appellate process, the Utah Attorney General's Office must respond at each level of appeal. Earl Dorius has argued the case on behalf of the state since the first appeal to the Utah Supreme Court. For the past seven years he has spent three months each year researching, writing, and arguing the Hi-Fi case and companion capital cases on behalf of the state. His salary during his first year in the Attorney General's Office, 1974, was $12,000. It is now $38,500. When he is working on these cases, he keeps two secretaries and two law clerks busy for most of the three months and once, faced with a barrage of writs filed by defense attorneys, required the assistance of five law clerks. The law clerks work twenty and sometimes forty hours a week and earn $6 an hour. The secretaries make between $10,000 and $16,000 a year. Photocopying alone for a single level of appeal, thirty copies of a two-hundred-page brief plus specially printed covers, runs over $500.

Since the day after they were sentenced Pierre and Andrews have been incarcerated in maximum security at the Utah State Prison. After being held in maximum for his own protection, Roberts eventually was transferred to the medium security wing where he is presently housed. Because it would be too costly and an unnecessary expenditure, the prison has never conducted a cost accounting to determine the expense of confining a single prisoner. The only method by which the approximate cost per prisoner can be calculated is to divide the total number of prisoners housed at the facility by the prison's fiscal budget. Since 1974 the population at the Utah State Prison has averaged each year just under 1,000, and the cost per prisoner for running the prison has remained between $9,000 and $10,000. For prisoners in maximum security this figure would be slightly higher. The proportionate cost of supporting Pierre, Andrews, and Roberts for the eight years of their imprisonment, then, is approaching a quarter of a million dollars.

In Utah, as in all states, public funds support judges and the judicial system, the prosecutors, the public defenders, the Utah State Prison, the Attorney General's Office, the county jails, and the city police. No agency, institution, or fund has been established to aid financially, emotionally, or otherwise the victims of violent crime. Except for the incalculable damage to his health and his potential, the loss of formative teen-age years, and the death of his mother, all of Cortney's expenses as a result of the murders can be determined to the penny, because as a victim he is solely responsible for their payment.

Byron Naisbitt carried extensive medical insurance with Blue Cross and Blue Shield, and Cortney was covered under the policy. As of 1981 the company had paid claims on Cortney of just under $75,000. A breakdown of the bill showed the sixty-six days at St. Benedict's to cost $21,562.30. One hundred forty-five days at McKay-Dee came to $35,241.42. And Cortney's fifty-six days at LDS Hospital ran $9,933.90. Twenty-seven physicians filed claims for services on Cortney, totaling $7,767.30. The claims would have been far higher but most of the physicians also carried insurance with Blue Cross and Blue Shield and were precluded from charging their usual fees. Dr. Rees, Dr. Hauser, and Dr. Grua charged nothing for their services.

Though the policy covering Cortney paid for physical therapy, it did not pay for such things as occupational therapy, speech therapy, or other professional services designed to help Cortney cope with his handicaps and lead a more productive and self-supporting life. In addition to the $75,000 paid out by Blue Cross-Blue Shield, Byron Naisbitt has paid out of his own pocket another $20,000.

Gary: I don't really think I had any feelings of anger or revenge. I have to admit, I avoided hearing about it on TV. I avoided talking to people in general about it as time went on. I avoided listening to the trial, though I often heard the synopsis during the ten o'clock news. The gory details and the pictures I wanted to avoid. I didn't want it to be thrown back at me. I was fortunate enough to cope with my feelings immediately, put them out of the way, and have been grateful ever since that I was able to do that.

I removed the result from the cause. That's how I coped with it, I just separated them. Mother's dead because she was murdered. It's not something I would have chosen. But she's dead. You can't bring her back, you can't do anything about it. You're helpless. When I separated the two, I put that particular murder in the class of all other murders, and, as with all other murders, the state has laws to deal with it. Knowledge of the details of how mother died makes it harder to separate the cause from the effect. If I associate a painful loss with somebody who willfully caused it, that excites a lot of anger. If I'm angry, what can I do about it? Not a lot. If every time I thought about her and her death, I ended up thinking about Pierre and Andrews, then that just brings back anger and feelings of revenge. And those are frustrating. Because you can't do anything about them anyway.

It's an emotional response. The mechanism that I did it by, I think is, first, dive into Cort. Exhaust myself staying with Cort, until I had to sleep. And then sleep. And then go back and exhaust myself again with Cort. And not get too involved in the funeral services until they happen. And in a sense, that was running away. After I got the thing pretty well encapsulated, my anger and my fear, why burst the capsule? I took my curiosity about the trial, and whether these guys are the guys who did it and so on and I said, "Look, if I satisfy myself that these are the guys, then one, it brings the details before my eyes, and second of all, it gives me an object for revenge." Now, none of this happened cognitively, it happened more subconsciously. And that's why I say I was blessed, because it was not something that I realized, planned and did. It more or less evolved.

I don't know the law. I will admit that every time I hear they are given a date for execution, I say, "Okay, I don't have to confront this another time." And then all of a sudden, in the same breath, they end up saying they've been given a stay of execution. I get a little confused and in a little bit of turmoil, and I say, "What's going on?" I mean, we say one thing and do the other. I'd like the privilege of that system if I were in their shoes. At the same time, it looks like it's a real screwy system. But I'm able to cope with that, it doesn't make me angry. I don't go around and slug the wall or anything like that. I just sort of shrug and say, "Oh well, one of these days something will happen." One of these days they'll finally either run out of appeals or else they'll have things found in their favor.

But in terms of revenge or whatever, I don't care. We have laws to do whatever laws do. They do their best to find them, and to prove they're the right ones. There are laws prescribed to do certain things with them. In this case the death penalty was possible. And I didn't really care. I wasn't real excited about having them back in society and having to live with them again. I wasn't very excited about having to support them. Personally, I think the death penalty is probably all right. There's no way you can have true knowledge that those are the right guys. Without absolute knowledge it's hard to judge. But by the nature of our society we have to have laws to live by, and those laws stipulate what to do in this circumstance. And I think that they're probably well-founded. You want to make sure that they're the right guys and you want to get them out of society one way or another. Those are the two basic objectives.

From what I heard while the cops were putting the case together, the case was pretty sound. And that was enough for me to decide, "Okay, I'll go along with that." I don't know any of the details. You have fingerprints and eyewitness reports and the guy gives you a description before you pick up the people, and he picks them out of mug shots and he picks them out of a lineup and their hair samples match, and blood samples match and the bullets match, and, you know, it's a pretty sound case. I understand they hit most of those points. I wasn't at the trial. It sounded like it was pretty solid to me.

I live with the rules and the regulations, and I'm willing to do that here. Even though there were only twelve people on the jury, everybody in society lives by the rules, and therefore they take their proportionate part of the responsibility. And I'm willing to do that. So, if they get the death penalty, fine. If they don't get the death penalty, that's fine with me, too. I knew that our law had not been tested. I knew that there were umpteen million ways they could try to get out of it. I know that if I were in their shoes, I certainly would want to have every possibility to get out and try to prove my innocence. Consequently, I knew it was going to take a long, long time. The chances of actually having them put to death, and I'm not even sold that that's the best thing to do with them, are, I won't say remote, they're pretty good, but it's going to take a long time. And so, what the heck. Whatever's going to happen's going to happen. There's no way to sit around and wait for them to get theirs. There's no reason for it. Just accept it that it's going to take a long time.

I feel like we have been very well blessed with Cort, and I feel that Cort has some sort of a mission somewhere, somehow to fulfill, and that's why he's here. And I think that with his physical problems he's either going to have to master them to prepare himself for another role, or that somehow those physical handicaps will play some sort of a part. Conjecture. That's my own personal faith. For some reason, Cort has been saved to work in some capacity, because medically he should have died. I think he is better off now than he had

*all rights to be, and I think if he'd really try he'd be better off than
he is now.*

*Mother's death had a strong impact, but it was over and done
with, that was the whole story. And it hurt, a lot. But at the same
time, although Cort was as bad as he was, there was still hope. And
it was such an intense hope that it kind of made Mother's death
easier. It was matter-of-fact, it was open-and-shut, she's dead. But
maybe Cort'll be better, you know, let's hope. Cort and hope. I really
think that's where most of the emotions went, and it's one of the
things that kept the family together.*

At Utah State Prison, Dale Pierre grows fat and wears glasses
with brown plastic frames, something he selected to be "commensurate" with his image. He varies his sleeping and waking hours,
but rarely misses the late morning, early afternoon "soaps" on TV.
One Life to Live is his favorite. He watches ball games, writes short
critiques of TV movies and educational programs, plays volleyball in
the yard, reads, braids his hair, tries to hypnotize himself, listens to
music. Once, he did a painting of a red bird on black velvet from a
paint-by-numbers set and sold it to a guard. His parents send him
money when they can. He is not liked by the other inmates in maximum, and more than one have threatened to kill him. For years he
studied books with titles like *How I turned $1,000 into $3 Million
in Real Estate, The Young Millionaires,* and *The Very, Very Rich.*
In June 1976 he wrote in a letter:

> I'm going to make history for myself. In effect, what I'm trying
> to do is accomplish what no other inmate in America has ac-
> complished. I intend to build a corporation with an annual
> earnings capacity of forty (40) million dollars. That may sound
> like an outrageous dream but if I can get the assistance I need
> I will accomplish my goals—the same way Carnegie, Wool-
> worth, Ford, Tiffany, etc. accomplished their goals. They all had
> one thing in common, "success" and that's what I'm after.

While incarcerated Pierre founded a company he called Poboi Enterprises Corporation, and on November 18, 1976, had the company

legally incorporated in the state of Delaware. He had no charter, no by-laws, no stock, no assets, and no officers except himself, but he was incorporated. With that done, he subscribed to investment magazines and wrote letters inquiring about classified ads that offered large, income-producing properties for sale. He signed the letters, "Dale S. Pierre, President, Poboi Enterprises."

-For two years, February 1977 to January 1979, Pierre kept a journal. Interspersed with observations on who was getting marijuana from the outside and to whom they were selling it on the inside, and who was engaging in homosexual activities with whom through the fence in the yard, Pierre wrote:

> I have come up with a simple idea for acquiring property without any down payment. I also took seven brown bombers—I want to purge myself. Nothing more.

> I have now formulated some specific plans for building a $250 million company.

> I have decided on a new name to use "Clayton Leon Cassiram".

> Andrews is fascinated by the amount of material I have collected on real-estate business and amazed at my persistence to see this corporation come to fruitation. I think that success is my destiny, I can feel it, especially for the last week or so.

> My mom dreamt that my appeals fell through and I was the first to go. What a sordid dream!! Anyway today is laundry day.

> Andrews' girlfriend wrote to him today. She warned him to be careful that he don't get taken by me. I *must* keep this in mind. People always get skeptical when I try to help. I wonder why . . .

> Hoorah! Hoorah!! The state has provided us with a television today. We got it hooked up quickly and it works beautifully. It's a Quasar, about 21″.

> I have decided to change my name again. This time its "Philbert Hamilton Bailey."

> I started back on my soap operas today. It seems as though I

have lost a lot of the story on "The Doctors" and "Ryan's Hope". But I don't seem to have lost anything on "All My Children".

I read up on Playboy's mansion west. If I am ultimately able to afford it I will duplicate his efforts on a smaller scale. 20 to 30 room mansion on 3-10 acres.

Success magazine has a very good article about Amway in it. It is the size of corporation I intend to build. The silver limousine, the yacht, the three corporate jets—yes sir—that's me.

I will try to borrow $50.00 to move the corporation. I definitely have to get it going. I am to build a corporation with combined assets of $1 billion. Acquiring at least $100 million within the first 24 months, expanding to about $500 million in 36 months.

My new name as chosen today is Cody Jaye Cavalho.

This has to be the most depressing day of my three year stay here. Athay called to tell me that the Supreme Court of Utah has turned down my appeal. . . . I may write a book called "Follow that Dream", about my personal views and feelings about being on *Death Row* and about my struggles to build my business empire.

I think I am getting depressed about everything. There is an article in the Deseret News about Andrews and myself. They are still trying to put a bad light on us. I am determined to dispense with these dirty tacticians and Mormon degenerates. I hope this doesn't sound violent.

I've started to read the Paul Getty books and it seems that being a business man is harder than I thought.

I have changed my name again. It is now "Houston Lee Hoyt"—after H. L. Hunt.

I go to court tomorrow. They have to set a new execution date for me.

Well, the bad, tough guys have rung in the new year with a most pathetic display of criminal stupidity. They all shouted "Drano" as the clock wound down on the television.

Andrews was telling me that the richest black man in America has a net worth of about $23 million. I intend to be worth 5 times this amount.

Ebony Artists Corporation will be my answer to Hefner's Playboy. I plan to make my corporate ventures open to all races. I am not planning to be an ethnic hero.

I have changed my name again. It is now "Del Ray Hoyt" for business and Del Ray Khanhai for legal purposes. [In all, Pierre changed his name twenty-seven times, finally taking his own middle name and making it his last, making his last name his first and his first name his middle. His legal name is now P. Dale Selby.]

Myself and Andrews had another argument about fornication, adultery and a mother's responsibility to her children. As can be expected my arguments were based on puritanical Bible doctrine, his was not.

This may sound very crass but I had my pre-execution physical check-up at about 1:45 PM today. The doctor says that my heart beat registers about 90. It is now about 3:40 pm and the warden has requested to see me. I went out to see him and he wanted to know how I wanted my body to be disposed of. . . . I saw the 6 o'clock local news. I got a stay of execution from the Utah Supreme Court. I don't feel very different except that the feeling of impending doom is not present anymore.

Andrews isn't doing a damn thing but watching television, listening to the radio, eating and sleeping. He doesn't seem to be interested in studying what is to be required of him as a tentative executive.

I must continue to make plans and plot my ultimate corporate destiny.

On September 25, 1981, Cortney turned twenty-four. He now weighs 190 pounds. A pulpy red scar runs from the left side of his neck, across his chest, and disappears in a roll of fat near his navel.

Smaller scars, little half-moon swirls, dot his chest and arms where tubes and needles once fed into his body to keep him alive.

Cortney can remember nothing of a period of four months, from late April to late August of 1974. He remembers nothing of his stay at St. Benedict's and nothing of McKay-Dee until one day when he felt as if he were awakening from a night's sleep to see two nurses, Ladora Davidson and Annette Wilson, at his bedside. But these two nurses never worked the same shift. Cortney's "awakening" was a gradual process of ever increasing awareness, images from the ICU blending into one scene until he was fully awake. He remembers clearly the Labor Day outing with his father, Gary, and Claire when he was told of his mother's death.

Thinking back to the day of the murders Cortney can recall none of his solo flight and only four isolated incidents that occurred that night at the Hi-Fi Shop. He remembers being stopped at the back door by a faceless man, shouting to Stan as they lay tied up on the basement floor, listening to the footsteps passing back and forth overhead. The last thing he remembers is hearing his mother's voice at the top of the stairs. Psychiatrists doubt that he will ever remember more than this.

Since his graduation in 1976 Cortney has continued to improve physically and mentally, though during this time he has hit plateaus when it seemed he was not improving at all. Then, almost suddenly, after six months or a year had passed, Cortney once again would exhibit signs of capabilities he had not exhibited before. His speech would become a little clearer, a little quicker, his gait more steady, his posture more erect.

After graduation from high school, Cortney attended classes at Weber State College, but his grades were poor and the number of hours he took not sufficient for him to advance onto his sophomore, junior, and senior years. Eventually, he merely dabbled at college work, taking two, sometimes three, courses a quarter, most of those some form of computer science. One quarter he surprised himself by making an A and two B's.

Each year since the murders Cortney has had an EEG and a C.A.T. Scan to test the functioning of his brain. Eight and a half years after he was shot, there appears to be no residual physical damage, no atrophy. Over the years his IQ has been measured and has climbed steadily. Most recently it was 123. But Cortney still has trouble performing intellectually. "He can't get it out," says his father. "It gets lost in there someplace." Dr. Iverson feels that the tremendous emotional overlay still existing in Cortney's mind is interfering with his intellectual functioning.

Cortney's friends from childhood all are married, and a few already are parents. From the summer after his graduation in 1976 until the summer of 1981, Cortney lived at his father's house, except for two short periods of time, one in a dorm at Weber State, the other in a halfway house for emotionally or mentally disturbed young people. Cortney did not fare well at either facility. He cannot handle stress as a normal adult, and the rigors of college life—the academic pressure and the responsibilities of independence—were more than he could cope with. At the halfway house, ironically, the relative mildness of his handicaps kept him from fitting in. Much of Cortney's life during the five years in his father's house was spent in front of a television or dawdling for endless hours with his home computer.

In the summer of 1981 Cortney took a major step in weaning himself from his dependence on his father. He moved into a small tract house alone, miles from his father's home. He has a job with the Department of Social Services in Ogden and makes enough money to pay for the low-interest government mortgage on his house. He washes his hair more frequently, talks less of computers, and is learning to cook for himself. He never complains of his handicaps. Each year he is capable of doing more things and shows a greater diversity of interests. He is alive and he is functional, and that alone makes his father very happy.

I think his recovery's been dramatic. I can't believe that he's alive and doing as well as he's doing. I'm thankful for that. I watched that kid pretty closely for all those months, pretty closely. I always had that feeling in me, no matter what the hell happened, that he was going to make it. And I prayed for Cortney. Whether it's an answer to a prayer or what, I don't know. But that's my feeling.

He doesn't remember anything. He can't remember any of that intensive care over at the McKay until the end of August. Can't remember any of the part where he was hyperalimented when his lungs were all full of crap and his belly was opened. He can't remember any of that stuff. Fortunately. I hope he doesn't remember. I hope he doesn't have to relive that terror. Put yourself in that situation. Why hell, somebody terrorizing you and torturing you and making jokes and threatening to kill you. They were joking, having a big time there. You betcha. Made the jokes about the cocktails they were going to feed them. What happened in that basement was an absolutely malicious, animalistic activity. And that kind of thing should not be tolerated in our society. We allow it every damn day of our lives, and I think it is absolutely stupid that we do. No one should be allowed to treat another person that way, and get away with it. No one will ever be able, no one will ever be able to know what terror, what pain and what anguish and what torture went on down there that night. Those two guys have no conscience about that one bit. It was a game they were playing, and it shouldn't be tolerated.

I never said a word to anyone during the trial, I never called anyone, I never talked to anyone, I never read the papers, I stayed free and clear of that whole thing. Never had an opinion on it. Because until that trial was over, those boys were innocent. But now they're guilty, now they're guilty and they're laughing, see. They're not only laughing at me, they're laughing at you, too. And people are going to get so tired of hearing about the Hi-Fi Murders and little Dale Pierre and all this ricky tick that by the time this gets settled they're going to say, "For hell's sakes, let's get this done, turn those boys loose and let's get this off our back!" And it's foolhardy. That little Ansley girl, pumped full of that stuff and then raped, for God's sakes, those guys ought to be . . . It's foolish to tolerate it. And we're still screwing around with them. They were found guilty by their peers and sentenced, and we're not doing anything about that, and it just irritates people and angers people to think that this can happen and nothing ever gets done about it. Maybe this is due process of law, but I think they carry it too damn far.

I was angry to think that someone would cause my wife any kind of trouble at all, and to go so far as murder her would be unthinkable. If anyone caused her any distress, it would anger me. What *the hell, she's my wife. And no one is going to cause her any distress as far as I'm concerned. Nobody. Not even for a day or a minute. She should have perfect freedom to come and go, think and do, whatever she wants to do. In perfect safety and perfect harmony, and anything that upsets that, upsets me.*

Cortney was upset about his own situation only one time. The thing that irritates him is that somebody killed his mother. He's more concerned about that. He can't understand why these guys aren't dead. "Didn't they get the death penalty?" "Yeah." "Well, didn't they get executed?" "No." "Well, uh, why not? They executed my mother. And two other people. And they tried to do it to me. And Mr. Walker. Why are we any different than they are?"

These guys know very well that there's no punishment. If they sit it out long enough, somebody's going to feel sorry for these poor little fellas down there. Their rights are always being infringed upon and nobody's looking after them. Well, who the hell's looking after Cort? I would like to have the same amount of dough it cost for that trial and the expense it's going to take to keep those boys in prison or whatever happens to them put in a trust fund for my son. But see, no one ever figures he had any right to be able to walk up and down this town and feel comfortable and free, and have a nice, normal life, unmolested and unchanged by anyone else. That's a right the Constitution theoretically guarantees him, but no one ever stops to think about that. They're so interested in the other side of this thing. The state and the taxpayers are paying for these guys, and no one gives a damn about what's happening to Cortney. But I do. And I know very well that in his later years, or forever, he's going to have some medical problems, and I'm not sure how he's going to be able to cope with those financially. But no one's guaranteeing him anything. At least Pierre and old Whatsie down there have guaranteed hospitalization, food, shelter, clothing—for life. As the perpetrators. But no one guarantees Cortney anything like that. As the victim. Who was perfectly innocent. And didn't ask for this kind of treatment, and certainly didn't want it. No one guarantees him anything.

I don't know what the answer is, but I know that the perpetrators get taken care of, and the victims get ignored. And many of those victims can't take care of themselves. Cortney is fortunate enough, hopefully, where he can get to the point he can take care of himself. But some victims can't take care of themselves. And I don't know how they manage. If I hadn't had medical insurance on Cortney, I would have had to sell a lot of stuff. But that bill would have been paid. It would have been paid if I had had to moonlight, or whatever I'd have had to do, it would have been paid. As it is, I'm out of pocket around twenty grand, and I can't even remember what it's for. But Cortney's not back to a normal life yet. And whether he ever gets back to a normal life I don't know. And as long as he's not back to a normal life then it always worries me, see. How is he going to get along in society?

I'm no attorney, I don't know anything about the law, but I've been watching a little more carefully since this happened, and I see no real justice. For the victims. I don't know. I think that everyone should have a fair trial, a good, honest, fair trial, and a chance to question that, to appeal it. After that I think that it's stupid to keep on with this appeal, appeal, appeal. What the hell are they doing? What are they accomplishing? It's been over eight years and we're still screwing around, one court to the next, one court to the next. What the hell, why don't they turn 'em loose? If they're going to do it, why the hell don't they turn 'em loose? I don't care what the hell they do, but they ought to do something. I think it's stupid to just sit. They were sentenced to die and they're still sitting around, fooling around, after eight years. If they are going to let those guys go, they ought to let them go. There's a point where a guy's had all the fair trials he's going to get. And just going on and on and on is just a damn stupid thing as far as I'm concerned. It's just a mockery of the damn law. If they don't have guts enough to carry out the sentence, why don't they turn them loose? See, it doesn't make any difference to me. I wouldn't give a damn if they turned Pierre loose this minute, forever. I'm not asking for them to kill him. I don't care if they kill him or not. They can turn him loose, it's not going to make one pinch in hell difference to me. But the law says that he should die as his penalty. And if that's what the law says, then that bugger should die. It's that simple. Otherwise, why in the hell have the law? If they don't want to execute people, then don't make the punishment. It's just a travesty of the law, just ridicules the law, and it's laughable. And that irritates the hell out of me. If it's right, then it should be done. If it's wrong, then it shouldn't even be there at all. And if it's for life then it should be for life, and not five or six years later say: "Oh, look how badly these people were treated. These people have been maligned here. Here they are down here and they really didn't mean to do it. They've had second thoughts about it." That's a bunch of bullticky. I don't give a damn how angry they are, no one has the right to take another person's life. Or torture them or do anything to them to change their situation. That's antisocial, and I don't give a damn what the cause is. But nobody wants to do anything about punishment, and I don't know why. They're trying to find excuses to give people the leeway to do whatever the hell they want to do. And that's stupid. No one forces anyone to do anything. And that's the same with those boys. They went down there with an intent, and they went down there knowing full well what the deal was. No one forced them.

I'm still irritated that the situation in this country is such that you can't feel comfortable to come and go in freedom. We should be able to do whatever we want, go wherever we want. Be perfectly safe and comfortable. And until that day happens, we're damn fools for tolerating things the way they are.

EPILOGUE TO NEW EDITION

September 1990

Nine years have passed since I finished writing the words you have just read. In that time much has changed and just as much remains the same. Byron Naisbitt, who turns sixty-eight this year, continues to practice medicine and deliver babies, and has been made a grandfather another ten times by his own children and those of his wife Sue. Gary finally earned his Ph.D. in biochemistry, and he and Annette have added three little girls to their family. Claire and Scott have two sons to add to their own three girls, two of whom have recently won national dance titles. Brett is a stockbroker at Merrill Lynch, and Natalie, the baby he and Diane adopted just before Carol was killed, is now a cheerleader at Weber High.

The most dramatic changes have occurred with Cortney and Pierre. In the many letters I have received from people who had read the book, I was always asked two questions: Has Pierre been executed? How is Cortney now? The answers are "Yes" and "Married, doin' okay."

In 1987, after thirteen years on the case, Earl Dorius, of the Attorney General's office in Utah—who argued every appeal on behalf of the state—finally resigned, turning over to his successor all of his files on Pierre and Andrews—seventeen archive boxes full of paper. When Dorius counts the victims in the case, he includes his own family and himself. "If you look at victims of the crime, in the periphery, I view each of my family as one of them, certainly, and me, in an indirect sense. My whole life changed, the whole direction of my law career changed, because of that guy. My oldest daughter is now twenty years old and married. She was born in 1969, so she was five years old when I got this case. It has gone to the U.S. Supreme Court, what, three times, on cert alone. I can remember working Christmas eve at the office until 10:00 P.M. one year, coming home, putting out the toys, and then the next day opening them in the morning and then going back to the office that afternoon, Christmas Day, to meet a deadline."

In 1987, Dorius spent 80 percent of his time on the Hi-Fi case. "I was also trying to run the division [of criminal appeals], and represent agencies and other appeals. It reached the point of absurdity." That same year, I asked Dorius if, given the opportunity, he would witness Pierre's execution. "I'm so jaundiced now I would love to see it," he said. "Just to know it's finally over and out of my life."

A few months later, on the night of August 27, 1987, Dorius drove by himself to the Corrections Training Center, which is across the freeway from the Utah State Prison at Point of the Mountain. From his office at the capitol he had just called each of the three families to tell them that Justice Byron R. White of the United States Supreme Court had denied the last of Pierre's eleventh-hour petitions. Before the calls, Dorius had watched Pierre's lawyers being interviewed on television as they stood outside the prison, so he knew that finally the appeals had ended.

At the training center were gathered government officials, the media, and a few parishioners from Pierre's church. In the main auditorium, Dorius gave a short press conference, then returned to a waiting room. "We waited until the appointed hour, which, as I recall, was either midnight or one o'clock in the morning. Seems like it might have been one o'clock. Then they put the Weber county attorney and myself in one vehicle with an escort and a driver and we went under the freeway over into the compound to this new maximum security warehouse building. I had not been advised of the route I was to take, and we got out of the vehicle and I went through one door and looked to my right and saw the holding cell where they had kept Pierre for the prior twenty-four hours. Continuing to walk forward I saw an acquaintance, who is now the warden at the prison. I had been the attorney for the prison years ago. He was in this room at the end of the hallway. The room was illuminated and I just thought he was in like an office or something, and that it was on my way to be taken somewhere else. So even before entering the room, I started to say, 'Gerry, it's good to see you . . .' not realizing that he was standing in the execution chamber, and that Pierre was on my immediate left, maybe three or four feet away, strapped to the gurney, saying his prayers."

In the six years since I had finished the manuscript for *Victim*, the appeal for Pierre and Andrews had slowly worked its way through the federal courts. In 1981 the Federal District Court in Salt Lake City had set aside the appeal while the Utah Supreme Court considered the case in light of a recent decision in another case. Two years later, the court decided the two men should remain under a sentence of death. The case then went back to the Federal District Court to continue its way through the system.

The Federal District Court denied the appeal and Pierre and Andrews moved one step closer to having their sentence carried out. In 1986 the Tenth Circuit Court of Appeals in Denver, a three-judge panel, unanimously ruled against them both. But whereas Pierre's lawyers then filed a standard petition for rehearing, counsel for Andrews entered a lengthy document, and the two cases split. The Circuit Court summarily denied Pierre's petition, and his appeal went on to the United States Supreme Court for the third time, where his writ of certiorari and then his final, formal petition for rehearing were both denied, the latter in June of 1987. Except for the never-ending habeas corpus writs, Pierre had finally exhausted all judicial appeals. His only hope was clemency.

In Utah, the power of clemency lies not with the governor but with the three-member Board of Pardons. In early August 1987, Pierre's lawyers filed his final appeal with the board, which agreed to hear ten hours of testimony, five on Pierre's behalf and five on behalf of the state.

On the first day of the hearing, Pierre did something I never thought he would do: he confessed to the murders. Yes, he had killed three people, he told the panel, but he didn't mean to; he had gone to the shop not intending to kill anyone. He had found the Drano in the basement and simply thought it might keep the people from talking. His explanation for the shootings was longer and more elaborate.

With little emotion and referring to Cortney as "the Naisbitt kid," Pierre unfolded a brittle story that began with the beatings he had received as a child, and progressed to the prejudice he had endured after arriving in the United States. He said that in Trinidad, where he lived for the first seventeen years of his life, he had not known prejudice. Not until he arrived in New York City as a teenager did he begin to feel the pain, the frustration, and the anger it causes. For the next four years, American society had discriminated against him, and hatred began to fester inside. The discrimination did not stop when he joined the Air Force. With this hatred well entrenched the night of the robbery, said Pierre, his head also was spinning from a combination of Valium, beer, and marijuana, and he had a tremendous headache. He had intended only to rob the Hi-Fi Shop, tie everyone up, and leave them in the basement. But then Carol Naisbitt had entered the shop, and she began shouting at him and shouting at him, and then she called him a "godless nigger," and with all of the pressure he had been feeling from the prejudice, combined with the pills, the dope, and the alcohol, that sudden outburst from Carol had caused him to whirl and shoot her and then rapidly shoot the others.

When he heard Pierre say this, Cortney, who was sitting next to his wife in a chair a few rows behind Pierre, reflexively crushed a plastic cup in his left hand. About a year before, Cortney had started having flashbacks about the murders, sometimes nightmares in which his legs would run as fast as they could across the sheets, and he would scream, "No, no, not with a gun!" And when he awoke he now would remember them.

Since I had married Cathy, I had begun to remember things. I remember Andrews had a carton opener and he would stroke it across our necks and say "How would you like to feel what it's like to have your throat cut?" And before Mr. Walker came in, I remember Pierre kicked Stan in the face. Then Pierre got up there and so very coolly explained what he'd done that night, and more just came flooding back, like the expression on my mother's face when she was shot. And she also had talked to me and I had talked to her. I said that I loved her and she said that she loved me, too, and that she would see to it that nothing happened to me, that I would get out of there alive. She also said that it was her time to go. He said that he shot my mother because she called him a "godless nigger." She didn't say that, I don't think she could have said that even if she wanted to, it wasn't her way. Everything he said about my mother and the way he played it up with her,

that's what really upset me, because nothing he was saying was true,
except that he shot her in the head and gave her Drano.

"Pierre played games with the facts to justify some of his behavior,"
recalled Dorius, "which was outrageous. He tried to make it appear
that he was provoked by Mrs. Naisbitt, when in fact she'd already had
Drano poured down her throat and couldn't speak: her mouth was
taped at the time he said she said that. He said he was under the
influence of alcohol and drugs, and there was no evidence at all. They
didn't even smell any alcohol on him: Orren Walker verified that. He
tried to say that they found the Drano there. He was playing fast and
loose with the facts. We were expecting him to mainly testify as to his
childhood, but we sensed that he might want to testify as to the crime
itself, and that's why we invited Orren Walker to be there, to rebut
that."

Dorius calls Orren Walker the Silent Saint, a man who has endured
the unimaginable both physically and psychologically, and tried to learn
and to grow so he could use his experience to help others. As he had
on the witness stand thirteen years earlier, Walker told the panel that
Pierre took his time, a long time, to shoot everyone, that he pranced as
he moved as if he were enjoying himself, that he, Walker, could smell
no beer on Pierre's breath. Pierre's story also failed to explain the rape,
the kicking of the ballpoint pen, the use of two guns, the talk about
German cocktails.

Dorius asked me to testify at the hearing, because I was the only
one who knew Pierre's background, his life in Trinidad. After Pierre's
testimony, Dorius wanted me to talk about two things: racial prejudice
in Trinidad and Pierre's attitude about alcohol and other drugs.

I sat at a small table facing the three-member panel. Behind me
and to my left, two or three feet away, sat Pierre. I hadn't seen him
since January of 1980, when, sensing our relationship was about to
end and being unable to think of anything else to discuss with him, I
asked him the question we had so lightly skipped over all those years:
how could he have done to those people what he had done? He acted
disgusted and said only, "What I do is my business," and I left.

In the interim, Pierre had read *Victim*. When a reporter from *The
Miami Herald* wrote to him to ask about the book, Pierre wrote back
that, yes, he had read it; someone seeking his autograph on the inside
cover had sent him a copy to sign. He wrote to the reporter that while

he had the book in his possession, he "took the liberty of reading it." Pierre told the reporter that the book was "amateurish."

To answer the lawyers' and the panel's questions, I talked and read from my notes about the tension I had witnessed between the East Indians and the Africans on the islands of Trinidad and Tobago. While researching there, I had heard many stories of teachers favoring Indian children, and of at least one Indian father who murdered his own daughter for marrying as African. As for Pierre's use of drugs, I had several letters from him and quotes in his interviews where he professed to disdain drugs and alcohol, except for an occasional beer. At the request of the government lawyers, I read from these.

In a tearful announcement a week later, the head of the Board of Pardons, Vicky Palacios, announced that the board refused to stay Pierre's execution. Since Pierre was sentenced to die in 1974, the state of Utah had repealed its old death penalty statute that gave the condemned a choice between the gallows and the firing squad. Pierre would be put to sleep with a needle.

When Dorius entered the execution chamber, Pierre paid no attention to him. "I could just see him talking to himself and staring up," remembered Dorius, "and he had an IV that had been started in his arm. His arms were wrapped tightly to the gurney, his legs were strapped to the gurney.

"This execution chamber was a square room. There was a room along the south wall of the chamber for the media, and there was a wall that divided them from another room on the south side for the guests of Pierre. Then on the west side of the room is where the executioner was. We could not see into that area, but there was like a one-way mirror on that side, and I noticed there were tubes leading out of that area that came through a little hole and ended up in Pierre's arm for the IV tubes. As I recall, there were maybe two or three of those. On the east side of the execution chamber there was nothing; that was just a solid wall. The north side was for all the government officials, and the only way for us to take our place was to walk through the execution chamber, and then back out again on the other side. I had not been advised of that, so when I walked in there I didn't realize I was walking into the chamber. I started to carry on this Hi-how-ya-doin'-old-friend conversation, and Gerry had this real strained look on his face, like, We shouldn't be talking. Then I looked to my left, and that's when I first saw Pierre, so I immediately quit talking. Although he was at somewhat of a diagonal, so that his head, as I recall, was facing right at me, he was preoccupied with his prayers. I don't know that he noticed me, again because he's strapped to the gurney, and there might have been a neck strap as well strapping him down. So all I saw was him talking, facing directly up to the ceiling. Anyway, I went to the other side and looked back and observed."

Outside, on a barren rise overlooking the prison, Dorius's adversary all those years, Pierre's attorney Gil Athay, stood among 150 death penalty opponents holding lighted candles in silent protest. Only a few feet away, another 50 people had gathered to ring in the execution and to mock death penalty opponents with chants and laughter. Before Pierre, Athay had never had the death sentence imposed on a client, and he had fought to have this one overturned. Along the way he had lost his bid for Utah Attorney General because he refused to compromise his beliefs, which made him an easy target for his opponent. During my research I encountered people who said they would have been just as happy to see Athay in front of a firing squad as they would Pierre.

Thirteen years later the sentence was finally being carried out, and Earl Dorius was inside the new prison warehouse, witnessing Pierre's final moments. "The warden was given the assignment to stay in the execution chamber and ask Pierre for his last words. I couldn't hear any of this. I watched him go over to Pierre and talk to him a little bit, and then he stepped back and gave a nod or some signal and that started the process. With respect to Pierre, I have to say, I think he was ready to die. There was no indication of any resistance at all from the time that I first saw him. He knew it was going to happen.

"The only noticeable change I saw is that first he went to sleep. Then I saw his chest heave, I believe once, like a crippling effect, a reaction to the drugs. And then again as if he were asleep. Other than that, the only way I knew he was dead was that I could tell from the reflection in the glass opposite me. I noticed that the soles of his feet turned from a pink color to an ashen gray. Apparently it's protocol for a doctor to take the vital signs and then wait five minutes and take them again, but she indicated that there never were any, so I'm sure that he was dead in a matter of seconds rather than minutes. Not a bit of pain. In fact, as the county attorney and I drove back over we discussed the fact that it was almost clinical. It's just as if they were sedating a patient to prepare them for surgery. That's the best way I can describe it. It's the most painless-appearing form of execution imaginable.

"I was later asked by a member of the media what some of my thoughts were, and I had to confess that my focus was on his feet, because of the way his body was angled. And the thought occurred to me as I was watching his execution, How could those little feet—and they were very small, they looked like they might be a size 6 or 7—do so much damage. I thought of the kicking of the ballpoint pen into Orren's ear, and that sort of thing, and it was almost like I fixed on his feet. And then there was the part of the trial transcript that talked about those feet walking up stairs—you know, the pattern of his footsteps, as if he were in a frenzy, running up and down the stairs and across the floorboards of the upstairs. That's how Orren kind of knew his whereabouts and remembered the difference between Pierre's footsteps and Andrew's. All I could think of was the pattern of the feet and the damage they'd done."

Pierre had been injected with three drugs to put him to sleep, to paralyze his lungs, and to arrest his heart. A little after 1:00 A.M., he was pronounced dead. His execution was the first in Utah since Gary Gilmore's death by firing squad in January of 1977, an execution that had ended a ten-year death penalty moratorium in the United States. Between Gilmore's execution and Pierre's, eighty-eight men had been put to death for their crimes. Pierre was the forty-eighth person executed in Utah, the second black man; the first black man was executed in 1926.

Poboi Enterprises never experienced the phenomenal growth Pierre had envisioned, nor did Pierre achieve his personal goal of owning a smaller version of the Playboy mansion. Just before he was executed, he bequeathed all of his money to Andrews, who suddenly became richer by $29. Of the 2,300 inmates now on death row in the United States, Andrews has been there longer than anyone.

I completed the manuscript for *Victim* in the fall of 1981. When it had undergone my and my editor's final review, I sent a copy as a courtesy to Byron Naisbitt. A few days later my phone rang, and when I picked up the receiver, I heard Cortney crying on the other end. *I had to sort of "con" the manuscript out of my father's hands because I wanted to read it and know what happened that night and about the four months in the hospital before I woke up.* Everything was in there, everything Byron had tried to tell him that day on the way back from the fish hatchery. But until he read the book you have just read, Cortney knew almost nothing about the murders or about his first four months in the hospital. Now he had read it all, and I listened while he cried about what he had read. When he could speak, he said, "I didn't know my family loved me so much."

When the book was published in the late summer of 1982, Cortney was almost twenty-five. But the young women he met through church groups and friends were still in their teens, most of them already engaged or promised to young men away on missions for the church. Once, at the urging of a nurse who worked for his father, Cortney went to the home of a young woman and talked for two hours with her mother, the young woman never speaking a word: she was under psychiatric care for a crippling shyness. Cortney called me one day in early 1985 to talk about some of his experiences. "Call it my imagination," he said, "but every time I meet a girl and I ask her her name and tell her mine, I can see her thinking and thinking, and then I can tell the exact moment she figures out where she's heard my name before, and I know she's going, 'Oh, you're some kind of freak, you're supposed to be dead.'"

About that time, Cortney received a letter from a young woman named Nancy, who lived in Boston. Nancy had read *Victim* and had been so moved by the story she wanted to correspond with Cortney. She wrote to Cortney, and even visited him in Ogden, and Cortney flew back to meet her family in Boston. But the relationship ended quickly after that.

I received many letters like Nancy's, some from as far away as New Zealand and Sweden. The letters were like little windows into the collective mind of the reading public, a public that all writers know exists, but only as a vague notion that rarely takes form inside the tiny cubicle where most of them work. Once in a while, when the mail arrives, the shade on one little window goes up. The most revealing peek I had, the one that made me realize that while I sat alone working on other projects, people were out there reading and being moved by the story, came through a letter from a thirty-two-year-old woman living in Seattle. The letter arrived in early September 1985. I have tried to paraphrase its contents, but I cannot, so l quote it here, only a few sentences short of its entirety:

> I've read your book *Victim*. I read it over a year ago and have pondered over it a great deal all this time. I've been wanting to write to you for a long time, but I'm not exactly sure what I want or need, perhaps, to say. I will try because it is important to me. I hope you will understand if it takes me a while to put this into words.
>
> I imagine you've gotten many letters from other victims of crime since the release of your book. I, too, am a victim. Not only of crimes committed by strangers, but from those who everyone expects and deserves love from.

The next paragraph contained a list of so much torture, abuse, and loss, so many rapes, beatings, and broken bones, that I thought for certain the woman was writing to ask if I was interested in telling her story for my next book. But she continued in another vein.

> I have been in therapy for the last three years and probably will remain so for years to come. I understand Cortney Naisbitt's mind. I am a could-have-been, too. I know the pain, fear, loss, misunderstanding, rejections, confusion, hatred, and rage. I know what it's like to have someone—several someones—actually want you dead. I suffer from so many phobias and all in the extreme, that I can't function in society without medication. I know the nightmares and the panicky awakening that accompanies it. Sleepwalking. Wanting to go outside and enjoy the day like most everybody else and be unable to. Spending every waking moment trying to stop yourself from suicide and forever asking yourself and God why you lived through the unlivable. Yes. I understand Cortney Naisbitt. I know how nearly impossible it is to find yourself a "safe" place and fit in, never really able to forget the very things you forced yourself to forget in the past when it was happening.
>
> Cortney is a survivor and for that reason I've often thought of writing to him to say "I know." But we victims often have too much

of our own pain and problems to be able to feel anything for anyone except ourselves. The aftermath of violence seems to last forever with us. I doubt Cortney would be comforted by or even want to hear from another victim. I'm not so sure I would be able to make him feel any better, anyway.

I guess that's where you come in. You took the time and the care and effort to write down clearly what no one who has never been a victim wants to hear and, yet, they must hear in order to face it and change it. Posttraumatic stress disorder is not something people should be turning away from. Victims need more than anything else support and people who identify and understand them. Once violated, a person's body is never going to completely heal. Victims lose an important part of themselves and you can't get it back. *You* spoke for us, for all of us, not just Cortney Naisbitt, in your book, and it means everything to me (for one). I often have a difficult time putting into words to my therapist, counselors, and doctors what I'm feeling, what is happening inside my head and/or body, but with your book I can turn to a certain page and say, "Listen to this, you know, 'cause it says what I'm feeling." Like Cortney, I get lost inside my head. Unless I can find something to identify my thoughts and feelings with, I can't communicate them to get help. I stay lost and unreachable.

At about the same time I bought and read your book last year, I also started "awakening" from my traumatized state, and your book was such a help to me in relating to others, including my therapist. That "awakening" is hell in its own way (my near-waist-length auburn hair fell out, I got/get overwhelmed by rage and emotional pain, the panic attacks escalated horribly, etc.), and I spent hours rereading parts of your book, telling myself that all I was feeling was appropriate for what I'd lived through. At times I'd call up my therapist and say, "I've found what I've been trying to say! Let me read this to you!" And I made a lot of "breakthroughs" because of the things you helped me to say so I could be understood and reached.

I'd like to thank you for writing *Victim* and saying for so many of us that who we are and what happens to us is important too. Because we survive, the rest of the world seems to be of the opinion that we're miracles of strength; however, we are just people. People who break in the midst of our own survival. We are due help and respect and sensitivity to our plight. We need to be heard. We need to feel safe, which only comes from being heard.

I'd like to thank the Naisbitt family, too, for caring and giving some light and life out of their pain and sorrow. It must have been one of the biggest "labors of love" in modern days, to say the least! And thanks to Cortney for surviving for people like me.

The letter was signed "Kathy."

When I received similar letters, I always made copies and sent them to Byron and to Cortney. I mailed a copy of Kathy's letter to Cortney, and I sent Cortney's address to Kathy. She wrote to Cortney, and he saved the letter. Here are some things she said:

There is a problem that I'd had all of my life, especially three and a half years ago when I got into therapy. I couldn't put things— thoughts, experiences, problems, differences, feelings—into words. I did not know how to express myself. I can't tell normal sensations and feelings from abnormal. And try as she has, Jane (my therapist) could only do so much. So I began to search for books that could say what I had to and couldn't. . . .

That's where you and your family and *Victim* came in. As I read the book, there it all was in front of me! Past and present! The thoughts, the torment, the fears, panic, shock, depression, loss. Everything! Somebody else knew and had put it down for me to read and communicate with! I began to use the book in therapy. I still do. I'll excitedly call up my therapist and say, "Hey! Jane! Listen to this! I'm feeling like this, again, or felt like that!" I mean, what is therapy if you can't communicate? If you can't or don't know how to say what's happening to you? My case, from what I've witnessed and understand from others, is relatively rare, because not only did I survive but I've put my guts and soul into changing it. There's been no violence in my life in four years. I am in drug therapy and I suffer many severe phobias, but I can talk, relate to those who are here to help me, in a world I've never known before. Your story was the greatest single source of help I've found.

It has helped me in another way too. It is very hard (at times, impossible) for me to cry out my pain and rage. If you can find something to start the process, it isn't long before you can just let go and pour it out! I found myself rereading parts of *Victim* that bring my pain and empathy with you and your dad to the breaking point. It sets me free from my confinement. I thaw. It's sort of like draining an abscess, I suppose.

You know, Cortney, three years ago one of the sisters at St. James Cathedral, here in Seattle, said something to me and I've put it forth as a goal to overcome some of my self-hatred. I was relating how useless I've felt as a woman since the hysterectomy. She told me that giving birth to a baby is only *one* way of *giving life*! You have really helped me understand much more fully what she meant. You and your dad, your whole family, have given life to me in a way no one else ever has. You can't imagine what that means to me! My case is not like other abuse cases, of which I've met many. But I don't feel so alone with all of it anymore, because of you and your fight to live. You really are there and I can hold the book in my arms and it's solid and real. I have hope and progress because you and your family opened up that tragic, emotionally agonizing part of yourselves, and I could hear and speak it too. Cortney, you've given me life! I use the book with Jane, with my church counselor, my doctors, and now even my priest! You've helped lead me to a new and healthier life through your pain and rage. That's the greatest gift one could ever give another. It's also the hardest, and most painful. I don't think there's any way I can possibly thank you enough. You've helped me make such great changes. . . .

For me to uncover you and your family, who, like me, have *had* to look at and deal with this terrible violence and not run or tried to hide, is a blessing, ironically. The fact you didn't die for it, Cortney, gives me a special kind of hope too. Thank you for being there and having the courage, strength, heart, and soul to reach out for people like me! I will forever be grateful and respect your nobility. I was lost and terrified and you gave me a voice! I will always love and appreciate you for that. You're an answered prayer. . . .

Please feel free to write or call me anytime. Because of my phobias, I only go outside when I must. And I can certainly understand not getting much motivation to sit down and try to put your thoughts on paper. I, too, have trouble with that. I would like to write once in a while and see how you're doing and let you know I'm still out here, alive and caring. But do let me hear from you (my phone # is at the bottom of this letter). Please do continue to take good care of yourself. You really aren't alone. Once again, thank you. May God bless and be with you always.

When Cortney read the letter he thought, *Finally, someone who knows how I feel.* He called Kathy's number, and they talked for four and a half hours. The next day they talked for nearly three hours. Over the next six weeks the two of them talked almost daily. Finally, Cortney, who was still working at Hill Air Force Base and had little annual leave remaining that year, persuaded Kathy to visit him in Ogden. At the end of a week of nearly incessant talking, they were married by a justice of the peace in Ogden on November 15, 1985. Two years later they moved to Seattle, where both of them receive counseling and Cortney attends catechism classes for his conversion to Catholicism. In 1991 they will be married again in the Catholic Church.

Cortney has now lived more of his life as a victim of the Hi-Fi murders than he lived before becoming a victim. Kathy told me recently, "Cortney keeps seeing more and more of the world, and the more he sees it, the more he likes it. He has more energy than he's ever had before. He's slowly coming out of his shell, and he's thinking beyond the Hi-Fi murders."

I did not attend Pierre's execution, nor did anyone from the three families. I forgot it was about to take place, until friends sent me clippings from the newspaper. I did not talk to Byron about it afterward, though I asked him recently if he could remember how he felt that day, and he said what I thought he would.

It was just another day, so far as I was concerned. My only thought was, well, the sentence has been carried out after all this fooling around.

He feels as I do that the moral dilemma should be not over the death penalty but over the emphasis placed on the murderer's welfare at the expense of the victim. His recent comments echo his sentiments from over ten years ago, when he spoke the words that became my coda for the epilogue. His feelings have not changed; nor have the laws in Utah.

Let's make a statement if you want to do it. We talk about justice. The only thing I can see that would be justice is if there was some way

Cortney could be taken care of, even on the same basis this guy in jail is taken care of. They've spent several million dollars on these guys' trials and retrials and all that sort of thing. But nobody cares what the hell happens to the victim. No one has given Cortney a thought. His rights have never been discussed, his problems have never been discussed, from a government standpoint. I've had people all the time ask how he is, but I'm talking about people who could really help. It makes me wonder what happens to people who are the victims of violent crime who can't take care of themselves. And he can't. I've decided that he's probably damaged a little more than I thought. At least under the circumstances, he's limited. If they'd put twenty-five cents on the dollar into a fund and just let him live off the interest and then put the money back into a general fund, that might have been justice to a person who's perfectly innocent in all of this. And they spend all this dough trying to prove whatever to these courts, and no one's given a pinch to what's ever happened to the victims. If you want to make a statement, that would be my feeling about justice—to make sure the victim of a violent crime is at least looked after somewhat. I don't know what is so important about all this appeal stuff, there hasn't been one single iota changed in this whole case. It just keeps going back and forth. I don't know how many judges have seen this now. Last time it was forty-eight; that's when what's-his-name was given the shot, and there's been a bunch more since. And then, see, assuming his sentence is commuted and he spends his life in prison, this other guy's guaranteed food, shelter, clothing, and medical care for the rest of his life. Nothing's guaranteed to Cortney. I mean nothing.

It costs, I understand, about thirty-five or forty thousand a year to keep someone in maximum security. And he's been there now sixteen, seventeen years [laugh], that's crazy, plus all of this ricky-tick, oh boy. That's the only thing that rassles me. It's not the sentence, they can turn him loose. I'll tell you what I did, I called the state's attorney general or whatever the hell they call them down there, and I said, "Listen, I want to make a deal with you. You turn that guy loose, just turn him back on the street, and instead of paying for him the rest of his life, pay Cortney what it would take to keep the guy in prison for the rest of Cort's life, which is going to be shorter anyway. You could save that much money." Thought I was crazy. "Why, we can't turn him loose." I figured what in the hell can I lose by doing it. I knew they'd just laugh. But I thought it might start someone thinking. I'd be glad to do that. Geez, if they'd do that I'd take that in two seconds. Turn that sucker loose and just pay Cortney for the rest of his life. I'm talking about Andrews. Hell, I'd've even done it with Pierre. I would really have done it, because I'm that much concerned. I would love to have made that deal. Turn that mother loose on the street. They're willing to spend millions of dollars on all this bullshit, but they're not willing to spend anything to take care of the people that were damaged.

I don't know. This has changed my life, there's no questions about it, for hell's sake. But I could be really comfortable if I knew that he was taken care of without it being a stress to him. I wish they cared as much about him as they do about that guy in prison.

A writer of nonfiction, of stories that dig deeply into human emotions, faces a constant dilemma: he must seek the truth, yet the source of that truth must be made to suffer again in the process; the writer must force his way past the pain. To draw the experience out, to make it real, he has to make people hurt, and while these people are hurting he has to tell himself that what he is doing is necessary to get at the truth, and that somehow if truth is set free, pain is justified. But there are times when truth itself seems trivial next to the pain you can imagine you are causing.

I met Byron Naisbitt one night in early May of 1975. That evening, during an hour of intense questioning by his brother-in-law Lynn Richardson and his nephew Brent Richardson, Byron only listened. I told the three men that I wanted to write a book about what had happened, that to do that I had to write about Pierre, I hoped they understood that, but I was there to try to convince the family to talk to me, to tell me the victims' side of crime, because to my knowledge no one had ever portrayed that in a book. I wanted to know, if they could tell me, how they dealt with this tragedy in their lives. At the end of that hour, Byron walked up to the front of the room and quietly shook my hand. He gave me two phone numbers, his office and his home, and then he said to me, "As long as Cort agrees, if you think that hearing his story will help someone else down the road, I'll do it."

Even now, I'm only beginning to understand that commitment.

10/7/03